WOMEN AT WORK

How They're Reshaping America

Edited by
HENRY MYERS

DOW JONES BOOKS

Published by Dow Jones Books
P.O. Box 300, Princeton, N.J. 08540

Copyright 1979 by Dow Jones & Company, Inc.

Printed and bound in the United States of America
10 9 8 7 6 5 4 3 2 1

Library of Congress Cataloging in Publication Data
Main entry under title:

Women at Work.

    Based on a series of articles originally appearing in
the Wall Street Journal, summer 1978.
    Bibliography: p.
    1. Women—Employment—United States. I. Myers, Henry, 1929—
HD6095.W684   331.4'0973   79-11635
ISBN 0-87128-573-8 pbk.

Introduction

Some of the most dramatic changes in the world around us take place so gradually that, even when we are aware of them, we tend to underestimate their extent, their impact and their importance. Such has been the case, over the past couple of decades, with the huge influx of women into America's paid work force.

The sheer number of U.S. working women today—41 million—is impressive indeed. Perhaps even more important, however, is the fact that about half the eligible female population now is in the job market—either working or looking for work. Furthermore, knowledgeable observers expect women's participation rates to keep climbing.

Reporting on such trends—going beyond day-to-day news developments and analyzing in depth the significance of important changes—has long been a major specialty of the staff of The Wall Street Journal. Over the past few years, the Journal has run many articles on working women, and late in the summer of 1978 it published an eight-part series on the subject.

This book, based on the series, on many of the other feature articles, on spot news reports in the Journal and on newly written material, goes even further. It offers a broad look at the whole subject of Women at Work. It presents many points of view: of men as well as of women, of professional economists as well as of women taking a job for the first time, of experts on child care and of people commenting on the changes around their own neighborhoods. It isn't a textbook; it doesn't make any pretense of discussing every occupation and every kind of situation. Rather, it takes up in considerable detail certain specific jobs and specific situations, on the theory that the reader will realize that much of what it reports about women lawyers, for example, also is generally true of women doctors and women dentists.

Women at Work begins with a broad-ranging section that provides an overview both of the book and, in many ways, of the whole panorama of women in the U.S. economy.

Then, a section entitled Gains Women Have Made reports on some of the fields in which working women have chalked up dramatic achievements. You will read about the growing squadrons of women lawyers; about the American women now working in overseas jobs and about the problems they face; about a woman trying to make a go of her own business—and, moreover, an innovative business; about women gaining entrance into the high-paying blue-collar jobs that once were an almost-exclusively male preserve; about women working in, of all places, coal mines; and about women succeeding in an auto exchange—a surprisingly tough line of work in which most men fail.

But not all women are taking up so-called nontraditional occupations, of course. As a section entitled The Old Standbys makes clear, many of the women flooding into the labor market do the kinds of jobs that women traditionally have done. They sell Mary Kay Cosmetics, or wait on tables, or help their husbands farm.

In moving into the labor force in huge numbers, women have fought many battles. Despite the antidiscrimination legislation passed under the impetus of the feminist movement, much bias lingers on. In Problems That Arise, you will read about the continuing problems caused by sexist behavior and, in the second chapter, about the difficulties faced by female airline pilots in gaining acceptance. Then, you'll find a discussion of sexual harassment on the job. In another chapter, you'll get more understanding of what it's like to be one of the first women—and a black woman at that —to head a big bank's branch office. You'll share the hard work as well as the achievements of a divorced woman who is both mother and breadwinner. The following chapter describes the difficulties faced by two women trying to find a good job after many years spent outside the labor force. And you'll delve briefly into the complicated subject of how and to what extent women, and the unborn, should be protected from chemical hazards on the job.

Although many of women's gains in the job market have been facilitated by antibias legislation, court decisions and agency directives, the legal battle is never finally, completely won. In a section called Fighting Back, the opening chapter briefly looks at just one aspect of the legal campaign against discrimination, and it shows how complex, and perhaps exasperating, such issues can become. The following chapter discusses the big, complicated scene at American Telephone & Telegraph Co. and the achievements—and failures—of a landmark affirmative-action program at the company. You'll also read about secretaries who are objecting to doing personal tasks for their bosses. And you'll visit some of the small firms that have prospered by helping women and minority groups find good jobs.

But not all the problems plaguing working women crop up at work. Many headaches, and often the worst ones, strike at home. Because the most obvious are the dilemmas faced by working mothers trying to choose among various child-care arrangements, the Coping With Life section of this book begins with a chapter on the pros and cons of day care. In addition, you will find chapters about the strain that sometimes is placed on a marriage when the wife works. And there are several chapters on the peculiar, but fascinating, problems afflicting marriages in which both partners are pursuing careers.

Besides affecting marriages, the growth in the numbers of working women is changing the whole economy. In a section entitled The Impact of Working Women, you will read how both companies and unions are being changed. You also will read how the money that women are earning is creating a large, high-class market to which companies are targeting sophisticated—and sometimes quite unsophisticated—marketing campaigns. You will be able to weigh both sides in a running dispute about whether working women are making rich families richer and thus increasing disparities of income among various groups of American families. And in a visit to

v

a typical suburban community, you will find how much life there has changed.

Although the careful reader will find a great deal of expert advice all through Women at Work, the final section of the book specifically aims to help the working woman get ahead in her job. Entitled "How to Get *Far* Ahead in Your job," it is written by Betty Lehan Harragan, an independent business consultant, lecturer, syndicated newspaper columnist and author of the much-praised "Games Mother Never Taught You: Corporate Gamesmanship for Woman." This section, which draws on Ms. Harragan's 25-year career in private industry, describes in detail what a woman should do to advance in a career. She assumes that you already have landed a job, and she gives some good answers to the next question: What do I do next?

Contents

Contents

Section I

Reshaping U.S. Society

With their help, the country survives $6,000 cars and $60,000 three-bedroom bungalows. They are one reason why schools are closing and child-care centers are jammed. Businesses court them, yet they have forced many a manager to rethink the rules of business. And in millions of homes, they have brought wholesale changes in everything from eating habits to the institution of marriage.

They are the nation's working women, 41 million strong and growing. As anyone who works in an office or attempts daytime deliveries in suburbia can attest, they are hardly an unrecognized phenomenon. But to many economists and sociologists, the steady flow of women out of the home and into the labor force is nothing short of a major event, one that is altering our society in ways still not fully understood.

Listen, for example, to the conclusions of Ralph E. Smith, an economist who closely studies the trend for the Urban Institute, a nonprofit research organization in Washington. The rise in the number of American women who work for pay, he says, amounts to a "subtle revolution" looming at least as large as the Industrial Revolution that shook Europe nearly two centuries ago. Yet, he adds, "it is slow-moving and there is no simple agreement on why it has been happening."

In 1890, when the government began keeping detailed records, 3.7 million women of working age had a job or wanted one. That number didn't include the millions of wives and daughters performing arduous farm chores in a then-rural America. Still, it was small, representing only 18% of all working-age females. However, as the population of working-age women rose, the number entering the paid labor force began to grow at an even faster rate. By 1900, one in every five women was in the labor force. By 1920, the participation rate had reached 23%. By 1940, it stood at 26%.

Late in World War II, with Rosie the Riveter in full swing, the participation rate reached 37%. With peace, many of these women returned home—but not for long. By the 1950s, the climb had resumed; the wartime peak was surpassed in 1956. Now, about half the eligible U.S. female population either has a job or is looking for one.

. At this rate, experts say, women who stay at home soon will be just as unusual as women who work in offices or factories once were. As evidence, they point to what's happening among women who, presumably, have the most reason to stay at home: mothers. Over 58% of women with school-age youngsters are working now. More surprising, so are over 41% of the mothers of children too young to attend school.

This trend isn't confined to the U.S. The Organization for Economic Development in Paris reports that the labor-force participation rate of women in countries such as Britain and France currently exceeds 40% and has risen to over 50% in Japan and several Scandinavian nations.

Here and in most other industrialized nations, it's generally agreed, both the migration to cities and the rapid growth of service industries have helped put large numbers of women on payrolls. Years ago, by contrast, women—particularly married ones—had many more reasons not to work. One of the most compelling was the fear of social ostracism.

In 19th and early 20th Century America, "women were simple not expected to go out and take jobs," says Howard Hayghe, a Labor Department economist who has studied the history of working women. "The idea wasn't accepted, and their role was viewed as being in the home." That dictum has been slow to die. As recently as the 1930s, says Fabian Linden, director of consumer research for the Conference Board, working women mainly "represented a population of the dispossessed, coming primarily from poor backgrounds."

Today, of course, a good job is as much of a status

symbol for a middle-class wife as it is for her husband, and even many affluent women now seek work for pay. Observes Betty Friedan, whose 1963 book, "The Feminine Mystique," presaged the modern women's liberation movement: "Evolutionary factors have been forcing women into the work force; women could no longer live within the limits of their traditional role" as housewives.

To understand the emotionally confining limits of those traditional roles, listen to the educated wife of a former corporation executive testifying about what she calls "the desperate search for identity that intelligent women go through in an urbanized, industrial society." She says:

"It is necessary to establish yourself as a person, not just as someone's wife. At parties and meetings and group-gatherings, people always ask, 'But what does he *do?*' They seldom ask what she does. It's taken for granted that the man does, and she just is. A neat trick, but not terribly satisfying. If you don't *do,* people assume you don't *think.* In fact, it was always better if corporate wives didn't think at all—except about houses, schools, shopping and moving. It amuses me now, but it used to infuriate me, that when I expressed a definite, divergent opinion to any of the men, they reacted with stiff backs, raised eyebrows, and immediately changed the subject. Some did take the time to point out to me the error of my thinking, with great affection and condescension. Artists and intellectuals and professional people take male-female equivalence for granted, but it is very difficult for a women in the business community to think of herself as a separate identity and not just as an extension of her husband. That's why there's so much alcoholism and breakdowns and kooky behavior."

Whether searching for a new identity, trying merely to augment the family income or entering the job market because of sheer economic necessity, women are not only going to work in increasing numbers; they are making a good deal of progress on the job.

Among the professions, they now account for about 12% of the nation's doctors, up from 6% in 1950, and close to 10% of its lawyers, up from 4%. Further gains are clearly on the way. According to the American Dental Association, for example, the first-year dental class that begin in the fall of 1977 included 880 women, 15% of the total and up from only 46 ten years ago.

· Women executives are getting ahead. Nearly one-quarter of management jobs now belong to them; that's nearly double the rate three decades ago. They sit on 25% of corporate boards of directors, according to a recent survey of 501 companies by Korn-Ferry, New York. The international executive-search firm adds that the female-director population jumped 13% in four years—although only 3% of the companies had a female director who also was an officer of that concern. In addition, more and more American women are being assigned to key foreign posts by U.S. multinational corporations. Jetting around the world to help negotiate major business transactions, they are doing work that, just a few years ago, would have been beyond their reach.

Many fields in industry, in fact, are opening up to women; among them, for example, is industrial sales. Computer Sciences Corp., of El Segundo, Calif., says it had only four female marketing and customer-service representatives five years ago. By mid-1978, one of the company's sales divisions had 50 women on a 200-person staff. At Xerox Corp., 419 of the 1,200 persons hired for sales positions in 1977 were women. International Business Machines Corp. says its female sales force has doubled since 1974. And some women are turning into entrepreneurs—taking big risks and working long hours in hopes of getting a new business venture off the ground.

Other women, lured by high pay, are tackling another kind of difficult venture: They are learning blue-collar skills and doing rugged work—jobs such as welding, carpentry and even coal mining—that always had been considered "man's work." In their pioneering, many of them have had to put up with a considerable amount of male harassment. But many of them also have had the guts to take the abuse and eventually have won the acceptance of their co-workers.

Of course, many of the women who have been flooding into the labor force have taken so-called traditional jobs— jobs always considered "women's work." Thousands of them still sell cosmetics, for example. Many more work as telephone operators, secretaries, store clerks, waitresses and, in some parts of the country more than others, domestic help. Nor has the farm wife disappeared—although her responsibilities have tended to expand, so much so that often she really is her farmer-husband's business partner rather than just someone stuck in the kitchen.

Whatever kind of job women take, they are quite likely to run into problems that men don't face. Many women complain of sexual harassment on the job. Many, working full-time and also putting long additional hours into raising children and keeping house, do practically nothing but slave and, fitfully, sleep. Many are women in their 40s who haven't held a paid job for years and find reentry into the labor force a difficult—and even terrifying—passage. And many say the hardest thing of all is to win acceptance from male co-workers.

In some ways, however, women workers are becoming a bit more like men. Female moonlighters, for example, are getting more common; a Labor Department survey in May 1978 found that 3.3% of the nation's female workers held more than one job, up from 2% in May 1962—while the proportion of such male workers dropped to 5.8% from 6.4%. And women are falling prey more frequently to occupational hazards, ranging from industrial accidents to maladies linked to toxic chemicals in the work place to stress-related ailments like ulcers.

Nevertheless, the feminist movement's drive to end sex discrimination in employment and pay still has a long way to go. The majority of women working today hold clerical jobs providing few chances for advancement. And as a group women earn, on the average, only about $6 for every $10 earned by men. That ratio hasn't changed much since 1955, when the government began keeping such data. Analysts explain that the high proportion of women taking entry-level jobs tends to keep the gap constant—despite lessening discrimination in pay. But discrimination clearly lingers on. According to a study of Labor Department figures by the nonprofit Scientific Manpower Commission, a white man who dropped out of high school had higher earnings on average in 1976 then a white woman with a college degree. It added that except for a few beginning groups, women's earnings are lower than those of comparable men "at every age, every degree level, in every field and with every type of employer."

Even the federal government—which through legislation and agency rulings has done much to reduce discrimination against women—isn't free of bias. In the fall of 1978, a Justice Department task force said government agencies discriminate against women in their own employment policies and are lax in enforcing sex-discrimination laws affecting the general public. The interim report to President Carter found that "sex discrimination isn't included within most agencies' primary civil-rights enforcement efforts." And in reviewing personnel policies and employment statistics of federal agencies, the task force said it "generally found the familiar pattern of men in top-level, policy-making positions and women in low-level jobs." Similarly, the Southern Regional Council says a study of federal courts in the area showed that although women accounted for 48% of the jobs, "the women are isolated largely in nonprofessional employment" as clerks and secretaries.

The problems that women have faced in landing good jobs and in getting promotions have led to much antidiscrimination legislation and to many court suits. Both in conjunction with various minority groups and in behalf of women alone, so many legal actions are under way at any one time that it is bewildering to any but the full-time observer. Moreover, the legal issues have tended, probably inevitably, to become more and more arcane as court decision has followed court decision and as agency rulings have multiplied. But there isn't a major corporation in the country that isn't painfully aware that antibias suits have resulted in multimillion-dollar settlements. And local governments also are vulnerable; a federal judge recently ordered the city of Chicago to pay nearly $3 million in damages to 225 women employes who charged the Department of Public Works with sex discrimination.

In fighting back against what they consider discriminatory or merely objectionable practices, women have not only turned to the courts and to federal agencies. On their own, secretaries have made an issue of making morning coffee for their bosses. Risking the inevitable jokes, female sportswriters have battled to get into male locker rooms for the post-game interviews essential to their reporting. And a whole new group of businesses has sprung up; many fledgling companies counsel women on how to find a job and how to get ahead once they have it.

The massive influx of women into the work force also has led numerous problems concerning child-raising and marriage in general. Many observers wonder what adverse impact the decision of a mother to work might have on her children. Day-care centers and outside sitters are poor substitutes for a mother's attention, one typical argument runs. A government analysis avoids any firm conclusion. But it wonders whether working mothers' absence from home may be "cutting off communications between generations and contributing to a state of alienation between young people and society."

In any case, it is believed that a link exists between the influx of women into the labor force and such developments as a doubling of the country's divorce rate within the last decade, fewer births among women of child-bearing age and later marriages. In 1950, for instance, 32% of the women between 20 and 24 years old hadn't married; now, the comparable rate is close to 45%.

(Some, psychologists believe delayed marriages are a decided social benefit, allowing couples to mature emotionally before making such a complicated commitment. On the matter of divorce, the Urban Institute's Ralph Smith observes that if a job gives a woman the economic freedom to bail out of a bad marriage, "what's so bad about that?")

Marriages seem to undergo the greatest strain if the husband objects to his wife working or if he refuses to share the burden of housework. Beyond those basic problems, some peculiar, sticky issues can arise, especially if both spouses have careers rather than just jobs. If husband and wife work for competing companies, for example, they can wander into conflict-of-interest situations by talking about the wrong subjects over dinner. One partner in the marriage may be offered a promotion in another city, but the transfer might disrupt or destroy the other's career. Sometimes such problems nowadays lead to solutions that in another day would have been unthinkable—such as living apart during the middle of the week and commuting hundreds of miles to spend weekends together.

Even apart from such unusual situations, the working woman has forced many corporations and labor unions to change their policies. Maternity benefits, for example, are rapidly becoming better and more common. A recent Conference Board study of 309 major companies found that 40% pay such benefits and that an additional 8% pay benefits only when maternity results in complications; 97% of the companies allow maternity leaves. Many companies also are permitting various arrangements for flexible working hours and hiring more part-timers—"mother's hours." And unions, after long looking askance at working women, are also adjusting to change. They are enrolling more and more women members; the number of female union members in California, for example, grew 11% in the two years ended in July 1977—while the number of male unionists dropped 1.5%. The implications haven't been lost on union leaders. They are negotiating for more benefits, such as those for part-time workers, likely to appeal to women. And women themselves, in turn, are becoming increasingly active in union affairs.

The impact of working women on the economy as a whole is hard to exaggerate, too. Because of their sheer numbers, there isn't any doubt that they help the economy prosper. Putting it another way, analysts say that if the ratio of women in the labor force weren't so high—four out of every 10 workers today are women—the U.S. simply couldn't maintain the $2 trillion gross national product—the total of goods and services produced annually—that the country currently enjoys.

For families, the benefit of a wife that works is also obvious: Two paychecks are indeed better than one, and can cushion couples from the squeeze of inflation and unemployment. "Without the enormous influx of women into the job market, the impact of inflation on our living standards would be far more servere," explains Geoffrey H. Moore, an analyst at the National Bureau of Economic Research. And if the husband or wife in a two-income family is laid off, the wages of the other become "a form of unemployment insurance," he adds.

Helping working women spend their wages is a profitable undertaking for many businesses. Mr. Linden, the Conference Board economist who specializes in consumer-spending patterns, gives clothing makers, cosmetics firms, convenience-food producers and restaurants as examples of businesses that prosper because so many women have jobs.

"Women who work tend to spend considerably more on their appearance than those who remain at home," he explains. He also notes that a Conference Board study found that families in which both spouses work spend 25% more in restaurants each year than those in which only the husband is employed.

The rise in the number of two-income families, in fact, has enlarged considerably the nation's "affluent" class, currently defined as those families with total annual incomes of $25,000 or more. Roughly 14% of all U.S. families were in this category in 1975, up from an inflation-adjusted 8% ten years earlier, according to Conference Board data.

This new affluence spurs demand for higher-priced cars, expensive furniture and appliances, and a number of other luxuries once available only to a rich few. "There's no doubt that the rise of the husband-wife working family has helped the vacation business," an American Express Co. analyst says. "Particularly, we find a rise in the number of families taking multi-vacations during the course of a year."

Working wives also keep the American Dream—the single-family home—a reality for many families. That's quite a feat; inflation has driven the average cost of a new dwelling over $60,000. Yet the housing market continues strong even though "most families have to have at least two incomes to afford a new house," says Michael Sumichrast, chief economist for the National Association of Home Builders. In the 12-month period that ended in June 1978, he reports, more than 47% of the families that bought new homes had two wage earners.

Not all the changes wrought by the advent of the working woman are so salubrious, however. Some economists, for instance, argue that these women aggravate unemployment, which despite three years of economic recovery still persists at a rate of close to 6%. The labor market, they say, simply can't accommodate all the women who want jobs. Furthermore, many analysts observe that the jobs wanted by many women—or, at least, the jobs open to many of them because of their low skills—are the same kind of low-pay, entry-level positions typically held by teen-agers; thus many of these women are competing with teen-agers in the labor market, and the unemployment rate for both groups is kept high.

On the other hand, a working woman pays some financial penalties that many consider quite unfair. As many working couples discover with deep chagrin every April 15, "two individuals who both work can be taxed more if they are married than if they are single," states a St. Louis Federal Reserve Bank study. That's particularly the case when both spouses have equal—and high—incomes. For instance, if a man and a woman each earn $25,000 a year and happen to be married, they'll pay nearly $2,000 more in taxes to Uncle Sam than if they were single, according to one Treasury Department analysis. And if a working woman's husband is a top-echelon executive, she is quite likely to have to pay out more than 50% of her earnings for federal income taxes alone.

Another irritant is the Social Security system, drawn up at a time when only the husband worked in most households. For instance, under its regulations, married working couples with the same total income as one-wage-earner families will receive smaller retirement payments. Though various changes in the law have been proposed, no new legislation appears imminent.

These are sticky public-policy questions, and they are likely to get stickier as time goes by. That's because most analysts believe that the long rise in women's labor-force participation will continue for some time. "I would expect over 44 million women to be in the labor market by 1980," says Ralph Smith of the Urban Institute. If he's right, that would amount to nearly 52% of the expected 1980 population of working-age females.

Such forecasts assume that barriers that tend to discourage some women from working will keep eroding. "As the balance of power continues to shift toward families with more than one earner," Mr. Smith says, employers as well as legislators will adopt more measures to accommodate working wives.

However, several developments, analysts believe, could inhibit further increases in the ranks of working women.

One is the prospect of reduced demand for schoolteachers, 70% of whom are women. After a long, sharp climb, teaching jobs are dwindling, and for a rather ironic reason: Too many other women are choosing to work instead of have children, thus drying up the needs for schools—and teachers.

Finally, a long drop in male labor-force participation may be ending. Above 85% in 1950, this rate has recently fallen to about 75%, largely because men have been retiring earlier than before. The trend toward early retirement may be subsiding, however; analysts cite recent legislation extending the mandatory retirement age in many businesses to age 70. If more of these men stay on the job, it's reasoned, there won't be any need for women who might want to replace them.

Section II

Gains Women Have Made

Toting up the gains made by women in the working world probably is easiest in the so-called learned professions, at least as far as sheer numbers are concerned, because bar and medical associations tend to keep meticulous records of their student and practitioner populations. And the gains have been striking. The legal and medical professions, plus accounting and engineering as well, have opened up their ranks to women as never before. Somewhat more nebulous, of course, is the gradual change in attitudes—particularly male attitudes—toward female professionals. So the chapter on Ladies of the Bar—which might just as well have been written about Ladies in White Jackets or Ladies With Pocket Calculators—puts much emphasis on the growing social acceptance of women in the professions.

The next chapter, on women who represent American multinational companies in foreign countries, carries a message both of hope and of warning. To the woman who secretly longs to take executive assignments in exotic places, it says that never before has there been so much opportunity; it also says, however, that it's still a tough way to make a living. The fact is that most foreign men are far worse chauvinists than American men, and in many countries a woman is in for a difficult time. In addition, a woman jetting around the world on business is going to face—just like a man—all the hassles of travel and of living out of suitcases.

Likewise, the chapter on The Venturer carries a warning. Do you want to start up your own business? Beware. You may have good ideas, be talented in many ways and be willing to devote backbreaking hours to your fledgling firm—and even then you are quite likely to fail. If you succeed, of course, the rewards, both emotional and financial, can be tremendous. But the story of Joan Massey and her struggle to make an unusual clothing shop prosper is fair warning to anyone, male or female, about the hazards of striking out on your own. At the same time, it is a story of grit and determination.

To the woman who hankers for a well-paying blue-collar job, the next chapter tells of heart-warming successes by many women now working in fields once exclusively male. But it also tells of another set of hazards. In the skilled trades, women confront two problems: the sheer physical demands of the work itself and the antagonism of many male co-workers. Furthermore, many women hesitate to enter these so-called nontraditional occupations essentially because they, like their menfolk, consider carpentry or welding or driving a locomotive "men's work." But aided by a push from government agencies, union apprenticeship programs and determined recruiting by many employers, women are increasingly entering such fields. They are succeeding in what they have set out to do. In this chapter, you will meet some of them.

Of all the blue-collar occupations, perhaps the most inhospitable to women is coal mining. All the problems typical of blue-collar jobs impede female coal miners, plus some additonal difficulties—the superstition against women underground, the mining companies' justifiable fear that the men may strike over the issue, the physical danger, the lack of toilet facilities. Yet the number of women miners, lured by the high pay, is expanding significantly.

This section of Women at Work concludes by telling you of an apparent oddity—a line of work that would seem quite likely to be dominated by men, but isn't. In fact, swapping cars in an auto exchange is handled far more successfully by women. The message here seems to be that, without giving people a trial, you never can be sure who will do a job best.

Ladies of the Bar

U.S. Supreme Court Justice Joseph P. Bradley declared in a 1873 opinion that "the paramount destiny and mission of woman are to fulfill the noble and benign offices of wife and mother. This is the law of the Creator."

The court thereupon upheld Illinois's refusal to grant a license to practice law to Myra Bradwell because she was a woman.

Almost a hundred years later, the American Bar Association Journal portrayed the status of women lawyers almost as bleakly, noting in a 1969 article that there is "widespread discrimination in the legal world against women lawyers." And even in 1975 Ms. Magazine asserted that the "law has been and still is a bastion of white male power."

Be that as it may, women have made some significant strides in this decade. Some observers now predict that law may become the first traditionally male profession to achieve full sexual integration. About 41,000, or 9.3%, of the nation's 441,000 practicing lawyers are women, recent data show, whereas in 1970 only 2.8% of the lawyers were women. The percentage is continuing to grow, and about 25% of all law-school students nowadays are women.

One woman lawyer recalls how the senior partner of a law firm told her in a job interview a number of years ago, "We'll hire a woman over my dead body." The woman adds, "Well, he was right." She was hired by the firm in 1973, after the man had died.

Women are gaining, too, as law-firm partners. One of them, Brooksley Landau, senior partner in the Washington, D.C., firm of Arnold & Porter, says. "It's only a matter of time before there's a significant change" in the number of women partners in large metropolitan law firms, at least. Partnerships, which usually aren't offered until the lawyer has been employed by a firm for six years or so, traditionally are stepping-stones to business and political power.

Although there still hasn't been a woman on the Supreme Court, Judge Shirley Hufstedler of Ninth Circuit Court of Appeals in the West is the second woman to reach the federal appellate level. (The late Florence Allen was appointed to the Sixth Circuit in Cincinnati in 1934.) Of the 394 permanently appointed U.S. district-court judges, five are women.

Some women lawyers have made spectacular achievements, particularly in government service. Jill Wine Volner, 35 years old, rose from a Justice Department prosecutor to a top post in the Watergate special prosecutor's office. She then became the first women to serve as general counsel to the Department of the Army. Rose Bird, 41, was the first women to become a chief justice of the California Supreme Court.

In 1973, the Manhattan district attorney's office had 14 women prosecutors out of a total of 166; five years later, 55 of the 229 prosecutors were women. The Justice Department says that, as of January 1977, there were 163 women among its 1,600 assistant U.S. attorneys, up from 43 out of 1,170 in October 1971. For a recent U.S. Supreme Court term, seven out of the 33 sought-after clerkships were filled by women.

On law-school faculties, the gains have been slower. Only five of about 60 full-time teaching positions at Harvard Law School are filled by women. And at Stanford Law School, which has 35 permanent teaching positions, only one woman is on the staff.

Discrimination against women lawyers in the past was also reflected in income levels. In 1967, a Michigan Law Review study showed that 9% of men lawyers and 1% of women lawyers earned over $20,000. Today, women law partners who have access to income data maintain that there isn't any disparity between men and women of equal experience.

Women attorneys took a big step toward parity with men when a group of female law students in New York in the early 1970s began a concerted attack against the large New York law firms by filing about a dozen lawsuits alleging discrimination. The suits were filed by the Employment Rights Project, a federally funded program at New York's Columbia University, on behalf of students and graduates.

The suits led to some substantial changes. In 1976, for instance, the firm of Rogers & Wells (of which former Secretary of State William Rogers is a senior partner) settled one suit by agreeing to a complex formula that guarantees, among other things, that the firm will offer over 25% of its positions each year to female graduates. In 1977, the Wall Street law firm of Sullivan & Cromwell settled a case on similar terms.

"In the larger law firms," says Ann G. Miller, a partner in the San Francisco firm of Lillick, McHose & Charles, "I think the blatant discrimination of 10 years ago has disappeared. What you (a female lawyer) may find is a subtle attitude you're uncomfortable with—a subconscious resistance you can't put your finger on because men aren't yet used to women in business situations. It's their social upbringing. All their lives, they've dealt with women as wives, girlfriends and the like: Suddenly they have to face a woman as a hardnosed adversary."

"You can't try to be one of the guys," adds Maryellen Cattani, a partner at Orrick, Herrington, Rowley & Sutcliffe in San Francisco. "You have to establish an asexual working relationship," she says, "and that is difficult."

Some women lawyers recall being turned down by law firms on the ground that "our clients wouldn't deal with a woman." Nowadays, female attorneys say that isn't often a problem. Lawyer Cattani says she has met resistance from clients on one or two occasions, but she adds, "The more sophisticated the transaction, the less likely you are to have a problem."

In the past, female lawyers generally found themselves shunted off into such fields as family law and probate work. Nowadays, women work in every phase of law, but increasingly in areas such as corporate securities, real estate and tax work. Ellene Winn, a partner since 1957 in Bradley, Arant, Rose & White in Birmingham, Ala., is regarded as a municipal-bond expert by fellow lawyers. Unlike most other women lawyers, she says, "I've never seen any discrimination. No one ever gave me the feeling they were doing anything but listening to my legal argument."

Lawyer Winn's self-confidence is echoed by some other women attorneys. Joanne Garvey, a tax specialist and partner in San Francisco's Cotton, Seligman & Ray, says "I never had any doubts that if I tried anything, I'd succeed."

Nearly all the women lawyers who made it into a partnership in a big firm were in the upper 10% of their class, and their associates rate them top-notch lawyers. As the ranks of lawyers grow more crowded, most men and women lawyers find their job options are restricted to joining smaller firms, going into government work or trying to set up a practice on their own. As one lawyer puts it, "If you're only in the mid-range in law school grades, you're going to have a real problem finding a job."

Indeed, a degree of unemployment in the legal profession has been acknowledged recently, providing a potential new obstacle for aspiring women lawyers—and men lawyers, too, for that matter. California offers figures on what current trends portend for the future of lawyers. The state bar says the state's population is expected to rise from 22 million in December 1977 to about 24.3 million by 1984. During the same period, officials say, the number of lawyers is expected to almost double from 58,000 to 90,000. Put another way, instead of the current ratio of one lawyer for every 380 people, 1984 will see one lawyer for every 270 people.

Foreign Assignments

When an American banker named Fredrica Chal-landes-Angelini went to Saudi Arabia to negotiate a loan, her first problem was getting a foot in the door. Literally.

Saudi Arabia generally doesn't allow unaccompanied women into the country—no matter who they are. So Miss Challandes—Angelini took a transit visa—indicating that she was only stopping at the airport before her flight carried her to another destination—and, when no one was looking, she walked out the airport door.

"Once in the country, I had no problems whatsoever," says Miss Challendes-Angelini, who is an assistant vice pesi-dent with Amex Bank Ltd., a London-based subsidiary of American Express Co. "I suppose that if your company has sent you there and you act in a competent mannner, they'll accept you." When the time came for her to leave, her Saudi customers took care ot the exit formalities.

The experience may have been awkward, but it wasn't unusual. It reflects a new development affecting even the most socially restrained parts of the world: Female managers are beginning to move into international business.

"Starting about 2½ years ago, there really began to be more women appearing," says Mary R. Gibbons, a vice presi-dent of Morgan Guaranty Trust Co., who arrived in London in 1974 and was the first woman in a prominent banking post there. "Before, I virtually never spoke to a female on the oth-er end of the line" when calling on business matters, she says. "Now, there will be women, and they will be the people to speak to."

In many ways, that's a predictable extension of the women's movement in the U.S. As more American companies have admitted women to management—either because of en-lightened corporate attitudes or the threat of lawsuits—some women naturally have moved into companies' international operations.

Companies have acted cautiously, however. When one

big American bank considered assigning its first woman over-seas, the decision was deemed so sensitive that it "went all the way to the top," an officer says. The move has worked out well enough that the bank has since sent several women to foreign branches.

Most companies publicly acclaim the wisdom of their decisions to post women overseas, and some prominently feature women managers in advertising campaigns. Henri Debuisser, executive director, personnel and organization, of Rank Xerox Ltd., says: "We have some very capable women executives, both in headquarters and in our marketing operations in Europe. They are well accepted, and we would very much like to see more women of similar caliber in our national and international managements."

However, many observers privately say women often are expected to be of higher caliber than men in similar positions. "She has to be exceptional, outstanding, dynamic, flexible, venturesome—a bundle all rolled into one—before they hire her," says Charles Mannel, director of the career services center at a leading business training ground, the American Graduate School of International Management in Glendale, Ariz.

Moreover, there still aren't many women in foreign posts. U.S.-based companies—which by most accounts are leading the trend—are only beginning to send women abroad, and most of these women are in what one describes as "lower-middle-management positions." Much of the activity has been concentrated in a few fields, such as banking, which generally have led in promoting women at home. It's all so new that neither women's groups nor international organizations have data on the number of women in international management. The trend is almost sure to accelerate, though, because more women are preparing for international careers. Mr. Mannel says his school has had a "phenomenal" growth in women's enrollment; women recently accounted for about one-third of the total, up from one-fourth a year earlier and from only about 2% in 1964.

But despite the changes, the feeling persists in many corporate circles that women can't operate effectively in many foreign economies. Some companies are reluctant to send women overseas for fear of losing business. "Maybe you could put a woman in London," says a male manager with a big American electronics company. "But in the Middle East? Forget it."

However, some big banks and companies *are* sending women to the Mideast—and to Africa, South America and other areas (including much of Europe) generally considered to be male domains. And many women are finding—as Miss Challandes-Angelini's experience suggests—that many presumed barriers to women are more apparent than real. They also are discovering that many of the real barriers aren't quite so formidable when a woman has the backing of a big bank or corporation.

"It's like driving around in a Rolls-Royce," says Yvette M. Newbold, an attorney with Rank Xerox, which is 51%-owned by Xerox Corp. "If you are working for a big and fairly glamorous multinational, it has got to count more than your sex."

Kimberly Albright, who is with Citibank's merchant banking operation in London, probably would agree. She has helped put together loans in Morocco, Turkey, Jordan and Iran, among other places, and says the people there "seem to accept the fact that they are dealing with Citibank and that I will deal with them." She adds that one "revelation" in her travels has been that some clients—such as the financial director of a government-owned development bank in Morocco —have themselves turned out to be women.

Miss Albright says she likes the fact that Citibank "actually will try these things out and test the hypothesis" that women can't work in such parts of the world. She adds, "I think the hypothesis tends not to be true."

Although women sometimes do run into unpleasant situations, Morgan Guaranty's Miss Gibbons, who is involved in syndicating Eurodollar loans, says, "Obviously, there are going to be a few people you're never going to get along with, but I don't think the ratio is any different than for a man in the same position."

Miss Gibbons travels the globe—in one year, she visited 13 countries on three continents—and she says her work experience has been "very successful." For instance, she helped coordinate a $1.2 billion loan to Mexico—an effort that took her to negotiations from London to Frankfurt to New York to Mexico City to Paris. "I believe anyone I come in contact with feels Morgan Guaranty wouldn't put me in the position if I weren't qualified," Miss Gibbons says.

Not all the stories are happy ones, however. One woman banker in Europe requested and received a transfer back to the U.S. because, a colleague says, "The pressures had become too much for her mentally—she had met resistance everywhere." Another woman quit her banking job in Canada because she was convinced that she wasn't being promoted as rapidly as her male associates.

Women often run into difficulties abroad because, except in the Communist bloc, they generally are even more of an oddity in most foreign countries than they are in the U.S. Many female managers are blazing trails—and doing so in countries where the women's movement hasn't had much visibility.

"Companies here haven't gotten to the stage, which they have in the States, of saying, 'We must look at ourselves under a microscope in this context and see if we are discriminating,'" says Anne Mackie, a commissioner with the U.K.'s Equal Opportunity Commission. "They still are at the stage of saying, 'We know there is some (sex discrimination) legislation passed, but we aren't discriminating at the present moment.'"

The state of things was illustrated in a study by the International Labor Organization—a Geneva-based agency of the United Nations—of female employment in Britain, France, Belgium amd Sweden. It found that women's work "generally remains rooted in traditional spheres of feminine activity" and said the recent increase in the numbers of working women "hasn't to any significant extent broadened their range of employment opportunities."

That's partly true in the U.S., of course, but many American women say the climate is worse overseas. "I couldn't believe the atmosphere when I came to London," says one women lawyer with a major American bank. Adds Fredrica Challandes-Angelini: "It's considered much more radical than in the U.S. to voice opinions about women's rights or even to do something as commonplace as calling yourself 'Ms.' Things I might say in the U.S., I wouldn't say here."

Some of the problems are cultural. One woman still smarts over an angry session with a male manager from one of her bank's African operations. The African had flown to London to help draft a corporate position for negotiations with a customer. He apparently hadn't been told that his co-worker would be a woman.

"From the minute I entered the room, he began fighting with me—*fighting* everything I said, in the rudest possible way." the woman recalls. "We couldn't get anywhere—he just didn't want to deal with me. Finally, I said, 'Hey, we're supposed to be on the same side.' "

And finally, after a full hour of arguing, the African "came around," the woman says, and the two got down to business. She thinks the problem was "completely because I am a woman." She explains: "From where he came from in Arica, he had never—absolutely never—had to deal with a woman in business."

Such a cultural lapse isn't all that surprising—just as it isn't very surprising that many women say they have found it difficult to work in male-oriented Japan.

But less predictably, women say the same thing about some West European men. such as the West Germans and French. "They're so chivalrous and so charming to women," one woman says of the French, "but doing business with them is very difficult. It seems to be a totally sexual kind of thing." And London's financial district—known as the City—gets low marks from many women. "The City is the last bastion," says Mrs. Newbold of Rank Xerox. When she worked for a law firm there, she says, "I had my bum pinched more times than when I was on the Italian Riviera."

By contrast, women working in Communist-bloc countries say they are taken seriously and treated well. Anna Ksiezopolska, an American who is Rank Xerox's sales manager for Hungary, says she has had "absolutely no difficulty" there. Working in Eastern Europe, she says, is "easier for a woman than it is in the West." (It isn't easy for an East European woman, however. "As far as work goes, she is treated as an equal," Miss Ksiezopolska says. "But she has two jobs—she is still a housewife.")

Sandra Beers, a second vice president in Chase Manhattan Bank's Moscow office, says the reaction of many customers there has been, "It's about time we saw American women coming over and handling our accounts." Miss Beers is the second woman to work for Chase in Moscow; she previously had traveled for the bank in Eastern Europe.

And Barbara Madgey, an assistant vice president in Crocker National Bank's London office who has worked on loans in Poland and Yogoslavia, says, "It's very easy working there. They have far more women in banking than in the West." She adds that in recent loan negotiations with a major Yugoslav bank, "They always had more women than men around the negotiating table."

Some places unaccustomed to native businesswomen are willing to accept foreign ones. Miss Challendes-Angelini has worked in the Ivory Coast, Gabon and Cameroon, and she says those African countries are "really quite pleasant and straightforward" in accepting Western businesswomen.

Women still have a long way to go, of course. As is true in the U.S., most women overseas aren't in top—or even upper-middle—management ranks. Miss Challandes-Angelini thinks "the real test" of corporate attitudes is "whether they'll but a woman in charge."

Many women think that eventually they will get top posts—and they are making long-range career plans. Citibank's Miss Albright, for instance, says she expects to spend "two or three years" in her London post, then perhaps serve in another foreign assignment. "In my mind, the Eurodollar markets still are growing at a tremendous pace, as the oil countries develop," she says. "To me as a merchant banker, that's where the action is."

The Venturer

Fayetteville, N.Y., a suburb of Syracuse, has its share of business. It has a Sears Roebuck store, a Household Finance office, a Chevrolet dealership. And it has Simply Splendid Studio Inc.

If Simply Splended isn't exactly a household name around the country, it isn't that well known around Fayetteville, either. It is an unusual kind of women's clothing store, and it has been in town just three years. It occupies a Civil War-era clapboard house on a side street near a shopping center.

Its owner is Joan Massey, a 51-year-old divorcee who has been running a nursery school in nearby De Witt for more than 20 years. Mrs. Massey hasn't any illusions about the school ever being very profitable, but she has great plans for Simply Splendid. It could blossom, she is convinced, into a large company with nationwide sales.

Every year, thousands of people—and many of them women—go into business for themselves. Some, like Mrs. Massey, have hopes of turning what they believe is a new idea into a major enterprise. Most, however, would be content to earn a decent living while enjoying the benefits of being their own boss. In either case, starting up and succeeding in a small business is far from being an impossible dream. Of the more than 10 million non-farm businesses operating in the U.S., 95% are considered small businesses by the Small Business Adminstration.

But statistics hardly give a clue to the tremendous effort required by anyone, male or female, to get a new enterprise off the ground. Nor do they hint at the odds against keeping it going any length of time. "Though the survival-probability rates are fragmented or dated, the evidence indicates that the risks have multiplied and the chances of making the grade have not brightened," said Bette Blondin and Rowena Wyant in a report for Dun & Bradstreet, the diversified publishing and marketing services concern.

Difficulties of raising capital, a lack of adequate information, government red tape and problems of day-to-day management all conspire against the entrepreneur. "Whether boom or recession, nine out of ten failures are traceable to managerial inexperience or ineptitude," Dun & Bradstreet says. The obstacles are such that it takes great initiative to strike out on one's own. "You definitely have to be the entrepreneurial type, compulsive, tenacious and a little on the weird side," Joan Massey says.

"Weird" isn't an adjective that those who know Mrs. Massey would apply to her. "Joan is go, go, go," says Miles E. McNeal, a Syracuse resident who is a retired partner of Ernst & Ernst, the big accounting firm. Even so, Simply Splendid has gone through difficult times, and its future is still very much in doubt. A look at Mrs. Massey's experience shows why.

In 1972, she came up with a new idea in women's clothing that seemed to bridge the gap between home sewing and ready-to-wear garments. In part, she was motivated by her own experience in buying clothes. At a shade under five feet, two inches, Mrs. Massey found that little girls' dresses were about the only clothes that came close to fitting her.

She decided to ask other women at a New York State fair if they had similar problems. Of the 2,500 women she asked, 54% said they couldn't buy properly fitting clothes. And 98% of the women who said they bought dress patterns admitted that they didn't know how to alter them for a proper fit. Mrs. Massey also learned that there was a shortage of quality fabrics available to women who sew at home in the Syracuse area.

Her idea has been to provide a selection of fabrics and classic clothing styes to enable customers to "play designer" and create their own coordinated wardrobes. At the Simply Splendid shop, they try on sample garments to get the correct size. At the same time, they decide on the style of neckline and sleeve they want and choose the fabric from large swatches. Using its own patterns, Simply Splended then makes up a package that includes parts of the garment pre-cut to size, the necessary decorations and instructions for sewing the garment. If the customer so desires, the store will put the garment together, but that increases the price 50%. "We're selling a service," not just clothes, Mrs. Massey says.

To many people, Mrs. Massey's approach has merit. "It's a good-enough idea that if she doesn't make it, someone else will," says Dick Davis, vice president of Monarch Fabrics, a New York wholesaler. Marjorie Dorr, a customer for several years, finds her trips to Simply Splendid a better way to shop than wading through clothing racks in a department store. "What you are getting for the same price is quality," she says. "In a department store, you find something for $100, and the seams are falling out of it."

Unlike the typical tale of a small business, Simply Splendid didn't get its start in a garage. That's because the garage and basement in Mrs. Massey's home in De Witt already housed her nursery school. So the showroom of the clothing business initially was tucked into a first-floor bedroom. To reach it, customers had to walk through another room, adapted as a production area. Closets in the bedroom served as display racks. An adjacent bathroom was used as a dressing room.

Most of 1973 was spent in researching the kind of product that the company would offer and in developing patterns. Nursery school mothers were recruited as advisers and models, and local seamstresses were hired to begin cutting the cloth from the patterns. By the end of 1973 the company was able to begin test-selling its product.

As sales increased, three full-time employes were taken on, and a part-time bookkeeper was hired. Costs were still relatively low, and Mrs. Massey was able to finance the business out of her own savings and her nursery-school earnings.

In November 1975 Mrs. Massey took over the mortgage on a $26,000, run-down, eight-room house in Fayetteville and put $20,000 into turning it into a store and production area. This outlay was partly met out of $27,000 in bank loans and partly with a $13,000 loan from her parents.

Mrs. Massey ran into many problems that she hadn't counted on, however. She had expected, for example, to find plenty of information about setting up and running a business such as hers. "I don't believe what's not available," she says. "I have encountered so many pitfalls along the way that could have been avoided if I had had professional services which most small businesses are in no position to afford. There is no organization you can go to. No road maps." Tracking down the information she needed was, she says, "like a detective story."

Other people report similar experiences. "I'm taken aback at the lack of resources that exist for entrepreneurs in what is supposed to be a free-enterprise society," says Beatrice A. Fitzpatrick, executive director of the American Woman's Economic Development Corp., a quasi-federal agency that aids businesses run by women.

Mrs. Massey did go to the Small Business Administration for advice, and she was impressed by what she describes as the agency's "super" brochures. But in terms of the direct assistance that she needed at the start, the SMA wasn't much help, she says. For example, the agency offers the services of SCORE, its Service Corps of Retired Executives who counsel small businesses. But the retired executive sent by the agency to help Simply Splendid was the former vice president of a major soft-drink company. "He told me that he knew as much about small business as he did about flying to the moon,'" Mrs. Massey recalls.

She also found little help at the New York State Department of Commerce. The department did send along a business consultant, but after a few months, he disappeared, the victim of a budgetary cutback.

So Mrs. Massey had to develop her own group of experts by asking for advice wherever she could. Her advisers ranged from Hovey Larrison, president of his own advertising agency (who came up with the Simply Splendid Studio name) to Robert Pietrafesa, president of Learbury Clothes in Syracuse, whose children had attended Mrs. Massey's nursery school.

"I've never seen so many people volunteer for work," says Mike Kisselstein, branch manager for Lincoln First Bank in De Witt, who provided financial advice. One reason was Mrs. Massey's persuasiveness, he says. Another was the vicarious experience of trying to make a new business succeed. "I suspect all of us would have liked to have done what Joan is doing, Mr. Kisselstein says.

Sometimes, though, the help proved costly. Once, an adviser, without consulting Mrs. Massey, changed the quality of paper to be used in a catalog. Mrs. Massey was shocked to discover that the change increased the catalog's cost to $1,500 from the $875 that had been budgeted. She also regrets spending $1,500 on a consultant who failed to find a source of capital.

But much of her free help did pay dividends. Fred F. Hoyt, the 81-year-old retired treasurer of Carrier Corp., plunged into puting Simply Splendid's bookkeeping in order (he says he was "looking for something to do"). He found that the company's bookkeeper, whose only previous experience had been keeping the books in her husband's drugstore, was putting down orders as sales. He also discovered there wasn't any system of cost control. "Generally the small business owner is irked by figure work," he says. "That happened here. You've got to know what costs are, but Joan didn't know what the cost of selling garments was." It was a long time, in fact, before Simply Splendid had a workable cost-control system. Only recently has the accounting and book-keeping setup been improved enough for Mrs. Massey to say, "We're finally getting a system with the information we need."

One of the big boosts for Simply Splendid came from Mr. Pietrafesa of Learbury Clothes, who, among other things, asked his cutting-room foreman, Leonard Annesi, to look at Simply Splendid's production problems. "We probably cut her piece-goods consumption by 30% or more by teaching her to cut more efficiently," Mr. Pietrafesa says.

Mr. Annesi also converted Simply Splendid's patterns from flimsy paper to paper a tenth of an inch thick. "They used to pin needles through paper on every pattern," he says. "With the hard paper, it was easier to fit the patterns to the material and easier to trace without pinning or anything. Before that, they were wasting a half yard per unit. In the course of a year, that adds up to thousands of dollars."

But the biggest problem for Simply Splendid, in common with other fledgling businesses, was the lack of working capital. At one point in 1976, for example, Mrs. Massey was forced to borrow $2,500 from a friend to meet her payroll, which has grown to five full-time employes, four part-timers and 10 seamstresses who are paid on a piecework basis. In the fall of 1977, Mrs. Massey was able to buy her fabric only because of timely investments, in return for stock, of $10,000 by Phyllis Sherwood, a local businesswoman, and of $5,000 by Mrs. Massey's mother. In that year, too, Mrs. Massey put up her house in De Witt as collateral on a $28,000 bank loan; she plowed some of that money into the business and used the balance for living expenses. If she runs short of money, she says, she will sell the house "if I have to." Mrs. Massey still hadn't drawn any salary from her company, although she says its balance sheet was much improved.

Initially, Simply Splendid's fabric orders weren't big enough for Mrs. Massey to worry about asking for credit. But as soon as she began thinking in terms of orders amounting to several thousand dollars rather than several hundred, credit became essential. "The minute you put in a $4,000 order," she says, "you'd be amazed how much trouble it is to get credit." At one point, Simply Splendid went to two factoring concerns (which provide ready cash by buying accounts receivable from manufacturers), but it was turned down flat. The reaction of one was that the company appeared, on paper, to be in bankruptcy. Mrs. Massey recalls.

For a while, Simply Splendid was chronically short of capital partly because the company was growing so rapidly— it needed money faster than money was flowing in. However, in the fiscal year ended in June 1978, another problem arose: The shorage of capital funds hobbled the company's growth. The advertising budget had to be cut in half, and as a result fiscal 1978 sales, which Mrs. Massey had hoped would rise approximately 40%, only about matched the $91,000 of the previous year. "We cut back on advertising because we weren't getting additional capital," she says.

"If I had $100,000 sitting around, this would be a whole different ballgame," she adds. But her efforts to raise large amounts of capital have come to nothing. For one thing, she is still looking for management talent to help her run the business, and she observes, "Investors won't invest if management isn't in place." Moreover, Mrs. Massey herself has little knowledge of money mangement. "Her understanding of financial statements is zero," says one man who has worked with her.

One solution, she says, would be to find a partner, "someone with capital, a feel for business and with skills I don't have." Right now she can't even afford to hire a business manager to take over daily operations. "I'd like to unload some responsibility so I can sleep nights," she says. As it is she devotes seven days a week to Simply Splendid. (The running of the nursery school has been delegated to others.)

Even so, Mrs. Massey is attempting to cut herself loose from the running of the Fayetteville store to concentrate on the company's future. One possible direction, she says, is a nationwide franchise operation. Another is to become the research and design arm of a large company that would distribute the product.

But she realizes that this is all a pipe dream until "we get our act together in Fayetteville." Mr. McNeal, the former Ernst & Ernst partner, observes that she clearly isn't about to settle for running a small clothing store. "She has big ideas, and knowing Joan I wouldn't bet against her," he says. And Frank J. Cleary, president of a graphic design concern in Fayetteville and one of Mrs. Massey's earliest advisers, notes, "I think she's at this point because of her drive. Without that energy, this thing would have blown away some time ago."

Blue-Collar and Happy

It is 7 a.m. at the Boston & Maine Railroad engine terminal in Boston. Dressed in workshirt and jeans, Sandra Bailey is driving a huge diesel locomotive into the repair shop. On the other side of Boston, in the shipyard of Bethlehem Steel Corp., Cherryle Parker is readying her welding torch. And on a construction job-site in Burlington, Mass., Eileen Murphy, who recently completed a carpenter's training course, is getting set to start another workday as an apprentice carpenter.

"For a month, I had a sore back," says Miss Bailey, leaning backward out of the window to follow her foreman's hand signals. "But I like this job. I'm never bored. And with my skills, where else could I earn $300 a week?"

Bostonians Bailey, Parker and Murphy are among women across the country breaking down the barriers in the skilled blue-collar ranks—the high-paying trades, crafts and assembly-line jobs once all but closed to them.

"We'll be seeing more and more women in these jobs, because of a push from the government and a pull from women," says Robert Buchele, an assistant professor of economics at Smith College who specializes in studying sex and race discrimination in employment.

Orchestrating the push from the government, the Labor Department has issued regulations ordering companies with federal contracts of $10,000 or more to meet specific goals for hiring women in all construction craft jobs, such as plumbing and carpentry; women must constitute 3.1% of the work crews in each craft by 1979, 5% by 1980 and 6.9% by 1981. The department also ordered companies and unions that run federally registered apprenticeship programs in these crafts to enroll women at a rate equal to half their percentage of the general work force in any area, or about 20% for most entering classes. And it is investigating 153 coal-mining companies for allegedly widespread discrimination against women and minorities.

The investigaton was prompted by Coal Employment Project, an Oak Ridge, Tenn., group representing a coalition of Appalachian women's groups. Citing statistics showing that 99.8% of all miners and 98% of mining employes are men, the group has filed an administrative complaint with the Office of Contract Compliance Programs in Washington. The complaint charges that the companies violated an executive order prohibiting federal contractors from discriminating, and it seeks an order requiring them to hire one woman for every three men in entry-level jobs until women constitute 20% of the work force.

In Washington, a spokesman for the Bituminous Coal Operators' Association, an industry group, says the coal companies "have been employing women and will continue to do so." But, he adds, "There could have been some problems (in the fields)—women want the jobs, and men want them, too." Arnold Miller, president of the United Mine Workers of America, pledges to support efforts to end any such discrimination.

At the heart of women's efforts in all industries is their push for what they consider a fair share of good-paying jobs. They now may often get equal pay for equal work, but they still have a long way to go in getting equal work. Studies by the Bureau of Labor Statistics show, for example, that craftsmen—95% of whom are men—earn up to an average of $9.39 an hour, while dressmakers—98% of whom are women—earn $3.62 an hour. Prof. Buchele at Smith College observes that women realize not only that skilled jobs "are good, well-paying jobs," but also that in the decade ahead skilled jobs will expand far faster than unskilled ones.

But Prof. Buchele and other observers say women haven't penetrated the skilled blue-collar ranks as much as the white-collar sector and probably won't in the future. Among the reasons is the economic fact of life that skilled blue-collar jobs aren't likely to grow as fast as white-collar employment, they say.

Elizabeth Waldman, a senior economist in the Labor Department, says that although discrimination is easing, particularly among companies, it still hampers women. "Not enough barriers have fallen," especially on the part of unions allowing women to learn these jobs, she asserts. High unemployment in many construction trades and deep-seated "male attitudes of what is appropriate work for women" have contributed to that problem, Prof. Buchele adds.

Both the professor and the government aide say, moreover, that working-class women haven't pushed as hard. "The women's movement is middle-class," Prof. Buchele observes. "So efforts in blue-collar are 10 years behind white-collar." Or as Miss Waldman puts it, "Women aren't thinking of jobs in that way yet."

Sharyn Bahn, a vice president and founder of Women's Enterprises of Boston Inc., a group that helps women land skilled blue-collar jobs, says working-class women have been trained from childhood that there are "men's jobs" and "women's jobs" and thus don't push to get into high-school "shop" courses and then union or company apprenticeships. She says the few women who have broken down barriers on the job find "a hostile, non-supportive environment . . . that can be lonely as hell." Or as Betty Jean Hall, director of Coal Employment Project, puts it: "We get tale after tale of what happens when women apply—the vast majority get laughed out."

Some companies actively seeking women say they can't find many candidates. Despite extensive recruiting in its own plants and in area schools, General Motors Corp. has only 600 women in its class of 16,000 trainees for skilled jobs.

Donald Pfeifer, GM's assistant director of labor relations, observes that many women seem content with lower-paying assembly jobs. He also notes that they often say husbands oppose the long hours of training and study for skilled jobs and that the women could fear male ridicule. Faced with filling a federal goal of about 20% women in the entering class, he all but throws up his hands. "It's unrealistic. No one but hairdressers can do it. We worked like the devil to get those we have," he says.

Other companies say most women just can't handle hard physical work. American Telephone & Telegraph Co., until recently under a consent decree to promote women and minorities, says women have had a "significantly" higher turnover and accident rate in tough outdoor jobs. Donald Liebers, AT&T director of equal opportunity and affirmative action, says the company now prescreens applicants for the necessary physical traits, allows pole-climbing trainees to learn at their own pace rather than keep up with a group, and uses lighter equipment, such as glass-fiber rather than wooden ladders.

"But it will be many years before we find women interested in and capable of performing these heavy jobs," Mr. Liebers says. Indeed, Lucy Cook, a solidly built 39-year-old, returned to her job as a telephone operator after a short stint as an installer. She says that despite a $100-a-week salary differential, she couldn't bear the tough outdoor working conditions, especially in the winter. She recalls, "I was climbing poles at 18 degrees with snow blowing."

But Miss Bahn, the Women's Enterprise's executive, retorts that companies and unions seeking women must bend over backwards to recruit and welcome them and avoid hiring ill-equipped women to fill quotas. "You can't find women by hanging an ad in the men's room," she says. "Once women believe jobs are accessible, they'll come in record numbers."

However, GM's Mr. Pfeifer says the auto company, for one, already is recruiting women from its own plants and area high schools to enter training programs. Often the company uses skilled female workers as "role models" to entice potential candidates, he adds. Yet Mr. Pfeifer says, "Many are called, but few accept." Change will come slowly, he thinks, and "it will take place in the lunchroom when one (skilled female worker) talks with" an unskilled worker.

To appreciate how difficult this process is, consider the case of Sandra Bailey, the Boston & Maine Railroad engineer. Miss Bailey, a tall, curley-haired 23-year-old, says that as a high-school student, she didn't know such jobs existed. "Counselors gear women for something to do when their children go to school," she says. But Miss Bailey, who is self-supporting, needed more challenge than that and wasn't making enough money as an $80-a-week waitress.

She got help from what may seem an unlikely source: the Boston Young Women's Christian Association. In a far cry from the days when YWCAs concentrated on "charm" courses for young girls, the Boston YWCA has initiated a number of programs introducing women and young girls to the so-called nontraditional occupations, the top-paying, skilled blue-collar jobs. The goal: to help women improve their economic status, according to Juliet Brudney, executive director. "Men with high-school diplomas have had the option of entering apprenticeships in the trades," she says, "but women have been relegated to jobs like sales clerks, factory workers and waitresses." So the Boston YWCA has offered federally funded 16-week courses giving women pre-apprenticeship training in four crafts—carpentry, electricity, plumbing, and painting and plastering—plus physical conditioning in pushing, pulling and lifting heavy materials and vocational counseling.

Of the 96 women who graduated in 1977, about 85% found "nontraditional" jobs, the Boston YWCA says—and one of them was Sandra Bailey. She says the course was the key to landing such a job. "I hadn't any opportunity to learn those things, to be pushed toward taking on a new direction," she says. "It takes incredible initiative (for a woman) to do it on her own." She adds that the Boston YWCA also helped directly in finding her job, because the Boston & Maine recruited women through the program.

Today, Miss Bailey is a $300-a-week "hostler," an engineer who moves cars in and out of the railroad yard. Says her foreman, John Doherty: "She's a good hostler. She fits right in with the crew, and takes her lumps like everyone else."

While Miss Bailey's work apparently pleases her foreman, she herself still doesn't feel completely at home on the job. She says that although she didn't run into any overt hostility, she felt at first that the men treated her "differently" and "talked among themselves." She adds that even now she "always stands out, so when I make a mistake, everyone knows." She says: "It's a strain being the only woman. All of the guys talk together and go out for a beer after work. But there's no support for me."

The help that the Boston YWCA gave to Sandra Bailey also has been extended to teen-age girls, in a course called

New Explorations. "The purpose," explains Patricia Wallace, coordinator-counselor, "is exploration, for girls to learn what's available out there." In vocational high schools, she adds, many girls "are still taking traditional 'girl' things. Why? Because of early conditioning at home. Because of fear of being the only girl in a class of 15 boys."

Eleanor DiRusso, a part-time counselor in the program, says most of the girls don't realize how many women are working today. She adds: "I'm shattering a lot of bubbles for them. What I'm saying is threatening. I'm telling them, 'You'll have to work; the sad reality is that many marriages don't work and even if they do, husbands often don't earn enough to support a family.'"

Much like the Boston YWCA, some companies and unions are offering women educational programs as part of the effort to gear up to meet federal hiring regulations. These programs attempt to break down stereotypical notions of men's jobs and women's jobs, give the women the pre-apprenticeship training that they never got in high school "shop" courses, and prepare them physically and emotionally for the job site. For example, the Massachusetts State Building and Construction Trades Council of the AFL-CIO, the trade group for all construction unions in the state, is sponsoring a federally funded program at three sites called Women in Construction Project. The 32-week program, designed to recruit card-carrying union members, offers pre-apprenticeship training in four crafts, physical training and vocational counseling.

Fred Hansen, secretary-treasurer of the council and a carpenter himself, says the unions sponsored the program because they realize that, under the federal regulations, women must get into the trades. "So the best way to deal with women in construction is to have a lot to do with how they get in," he says.

Susan Scully Troy, director of Women in Construction Project, says that 19 of the 104 participants soon dropped out, because of frequent absences, lack of interest in the work or unwillingness to make a further commitment to enter the unions' apprenticeship programs. She says 13 are college graduates—hardly the uneducated and unskilled heads of households that the program planners most wanted. She says, moreover, that some union business agents have had "reservations," although none have been "obstructive." (Indeed, Mr. Hansen says, "Put yourself in the place of a man out of work for a while—now he has to compete with women.")

For their part, some women have balked at the counseling, which they say is condescending and "causes anxiety" where none exists. But Women's Enterprises, under contract to handle the counseling, defends both the biweekly individual sessions and the weekly group sessions, which center around topics such as how to handle an interview or deal with ridicule. Says Mary Keefe, a counselor for the carpenter's training project: "We're here as guides. Women are made fun of on the job, and it begins to get to them. We're saying, 'Give each other support.' "

Despite problems, Women in Construction Project has helped women like Eileen Murphy, 27, the apprentice carpenter. Mrs. Murphy, a divorced mother of two daughters who had been on welfare for eight years, had been hunting unsuccessfully for a job that would pay enough to justify forfeiting a $304-a-month welfare check. She then spotted a newspaper ad for the program that said: "Women build your own future."

A woman with only a high-school education and no skills, Mrs. Murphy decided to build her future in carpentry. She completed the training course (six weeks earlier, she went off welfare) and then entered the union's four-year work-and-study apprenticeship program. As an apprentice carpenter, she is earning $5.38 an hour.

"Men think they have a corner on skills, but it's all practice and logic," she says. "Sure, I feel a little apprehensive about going out on the job. But I have the right to earn a living, too."

Mrs. Murphy can take heart from women like Cherryle Parker, 24, the black welder with Bethlehem Steel. Miss Parker, also a divorced welfare mother of two daughters, had entered a program sponsored by the Boston YWCA. She then enrolled in a welding-trainee program, passed with flying colors and landed her job for $6.26 an hour. Shortly afterward,

Miss Parker marched into the welfare office, presented four pay stubs and canceled her $295 monthly welfare payments. She says she has plans now for "working on my career" to advance to first-class welder.

Deep in the Mines

A huge hydraulic mining machine bites its whirling teeth into a seam of coal while a crew of sweating miners heaves timbers and two-by-fours up against the low, sagging roof. It's 3 a.m. on the "hoot owl" shift, 350 feet underground at Bethlehem Steel Corp.'s Beth-Elkhorn Mine 29 at Jenkins, Ky. And the scene is typical in its dirt and danger.

Without warning, walls tremble and timbers collapse as an avalanche of coal comes crashing down, sending up a roaring cloud of dust. Some miners scatter in all directions, but one of them, a young woman by the name of Sandy Bailey, holds her ground behind a still-intact pillar of coal, "You were lucky this time, Sandy. That rock fall just about killed you," Willis Roberts, one of the foremen, banters across the tunnel.

Mrs. Bailey, covered in dirt and perspiring heavily, gives a grin and says, "I was too tired to budge."

She is, of course, not a typical coal miner. But neither is she a novelty. It's estimated that several thousand women in the U.S. are carving coal out of underground seams. Although these women represent only a fraction of the nation's 150,000 underground coal miners, they are beginning to make themselves felt in an industry that until five years ago was close to being an exclusive male preserve.

In recent years women have established themselves in many traditionally male jobs, from driving trucks to police work. But until quite recently most women simply accepted the notion that an underground coal mine wasn't a "proper place for them to work," in the words of Brigid O'Farrell, a researcher at Wellesley Research Center on Women, Wellesley, Mass. "A coal mine was thought of as a dank and dismal dungeon into which women dare not venture," she says.

Though this view is changing rapidly, "many mining communities still consider underground mining unsafe and unsuitable work for women," according to Helen Lewis, a sociologist at Clinch Valley College in Wise, W. Va. "They still believe that a woman's place is in the home, not in an underground mine." Indeed, resistance to women's working underground can be found in much of the U.S. In several coal-mining states, including Pennsylvania, Ohio, Illinois, Indiana and Wyoming, laws have prohibited women from working underground, although they have become academic because of federal legislation against job discrimination. "A lot of coal companies really don't want women working underground. They feel they have enough labor problems without adding further dissension and conflict," Mrs. Lewis says.

Coal companies don't deny this. They say that strong, century-old superstitions against women working underground persist in many coal-mining areas. "There are still a lot of mines where the men would walk out if a woman went in," says a spokesman for Pittston Coal Co. in New York. "Women have been accepted in some places, but certainly not as far as the industry in general. In many places, it's still like the old days on sailing ships, where women on board were a jinx."

The majority of women miners are clustered in the largest coal companies. These companies, many of them owned by steel or oil concerns, have hired women as a result of intense government pressure to comply with anti-discrimination legislation. But these companies have been criticized within the industry for their compliance.

Bethlehem Steel, for example, was rebuked when it became the first major concern to break with tradition and send women underground at its Beth-Elkhorn subsidiary in Jenkins. "We were told quite bluntly by some operators that they thought we were going too fast in implementing the laws," says Dave Zegeer, manager of Beth-Elkhorn's mining operations.

Bethlehem Steel is now the largest employer of women miners in the U.S., with women working underground at its mines in Kentucky, Pennsylvania and West Virginia. Most of the women are divorced, widowed or married to disabled miners, and many of them provide the sole means of support for their families. The relatively high pay, the improved fringe benefits, job security and better opportunities for advancement are the main reasons why women choose to work underground, according to Bethlehem Steel.

Before 29-year-old Sandy Bailey went to work at the Jenkins mine, she had driven a bus for senior citizens and had worked in a shoe factory. "When I became a miner, I just about tripled my income," she says. "There just aren't any other jobs around here that pay that kind of money."

Mrs. Bailey's husband, Robert, who runs a carpet-cleaning business, says he earns less money than his wife and has been trying "to get into the mines myself." However, the mining companies, except in the case of women, will usually only hire miners with experience.

But Mrs. Bailey earns her salary, both in the work that she does and in the life style that her job forces on her and her family. The Baileys have three young children and live in a trailer in Cram Creek, Ky., about a 40-mile drive from the mine. Because she works on the midnight to 8 a.m. shift, her time with her children is limited. Fortunately, her mother lives next door and her sister nearby.

Despite increasing mechanization, underground mining is still hard, backbreaking work. Mrs. Bailey is employed as a GI, or general inside laborer. Working inside tunnels, commonly only four feet high, she is routinely called on to shovel coal onto conveyor belts, to lay track for the coal-hauling shuttle cars or to drag mining-machinery power cables. She also sprays the mine walls with limestone to hold down dust, and she builds brattices, or partitions made of convas or plastic, to channel filtered air through the tunnels into work areas. In addition, she is assigned to general cleanup—about the equivalent of an "underground garbage man," she says.

The danger in Mrs. Bailey's job is greatest when she is assigned to "pillar work," which involves removing the columns of coal supporting the roof (which have been carved out by the mining machines) and allowing the roof to fall in. The surrounding roof is shored up with heavy timbers. "You can't control everything. Rock falls can kill you no matter how cautious you are," Mrs. Bailey says. No wonder her husband says that "sometimes I wake up at night and worry whether she's been buried by a roof fall."

"It's hard work for a man, let alone a woman," says

Joe Adams, the foreman. But Mrs. Bailey is stocky—150 pounds and five feet, four inches—and she's "not the timid type; she'll try anything," Mr. Adams says. "Sandy hangs in there with the best of them. She's got good sense and a lot of guts. I'd say she's a real fine worker."

Mrs. Bailey is modest about doing a job that few men, let alone women, would relish. "Sometimes I feel like my job is no different than household work,." she says. "A GI picks up after everybody else has made their mess. That's about all that I do at home, too."

Down in those dark, narrow tunnels, the normal niceties of sexual distinctions become blurred. There are no toilet facilities, for example. Instead, Mrs. Bailey says, "you look for some privacy—it was embarrassing at first when I didn't know my way around, because I'd have to ask the foreman to direct me to a place where I could have some privacy."

Mrs. Bailey could improve her working conditions by applying for the more highly skilled and better-paying jobs in the mine; such jobs are awarded on the basis of seniority and qualifications. But, she says, for the present she is content to be a GI because she doesn't want to be stuck in another job that she might not like as well.

Perhaps a more important reason why she hasn't sought another job is that it might require her to transfer to another crew. That is an important consideration for a female miner. "I'm accepted here," she says. "But if I was on another section, it might be different. Some miners might not be so willing to accept a woman."

Generally, the men have treated her well. There was a miner, she says, who in her early days underground, snarled, "What the hell are you doing here?" But, she says, "I really told him off, and after that we really became good friends." Actually, her worst experience was her best. The miners painted her face green as an initiation rite. Says Mrs. Bailey, "If they don't do these things, you know you're not being accepted."

Other women miners haven't adjusted so well. "I was afraid I was going to be resented and mistreated here," says Loretta Ruth, who at the time had worked at the Beth-Elkhorn mine only a few months. "I haven't been yet, but I still have apprehensions about it," she says.

Such fears aren't entirely unfounded. In December 1973, when Beth-Elkhorn hired its first women miners at Mine 29, the company decided to use part of the men's bathhouse as a temporary shower facility for the women until a permanent facility could be built. But the miners apparently weren't in the mood to accommodate the women and walked off the job in protest. "We finally ended the strike, but only after the men got their lockers back," according to one of the foremen. "The men felt the women were intruding on them, and I agree. After all, they were here first."

Most companies try to keep such conflicts to a minimum. At first, Island Creek Coal Co. had all 15 of its women miners working one mine near Richlands, Va. Thurston Strunk, president of Island Creek's Virginia Pocohantas division, explains why: "It's a matter of facilities. Rather than build facilities for the women at every mine, we have them at one mine." Also, he says. "You never know what the reaction of the men will be. If there's resentment; we'd rather have it concentrated at one mine than all mines."

Indeed, there is resentment. "Women don't belong here; they're nothing but bad luck," grumbles an old miner at Mine 29 as he spits out a wad of chewing tobacco. "They're just a bunch of goldbrickers out to make a fast buck," adds another miner.

Some of the hottest opposition to women working underground has come from miners' wives. At a rally in Logan, W.Va., a group of wives protesting the proposed hiring of women miners in the area picketed a nearby mine, and it was forced to close for a time.

One of those who participated in the protest, Beulah Whitman, says she thinks it's "immoral" that women are working underground. "No decent woman would want to work there," she sniffs. "There aren't even toilet facilities." She also notes that miners often use language "not becoming to a lady." She adds, "Distance is decency."

Charles Gilliam, a state legislator from Logan who has led efforts to bar women from mines, concedes that the wives' opposition may partly stem from jealousy. "I suppose some of them think there may be something going on down there with their menfolk," he says. He says he opposes women in the mines "because they're going to take jobs away from the men and cause coal prices to go up, because it will take two women to do the work of one man."

There aren't any studies to indicate this is so. To the contrary, some coal companies say they have experienced less turnover, lower absenteeism and even improved production in mines where women are working. They also contend that women miners are more ambitious than men and more conscientious about their work.

"Women are a very welcome source of labor for us," says Howard Frey, executive vice president of Westmoreland Coal Co. In fact, some of the women miners at the company's Stonega division enrolled in training programs to become foremen. "They want to learn to become first-rate professional miners," Mr. Frey says.

Yet the opposition remains. And it has touched Sandy Bailey in a very personal way. She says some of her own relatives have given her the cold shoulder for working in the mines. "I have two brothers-in-law who won't even speak to me anymore," she says. Mrs. Bailey's husband, Robert, also has been ridiculed. "I get asked all the time, 'How come you let your wife work in there?'," he says.

Even Edna Meade, Mrs. Bailey's mother, feels the criticism. "One time I was boasting to one of the women hereabout how proud I was of my daughter, and I was told real quick, 'Your daughter has no business in the mines,'" Mrs. Meade recalls.

While Mrs. Bailey may not be accepted in the community, she is making inroads in the union. Roger Bates, president of United Mine Workers Local 1812 at Mine 29, says Mrs. Bailey already is serving on various local committees, and she even drafted a resolution calling for a maternity-leave policy that was adopted at a UMW convention.

At first, the miners were wary of having a woman present at Local 1812's meetings, Mr. Bates says. But apparently they have come to appreciate her. "She attends all the meetings and brings up good points. When Sandy says something, the men listen," he says. At a meeting, for example, Mrs. Bai-

ley said that when Mr. Bates recites the union's "oath of obligation" to uphold union principles and never wrong a
"brother," he should also say "sister." She explained, "I have
a right to expect people not to wrong me, too." Her suggestion was dutifully adopted.

But there is one veteran woman miner who turns up
her nose at the new crop of miners. She is 73-year-old Violet
Smith, the tobacco-chewing, chief operating officer of the
family-owned King Coal Co. in Hesperus, Colo. Mrs. Smith,
whose husband is second in command at the company, declares, "I've been working 49 years in the mines—five of them
underground—and I ain't found a man yet who can do the
work I can. So why should I think these libbers can do any
better?"

Swapping Cars

Certain trades in this world are notoriously macho—professional football, for instance. Then there is automobile sales.

Car salesmen are aggressive, demanding, always in a hurry and sometimes hard to get along with. Most of all, it seems, they have a hard time getting along with other car salesmen. They tend to be men.

All of which makes it noteworthy that—and helps explain why—a little firm here called Dealers Exchange is staffed almost entirely by women and occupies a prominent if specialized niche in the auto industry. It is the only national company arranging swaps of cars and trucks between dealerships, and all 41 of its field representatives are women.

"To say that men are less capable than women at this job is a bit of an understatement," says Jean Alderson, one of the representatives. "They're totally helpless at it, bless their hearts." The exchange has tried. In recent years it has hired seven men, but they couldn't cope with impatient and sometimes abusive auto salesmen seeking a certain car for a customer who wouldn't wait. Two of the men had to be fired, and the others quit after less than two months.

It all stems from the staggering variety of models, engines, colors and options now available on American automobiles; theoretically, at least, there are more than two million permutations offered at Ford Motor Co. alone.

Let us suppose that Morey Sharkskin at Belchfire Motors has a customer who wants—insists on—a dove-gray Lincoln Mark IV, a Cartier designer model with lumbar massage seats and quad stereo. A rep for the exchange gets a panic call from Mr. Sharkskin, who doesn't have the car in his lot and sees a healthy commission vanishing. The exchange's rep scans the weekly inventory sheets from auto makers showing which dealers in their area have what, and finds an auto at Bonanza Motors that more or less meets the needs of Belchfire. The field rep then calls Bonanza to make sure the car hasn't been sold, and tries to secure it for Belchfire (reminding Bonanza, if necessary, that it has received special favors in the past). The dealers settle the details between themselves.

The only man around the exchange is James Smeed, who carries the title of president but in practice concentrates on his duties as chief executive of Dynasonics Corp., the parent concern of the exchange. The exchange is run by vice president and general manager Claire Holmes, a slender ex-dancer who wears crisp polka-dotted dresses, speaks in the lilting inflections of a finishing school headmistress and calls the employes "my girls."

The girls have done well by Mr. Smeed. In 1977, the exchange, operating from 20 offices nationwide, swapped more than 180,000 cars and trucks for some 1,650 dealerships and turned a profit of $192,000 on revenue of about $1.2 million. The exchange charges subscribing dealers a monthly membership fee ranging from $15 to $27 and gets a few dollars per trade on top of that.

Dealers are grateful for the service that can make them hundreds or thousands of dollars on a sale. But trading doesn't always go smoothly. "When they call, they have customers and commissions at stake," says general manager Holmes. "They could be angry. They could be frantic. They are exuberant, aggressive people. It's important to talk to them with a smile in your voice."

To this end, Mrs. Holmes trains employes in grammar, voice modulation and the arts of persuasion and conciliation. The latter often is necessary, as some dealers are suspicious of each other. Exchange president Smeed says that some time ago Ford dealers in the Chicago area were notorious for feuds that lasted for years, often sparked by trades in which some dealers got cars with missing hubcaps, lighters and other small accessories.

At one point, he adds, a third of the Ford dealers in the region refused to trade with one another—until exchange reps shamed them into it by offering to guarantee that cars they traded would be fully equipped or the women would pay for missing parts themselves.

Male employes at the exchange haven't been able to develop the pleasant unflappability essential to the job; confronted with an aggressive client, they get aggressive right back. One man was fired after blowing up at a pushy auto salesman and showering him with epithets.

Dealers say they would rather do business with women anyway, as some male exchange employes have discovered. One hapless recruit kept fielding phone calls only to be told by the salesmen that they wanted to talk to one of his female colleagues. He quit after a few days, unable to make a single trade. "I'd rather talk to a woman than a man," says Jay Alberstein, sales manager for Mahoney & O'Dell, a Ford dealership in Visalia, Calif. "They work harder, are more fun to talk to, and they're more patient than men."

They've also done a better job at running the exchange. In 1970 Mr. Smeed sold the business to Dynasonics, which put three men in charge of exchange operations. But within six months, he says, profits plunged 80%, and he began a legal battle in which he eventually regained control of the exchange and Dynasonics as well.

The women who handle the exchange phones have varied backgrounds. Edie Smith in Dallas was a cosmetologist, Mary Risheberger in Cincinnati was a singer and Amy Wartman in Cleveland was a nun. A good field representative can make $11,000 to $13,000 a year in salary and bonuses for trades, plus extras like flowers and candy from customers. (Offers of dates from salesmen must be rejected under exchange policy.)

In time, the field reps often develop friendships with salesmen and dealers. "You really care whether they get their cars or not," one woman says. Sometimes they don't, particularly when they make a mistake in ordering and ask the exchange to unload the results.

One Southern California dealer ordered five huge Lincoln sedans bristling with extras—but without air conditioning. No one was willing to trade. Another dealer, who found himself with three big station wagons also loaded with options but lacking automatic transmission, was luckier; he eventually sold them to three Texans who loved the luxuries but wanted to grind the gears themselves.

Dealers Exchange, which mainly has been servicing Ford dealers, now is expanding and doing business with General Motors dealers and others as well. It's possible for dealers to locate cars for trade themselves, of course; Ford, for example, provides dealers with microfiche shipment reports of their own. But many dealers find it easier and quicker to work through the exchange. "They can invent any system they want." Mr. Smeed says, "but you can't take the people out of the auto business."

Section III

The Old Standbys

Not all working women are breaking new occupational ground, of course. Thousands upon thousands of them still fill jobs traditionally considered women's work—such as secretaries, nurses, domestic help, schoolteachers, store clerks, telephone operators.

But even some of these occupations have been changing significantly over the years. In this section of Women at Work, we examine three of them.

The first chapter describes what is involved in selling Mary Kay cosmetics. That work may not seem, at first blush, very sophisticated. However, as you read the description of how these women actually sell the cosmetics, you are likely to conclude that selling cosmetics can be very sophisticated indeed and that a woman who succeeds with Mary Kay probably could succeed in many other kinds of sales work as well.

The next chapter, Tips for Experts, is about cocktail waitresses. People in the cocktail-bar business have come to realize that a truly expert waitress is practically worth her weight in caviar. So now schools have been set up expressly to teach beginners the fine points of a job that's a lot harder than it looks—if done well.

And in Up on the Farm, you meet a modern farm wife. Although city folk may get an instant vision of someone hopelessly mired in the past, that notion is wrong. Donna Keppy, who helps her husband farm 235 acres in Iowa, plays a far wider role than did millions upon millions of her predecessors through history. And while the brute physical work of farming hasn't been completely eliminated, it isn't as relentless as it used to be; meanwhile, the need for managerial talent is growing constantly. Because of those changes, Mrs. Keppy does far more than cook meals, raise children and tend the garden. She has become, in fact, her husband's business partner.

Selling for Mary Kay

Inside the Dallas Convention Center on Mary Kay Cosmetics Awards Night, the tension is pore-tightening. The eyes of 7,500 Mary Kay beauty consultants are on the glittering black and silver stage set, dark except for a mountain of lighted stairs at stage center.

Then a sudden drum roll, and to the squeals, cheers and ecstatic applause of "her girls," Mary Kay Ash, company founder and chairwoman, rises slowly out of the top of the stairs on a hydraulic platform, like a golden figure emerging from a neon cake.

"Each of you can have all the applause," promises the round, blond-wigged woman whose smooth face belies her 60-some years. "Each of you can have the spotlight." Dozens of the company's top saleswomen from the U.S., Canada and Australia then proceed to claim just that onstage, along with expensive prizes—mink coats, gold and diamond jewelry, trips to Acapulco, and the use of new pale-pink Cadillacs and Buicks.

As she watches Mary Kay crown the Queen of Sales with a diamond tiara, a tearful consultant in the back row vows that she will be on stage next year. "I'm going to go home and sell Mary Kay to everything that moves," she says.

Colorful pageantry, costly incentives, and dabs of behavioral psychology are basic at Mary Kay Cosmetics Inc., which spent more than $1 million on its extravagant three-day sales seminar to inspire and teach its independent beauty consultants—whose numbers total 40,000—to sell more of the company's skin-care products. Such techniques sell $48 million of cosmetics a year to some seven million customers and make Mary Kay Cosmetics, along with Avon and Tupperware, one of the few successful direct-selling companies still homing in on sales in America's living rooms.

The Dallas company was founded in 1963 by Mary Kay Ash, then a retired saleswoman equipped with $5,000, plus a product whipped up by a hide-tanner and a sales plan that worked without a wrinkle. Having no franchises, no distributorships, and no advertising budget, the company earned a tidy $6 million in 1977 and paid for its chic $7 million headquarters in Dallas as it went up.

The foundation of the company is its sales force, the "consultants" who soft-sell the company's skin-care products at home demonstration shows using charm, positive reinforcement and subliminal persuasion.

In a living room in North Dallas, Zoe Hall, an 11-year veteran of Mary Kay home beauty shows, is telling three women how Mary Kay Cosmetics evolved from the experiments of a tanner who used hide-tanning principles on his own skin and, at age 73, was said to have a remarkably youthful appearance.

Nicki, a perky Dallas woman, has come to the show at the urging of friends who were "overjoyed with the product," she says. Hazel and Dixie, two skeptical women from nearby Irving, Texas, were invited over their CB radio in a highway conversation with another Mary Kay consultant.

In front of each woman is a mirror and a square Styrofoam palette with blobs of cream, different shades of foundation and rouge, and little heaps of colored powders. As Mrs. Hall gives instructions, each woman uses the cleansing cream, the oatmeal masque, and the skin toner, and applies her own face and eye makeup. (Consultants don't apply makeup to their customers, because of cosmetology licensing requirements in some states.)

Mrs. Hall has diagnosed Dixie's skin as especially oily, and prescirbes Mary Kay's special water-based products. "Oh, this is your lucky day," she exclaims, patting Dixie excitedly on the arm. Mrs. Hall hasn't any doubt about the outcome of her sales talk. "You're going to be so pleased when you take this home," she tells Dixie.

Assuming a sale is part of the positive psychology the consultants are taught by their sales directors and their Mary Kay handbooks. "Nod your head yes when you're talking to your customers—it's a mild form of hypnosis," Beverly Sutton, a senior sales director from Tulsa, tells 300 consultants at a seminar class on selling techniques. "Look them in their right eye because the right eye controls—that's also a form of hypnosis. Phrase questions to get a yes answer. Touch the customer often to show you care. And when it comes time to sell, give them a full, complete set of all the products. If they hold it all, they'll want it all."

With Mrs. Hall's help, Nicki, Hazel and Dixie have finished making up their faces, and with Mrs. Hall's help, now are making up their minds which Mary Kay products they can't live without. "You can really feel the difference in your skin, can't you?" Mrs. Hall asks, nodding.

Hazel nods back. She buys $54 worth of Mary Kay products, and wants to buy more, but can't afford to. Mrs. Hall tells her she can earn the money for more by inviting Mrs. Hall to come to her home in Irving to give a show to six of Hazel's friends. Hazel agrees. As the hostess, Hazel will get 10% of Mrs. Hall's sales at that show—15% or 20% if she can get one or two of those friends to host shows, too. Mrs. Hall will get access to six new customers, plus a chance to book more shows.

Nicki is so impressed that she is recruited to be a consultant herself. She buys $32 worth of Mary Kay and agrees to talk with Mrs. Hall later over coffee about the Mary Kay opportunity.

Dixie alone is unconverted. She says no, she doesn't think she'll take anything today. But to Mary Kay consultants, no isn't a final answer. "Remember," reads the Mary Kay consultants' handbook, "When a woman says 'No,' she means 'Maybe,' and when a woman says 'Maybe,' she means 'Yes.'" "O-Oh," Mrs. Hall says ruefully to Dixie, "and the special cream did *such* nice things for your problem skin. Isn't there some way you could take this home with you so you can get started on good skin care right away?" Alarmed by Mrs. Hall's tone of emergency, Dixie sneaks a worried look at herself in the mirror, and says, "Well, maybe. . . ." She takes $37 worth of special skin products home with her.

A customer gets no time between payment and delivery to change her mind. Consultants like Mrs. Hall pay cash in advance for enough inventory of the company's limited product line to fill any customer orders on the spot. "Women are impulse buyers," says Mary Kay. "They buy more when they can have it right away."

At Mrs. Hall's afternoon show, she sells $123 of merchandise retail. She will keep 50% of the total—$61.50 for three hours of work.

The generous sales commissions are what recruit most consultants into Mary Kay. Salaries for an active consultant range between $600 and $800 a month for about a 20-hour work-week. Established consultants needn't hold daily shows —almost 35% of their sales volume is reorder, and hundreds of consultants live on reorder sales alone. "I earn as much in eight hours as a Mary Kay consultant as I used to make in a week as a bank teller," says Robin Hiebel of San Antonio, who has worked selling Mary Kay for only five months.

Like Mrs. Hiebel, most consultants are younger women, married with one or two children, and working to supplement their husbands' middle-income salaries. The company also has a few hundred male consultants, as well as several husband-and-wife consultant teams.

The 17 national sales directors—the company's top saleswomen—average $56,000 annually, according to Richard Rogers, Mary Kay's president and Mary Kay Ash's son. And because the consultants are independent business people, they are entitled to tax deductions on rooms in their home used for business, depreciation on their car, clothing, travel, child-care, gasoline, and other job-related expenses.

Recruiting new consultants is profitable as well. By adding Nicki to her unit, Mrs. Hall increased her chance to win the use of a new pink Cadillac for a year. Her unit must have a wholesesale volume of $30,000 for two consecutive calendar quarters to qualify for the luxury car, then maintain that sales level or take over part of the leasing payments. The company currently has 380 pink Cadillacs under lease, and, says Mary Kay, "They're the best advertising we have. The company depends on word-of-mouth for publicity. "It works," Mary Kay says, "The three ways to get word out fast are telephone, telegraph, and tell a woman."

The key to success in Mary Kay is self-motivation. To give them courage and energy, consultants are offered inspirational poems, tapes, books and classes. At a seminar class entitled "Controlling Attitude and Motivating Self," sales director Luella Gunter suggests daily Bible reading and practicing thought repetition.

"I have learned through Mary Kay to control my thoughts," she tells her students. "To stop procrastination, repeat 50 to 100 times a day: Do it now. Do it now. Do it now. After one week, you will have an indelible tape on your brain that will automatically snap on whenever you put something off. Isn't that a comforting thought?"

Consultants also get motivation at weekly meetings of their sales unit, where they try role-playing to discover how to overcome objections, listen to little sales sermons, receive ribbons for their sales accomplishments, and sing spirited songs. At a recent meeting of part of Dallas sales director Helen McVoy's "Mighty Macs" unit, about 175 women were jumping up and down enthusiastically, and pointing to appropriate parts of themselves as they sang:

I've got that Mary Kay enthusiasm
Up in my head,
Down in my heart,
Down in my feet.
I've got that Mary Kay enthusiasm
All over me
All over me to stay-ay-ay.

"When I first started with Mary Kay eight years ago, those silly songs nearly did me in," says Mrs. McVoy, a gracious, likable woman who in 1977 led the company with a salary of $118,000. "But you know, it works. Enthusiasm is part of the Mary Kay sales plan."

That plan includes keeping the product line limited and portable, selling direct to the consultant, and giving commissions on retail sales only. There aren't any territorial limits on where a consultant may sell or recruit. All a new consultant needs to start is a $65 beauty case; advancement is made on the basis of sales volume and recruiting skill alone.

Mary Kay Ash devised the plan herself on the basis of her 25 years of direct-selling for Stanley Home Products, a housewares party-plan company, and World Gift, a decorative-accessories company. She was a top salesperson in both companies, and when she left World Gift in 1963, was making an annual salary of $25,000. (She now draws a salary of $100,000 a year, and owns $7.5 million in Mary Kay stock.)

She retired, intending to put her acquired sales techniques into a book. But, instead, she put them into practice. For 10 years, she had been using a private-label skin treatment, purchased from the tanner's granddaughter. Mary Kay bought the formulas and started business with 10 beauty consultants.

"Cosmetics was a perfect business, because every woman at 20 is an expert at make-up," says Mary Kay. "I wanted to establish a company where any woman could have the opportunity to share in the great American dream, yet still be free to do what comes first for women." Consultants are taught that their priorities must be God first, family second, and career third. "I'm chairman of the board at the office," says Mary Kay. "But I'm Mel Ash's wife at home."

Tips for Experts

You have to have the memory of an elephant and the hide of a rhino to do the job well—but no physical resemblance to either, please. If you qualify, you can easily become one of the highest-paid hourly workers in the labor force and probably hide most of what you make from the Internal Revenue Service.

The job is cocktail waitress, and the pay can range up to $25,000 a year, almost all of it in tips that are often underreported to the tax collector. There isn't any shortage of women who want to be cocktail waitresses—clubs and bars are regularly deluged with applicants, who run heavily to divorcees and college students—but there is an acute shortage of skilled ones.

"It's very hard to find anyone good at it," grumbles Jack Gibson, an assistant manager at the Don Jose Disco-Restaurant in Fullerton, Calif. Charles Chop, president of the U.S. Bartenders Guild, says only 5% to 10% of the cocktail waitresses now working are competent.

To plug this yawning gap in the labor force, some entrepreneurs are setting up schools to teach aspirants how to order drinks, dodge passes from lecherous topers, and keep booze flowing as rapidly as possible down as many gullets as they can. One is Southern California Cocktail Waitresses Inc., located in Irvine, Calif., and owned by former Playboy bunny Peg Dameron. A bar owner previously, she hired "one turkey after another" to serve drinks and decided to open the Irvine school after her own place had burned down.

The two-week course costs $150, and there is much to learn—including the contents of some 200 mixed drinks, the order in which they must be given to the bartender and the abbreviated jargon used in the trade.

The goal is speed . An efficient and genial waitress can "make or break a bar," says a personnel manager for Host International Inc., which operates many at large airports.

Lynne Jorgensen, another former Bunny, makes the difference at the Saloon, a Beverly Hills watering hole; when she is on duty, bar volume increases about 50%. says Howard Rosov, the owner. "She's the best cocktail waitress in Los Angeles," he crows.

At Miss Dameron's school, which includes a somewhat dingy simulated bar, aspirants continually shuffle through three-by-five cards listing drink ingredients; they must know them because the bartender's glassware and liquor stocks are arranged in a certain way, and drink requests must be given so as to save him as much movement as possible. Besides standard cocktails, trainees have to learn about such exotica as the Skip and Go Naked (a potent combination of gin, beer and sweet and sour mix), the Dirty Mother (brandy and Kahlua on the rocks), and the Freddy Fudpucker (tequila, orange juice and Galliano).

The orders are given to the barkeep in a staccato stream of bar argot, again to save time. A party may, for example, order a weak Jack Daniel's with water, a margarita without salt, a Harvey Wallbanger, a Scotch and soda, a Scotch and water, a Presbyterian (bourbon, soda and ginger, with a lemon twist), and a Perfect Manhattan (bourbon and sweet and dry vermouth, with a lemon twist). The bartender hears this: "Tall Dan water, Scotch left and right, a Press, a Perfect Man, a topless Maggie, a Banger."

Written orders are verboten; too much time is wasted. Instead, candidates are given extensive memory training so that they can keep a score or more of orders in their heads and remember who ordered them.

Charley Brandon, who now worked part time as an instructor at a Dameron-franchised school in San Diego (there is one other franchise, in Long Beach), is famed for her recall. Claude Waymore, a banquet manager at Culpepper's, a dinner house there, says the former hoofer for the Bob Hope USO troupe took 45 orders at once at a luncheon for golf pros and brought a second round later, all without a single error, She got a $100 tip.

Waitresses are taught to circulate constantly among their tables, looking for empty or near-empty glasses and getting more orders. Psychology helps; if a hardened imbiber in one party finishes his first drink long before the others, a waitress may say, "You're not going to let him drink alone, are you?" If a couple are waiting for dinner and have had one drink each, a canny waitress will ask whether she can "freshen" their cocktails rather than baldly ask whether they want another drink; they may feel guilty about having two. "Sometimes you'll freshen one cocktail 10 times," Charley Brandon says.

All the brains and energy in the world, however, won't help the aspirant with a frightful figure and a face only a mother could love. The keystone of the bar business is still the affluent male, and part of the training at the Dameron school is concerned with diet, beauty tips, and how a waitress can best display her attributes.

The waitresses are taught, however, to move too fast for most passes to land. If they do land, waitresses are instructed to call the manager and never try to handle the situation themselves. Waitresses without training often try to cope with other problems themselves, at their peril. At the Palomino, a country-and-Western club in North Hollywood, one besotted member of a singing group recently took offense at a waitress's announcement that the bar was closed, and took a drunken swing at her—after she had poured a pitcher of beer over his head. He missed.

Some customers view cocktail waitresses as floozies, and the women are affronted. "It's almost as if the people equated the job with prostitution," says Janie, who left a position as a dental hygienist because she was tired of "inflicting pain." She adds: "I gave up a high-paying job for this one, and it takes a lot of know-how, a good personality and quick wit."

Janie, a graduate of the Dameron-franchised San Diego school, now makes $50 to $60 a night per four-hour work turn at a popular bar-restaurant there. Most of the income is unreported. "I like escaping the IRS," she gloats. "For the first time in my life I'm getting away with something." Says one IRS official: "I can't imagine a worse employe group when it comes to reporting true income."

Miss Dameron's graduates haven't had any trouble finding work, and neither have those from an even newer school in Los Angeles owned by hefty, gravel-voiced James Scarborough, proprietor of the Major School of Bartending there. together, the two have turned out more than 500 graduates and assert that all have gotten jobs, most of them immediately. Both Miss Dameron and Mr. Scarborough now plan big expansions through franchising.

Most employers seem pleased with the graduates they have hired, though a few grumble that some of the women, though well-trained, are "flaky" or unreliable. Miss Dameron concedes that some waitresses occasionally live up to the occupational reputation for "taking off with any guy with a motorcycle and a six-pack. Some do exactly that, and I could break their necks. It doesn't do business any good."

Up on the Farm

The tractor's roar breaks the silence of the sunny Iowa day. Ignoring the din, the driver concentrates on plowing a muddy cornfield. Suddenly, the tractor becomes stuck in a quagmire of manure and mud. The driver shifts the throttle, raises the plow and twists the steering wheel about.

But the tires grind deeper. The stench is overwhelming. Finally, after lip-biting effort, Donna Keppy frees the tractor. "I knew that as long as we kept moving, we'd make it," she says.

The statement fairly sums up 40-year-old Mrs. Keppy, too. In her busy, expanded role as a modern farmer's wife, she helps her husband, Allen, run a prosperous hog and grain farm at Wilton, Iowa. Mrs. Keppy is much more than a field hand, however. Though the roles of America's two million farm wives vary widely, Mrs. Keppy perhaps typifies a new breed. She's her husband's business partner, involved in nearly all aspects of their complex farming operation—from planting to harvesting their 235 acres and from breeding to marketing 2,500 hogs a year.

Some agricultural experts believe the long-term outlook for family farms like the Keppys' depends on whether more food producers have partners in marriage who are also partners in farming. Mrs. Keppy represents "the type of farm wife we're going to see more of in the future," says Keith Hefferman, a friend of the Keppys and director of agricultural promotion for the Iowa Development Commission. "That's the only way the family farm is going to make it."

The role of the contemporary farm wife is a far cry from that a generation ago. Back then, homemaking, raising children, growing and canning produce and possibly feeding chickens consumed most of the farm wife's time. Heavy farm chores were "men's work," as were business decisions such as crop plantings, marketing or equipment purchases. And a farmer's wife who "kept the books" was more likely to handle family photograph albums than farm bookkeeping.

Today, "farm wives are working more with their husbands and at a more sophisticated level," says Calvin L. Beale, who directs population studies for the U.S. Department of Agriculture's Economic Research Service. A poll of 12,000 Successful Farming magazine readers confirmed his view; it found, for example, that three-fourths of the wives participate in farm business decisions. And the role of women in farming seems likely to increase even further. As total enrollments in the agricultural schools of the 72 land-grant colleges have soared, so too have the numbers of female students at these schools. By the fall of 1977, female ag students had risen to 30,989, or about 30% of the schools' total, from 13,953, or about 19% of the total, four years earlier.

Effects of these changes are rippling throughout agribusiness. Farm-equipment makers say women's greater role in field work is one reason tractors are being made easier to operate and more comfortable, with such options as power-assisted clutches and air-conditioned, carpeted cabs. Many equipment dealers, now catering to female customers, are setting up ladies' waiting lounges stocked with women's magazines. And some farm wives have become political activists, promoting agriculture and pushing, before legislators and television cameras, for what they consider fair crop prices.

The widening horizons of farm wives reflect, in part, changes in agriculture generally. More and more family farms have reduced their hired hands, gone heavily into debt to expand and mechanize, and emerged as highly specialized businesses. As the number of such operations grows, more of the total food supply is being produced by large farms. And this growing complexity and replacement of brute force with managerial talent are contributing to farmers' greater reliance on their wives. In turn, farm women have more time to help farm because modern household conveniences and smaller families have simplified "traditional" homemaking duties.

A day in the life of Donna Keppy illustrates these changes. The clock radio clicks on at 5:15 a.m. in the Keppy's small white ranch house, where they have lived for six years. Previously, for 10 years, they rented a 143-acre farm from Mr.

Keppy's father. Both Allen's and Donna's parents and grand-parents lived in eastern Iowa, near where the family presently farms with only part-time assistance from Mr. Keppy's brother. The home is full of evidence of the Kepps' livelihood: posters of smiling hogs, piggy banks, "Pigs Are Beautiful" buttons and pig-shaped soap holders.

Mrs. Keppy dresses quickly for her chores: corduroy jeans, black rubber boots, gloves, a beat-up ski jacket and head scarf. By 6 a.m., she is working outside with her husband. She shovels manure and feeds, waters and checks the health of the animals in the farrowing house, an old barn where pigs are born and raised for six weeks.

Her duties as "sanitation supervisor," as she jokingly refers to herself, represent the most physically demanding of her chores. "Sooey!" Mrs. Keppy yells, slapping the puppy-sized pigs out of the way so she can pitch 30-pound forkfuls of manure-laden straw out of the barn.

Then it's time for breakfast. As the Keppy daughters serve the meal, Mr. and Mrs. Keppy discuss whether to sell hogs to cover feed-corn purchases and to meet a payment on the farm. But, as it happens, hog prices are rising; so they consider taking out a loan rather than selling hogs at lower prices now. They decide to sell just a few and hold the rest in the hope that hog prices climb further. (Weeks later, they find their timing was right; hog prices increased $5 a hundred pounds. "We paid back the 30-day note to the bank and made money at it," Mrs. Keppy says.)

Breakfast at the Keppys is a simple fare of cornbread, sausages and orange juice. Mrs. Keppy says she can't take time to fuss with meals. An exception is the noontime dinner, for which she usually bakes and prepares steak or a ham. It isn't unusual for supper to consist of frozen pizza. By contrast, her mother-in-law still cooks five complete meals a day for her farmer-husband. When Viola Keppy's seven sons were growing up, "my responsibilities were centered around the home," she recalls. "(Donna's) responsibilities are spread out more."

Breakfast is also when "Donna gets her assignments for the day," Mr. Keppy says. While he regards his wife as his business partner, he gives the work orders. "He's the boss,"

Mrs. Keppy concurs. This doesn't diminish her importance, Mr. Keppy, a strapping 200-pounder, hastens to add. "Without Donna, I'd need an additional full-time man here," he observes. "The timeliness of having a wife in the house to take phone calls, or run a tractor or help load pigs is much more valuable than her trying to add $3 an hour to the family income with a regular job." In fact, when the four Keppy daughers were infants (now they range in age from 10 to 18, with the eldest away in college), Mr. Keppy found it cheaper to hire a babysitter than to replace his wife with a paid field hand.

By 7:30, the farm couple is back outside in the brisk spring weather, inspecting the muddy fields. Mrs. Keppy expresses doubt that the ground is ready for plowing and concern that, if the pace of field work doesn't pick up soon, planting will be delayed. "I agree that the fields don't look quite fit," Mr. Keppy tells her. "But I think we should go ahead anyway."

She plows for nearly three hours. Her ruddy face and stocky, five-foot-eight-inch, 150-pound frame indicate that she has done her share of farm work since learning to drive a tractor at age 12. As she plows, pop tunes and the morning commodities report blare from the vehicle's radio. The work seems monotomous and bonewearying. Yet the dark-haired woman drives the vehicle with the careful attention of someone who loves the land. "I get satisfaction from turning over the old to start the new," she says.

It's now 10:30. Mrs. Keppy bathes and changes clothes because she must take 36 hogs to market. Mr. Keppy's brother has helped him tramp through mud to select and herd the squealing, 250-pound animals onto a hauler's truck. This messy job of "running the gate" is Mrs. Keppy's when she isn't plowing.

"You know, marketing is our bread and butter, the final end of the product," Mrs. Keppy observes as the truck pulls away. "It's good to know this group (of hogs) made it through without being sick." One year, a dysentery-like disease killed 20% of the Keppys' pigs.

She delivers the hogs to an Oscar Mayer & Co. meat packing plant close to Davenport, 25 miles away. At the plant, her friendly kidding with the weighing-office workers suddenly ceases when the hogs prove overweight. That usually means they have too much fat. Lines crease her forehead. But because Keppy animals enjoy a reputation for having a high proportion of valuable lean meat, the packer pays her the full price. She leaves happy.

Since genetics and nutrition are key factors in maintaining livestock quality, Mrs. Keppy keeps informed of latest hog-breeding developments by reading industry publications. This know-how comes in handy each fall when the Keppys shop for a boar, which can cost $5,000 or more, as well as every few weeks when they choose certain young female hogs to breed rather than market.

A no-nonsense attitude characterizes Mrs. Keppy's approach to farming. She refuses to use the phone for idle social chats, and she gets angry at equipment dealers who lack needed parts. Dealers "aren't business-minded enough around here," she complains. "Our philosophy is that time is money and money makes money."

So, as the empty truck lumbers past grazing hogs, she wonders how farmers can succeed with such old-fashioned pasture feeding (the Keppys own a $62,000 automatic feed-grinding facility). "Their end-product isn't much different from ours," she muses. "It's just not as efficient a way to get the hogs to market."

Mrs. Keppy knows what she's talking about. The Keppy farm's sales exceed $230,000 a year, and in 1974 Mr. Keppy was named Iowa Pork All-American—meaning that he is regarded as one of the state's best hog farmers.

Following midday dinner, Mrs. Keppy returns to plowing and then harrowing. Her work ends at 6:30, more than 12 hours after it began. "It's been a slow day," the farm wife says, wearily climbing down from the tractor.

Even though field work wears her out, Mrs. Keppy's farm heritage has instilled in her a strong sense of purpose. "Farming is hard work, but it's got its rewards, and they're not all monetary," the usually soft-spoken woman says forcefully. "There's a lot of self-satisfaction, too."

Mrs. Keppy's work frequently continues through the evening. When the weather gets warmer and the ground dries, she plows until 9:30 at night. Otherwise, she may spend her evening working on farm records, preparing animal entry forms for state fairs or typing business letters.

In view of the modern efficiency of most of their farming, the Keppys are ill-prepared for record keeping, Mrs. Keppy believes. Her "office" consists of a desk in the master bedroom and a file cabinet in the kitchen. To get peace and quiet while discussing grain prices on the telephone, which is located in the busy main hallway, she frequently steps inside the bathroom. Thus, one of her high priorities is a full-fledged office. "We need one if we're going to run this farm like a business," she says. But the building of an office keeps being postponed because the Keppys repeatedly spend their money on better hog facilities instead. Another purchase that shows where their real priorities lie: They traded in a 15-year-old, 70-horsepower tractor to buy a $28,000, 120-horsepower model with an enclosed, air-conditioned cab.

Donna Keppy has been busy in other ways. She has served as state president of the Porkettes, a women's auxiliary of the National Pork Producers Council. Her leadership helped the auxiliary evolve into a group of promotion-oriented "pork pushers," as she calls them. For example, along with other Porkettes and their husbands, the Keppys have traveled to supermarkets in several states, handing out pork recipes, chatting with shoppers about farmers' problems and appearing on television talk shows. Later, Mrs. Keppy was named to the Iowa Development Commission, a state promotional group.

Her hectic, broadened and more public role as a farm wife developed without any assistance from the women's liberation movement, Mrs. Keppy says. She thinks feminists don't realize how difficult equality of the sexes can be. "You know, we say that a woman's libber never lived on a farm," she observes. "I do a man's job when I'm out there scooping manure or lifting 50-pound bales of hay in the summer." But then she adds with a smile: "Maybe we're the first generation of women's libbers."

Section IV

Problems That Arise

Previous sections of Women at Work have mentioned many of the problems faced by women on the job. In this section, we will investigate in detail some of the problems that arise most frequently.

The first chapter, Sexism Lives On, primarily concerns attitudes—mainly but not exclusively male attitudes—that set obstacles in the path of working women. Whatever the antidiscrimination laws may say, a great gulf still lies between the recently improved opportunities for women and true equality. That women's employment opportunities have improved is undeniable. However, it is just as true that many attitudinal problems linger on. Many men still resent female competition on the job. Many husbands still refuse to acknowledge that their wives are intelligent people, still belittle their accomplishments and still won't help an obviously overburdened working woman with the housework.

Then you will read how sexism hampers women in a specific industry, the commercial airlines. Female pilots have scored big gains in recent years, but often at the cost of considerable harassment from male pilots and from passengers, including some women passengers.

The following chapter concerns another kind of harassment—specifically sexual harassment on the job. Although women are trying to help each other combat such hassles, the problem—the notorious "casting couches," the threats of blocked promotions or dismissals if sexual favors are denied, and similar tactics—is a long way from being eliminated.

In addition to such overt manifestations of sexism, there is another, more-insidious kind—the way in which a

woman often has to offer unusual talents or expend unusual
effort to gain the recognition that an average man probably
would achieve with average effort. In a chapter entitled "No
'Banker's Hours,'" you will meet Challis Lowe, a black
woman who has carved out, with great effort, a successful career at a Chicago bank. The difficulties that she has faced tell
a lot about the difficulties faced by many career women.

Such difficulties tend to be compounded, moreover, if
the woman is a mother with children at home as well as a
breadwinner. A widow or a divorced woman often is further
hampered by lack of enough money to do more than simply
scrape through financially from one day to the next. The demands on her time tend to be staggering. In Mother and
Breadwinner, you will follow the career of one such woman,
Liz Gude.

One of Mrs. Gude's key difficulties was her lack of
preparation for a working career—a difficulty hobbling many
women. In Hunting for a Job, you will meet two more such
women. Both of them had been out of the labor force for
many years, and in trying to get back into it, they have strug-
gled with many problems typically faced by job-hunters in
their late 30s and 40s. Among them: lack of specific, job-ori-
ented training; lack of recent working experience; lack of understanding of what often is involved in a job, such as office
politics, and even lack of self-confidence. In addition, some
women unconsciously increase their difficulties by bad habits
such as chronic tardiness, by demanding too much money for
a beginning worker and by laying down too many incidental
conditions, such as rejecting a job because the office isn't at-
tractively furnished.

The final chapter, Protecting the Unborn, takes up a
particularly difficult problem affecting women in some industries. In many chemical companies, for example, some substances present in the workplace have been found to endan-
ger the human fetus or to cause genetic damage in workers.
The problem becomes complicated because the obvious solution—keeping women out of such factory areas—also would
deprive them of an equal opportunity to work. Whatever the
eventual answers, it's a sticky problem likely to be debated,
and litigated, for years to come.

Sexism Lives On

Ann Standerfer, a poised young career woman who has worked her way up from file clerk to personnel officer at a Denver bank, now has duties with a twist of irony to them. She handles the salary—administration program—and has learned that many male peers make a lot more than she does for similar work.

She says that greater male seniority accounts for some of the difference, which affects other women at the bank as well, but that seniority doesn't account for all of it. Though sometimes nettled, she isn't pounding on any desktops. "I have some power to make changes, but I'm not in a hurry to make myself obnoxious," she says. "I want to make things right."

That may take a while. "I've found oldtime bankers very reluctant to change," she concedes. "They talk about equality, but in their hearts they don't believe it. The greatest change will come when we have a generation that really *does* believe it."

Around a table in a meeting room, 10 other Denver-area women nod and murmur assent; most have had similar experiences that reveal the gulf still yawning between opportunity and true equality with men. A varied group, the women range in age from the 20s into the 50s, in occupation from homemakers to professionals. Some are single, others married, still others divorced.

All have been invited through William R. Hamilton & Staff, a Washington, D.C., polling concern, to discuss their convictions and feelings about women at work and the effect of work on their own lives. The impact is a forceful one, streaked with joy and pain, that can't be measured in figures or lines on a graph.

All firmly agree that these are frontier times for their sex. Opportunities for women have indeed expanded enormously, they say, and they are a little awestruck at the breadth of the horizons now before them. Among other things, the changes take some of the economic urgency out of the search for a husband.

Cynthia Giguere is 24, single, studying for her M.B.A., and in no hurry to wed. "Ten or 15 years ago, you didn't have many choices," she says. "You got married after high school or you went to college and probably got married after that. But women going into high school today can be anything they want. In a way it's more difficult for us now; there are just so many new options open."

The opportunity explosion is also creating a restless stirring in the suburbs. Aroused by the heightened sense of their potential, women are growing unsatisfied with the traditional housewife's role. Ann Schum, a secretary-receptionist at a women's counseling service, sees them coming in for advice on jobs, schooling—anything to satisfy a formless urge to do more, grow more. "A lot of women are running around feeling unfulfilled because they've been told they should be feeling unfulfiled," one panelist notes wryly.

So great has the pressure become that now it's not only more acceptable among women to get a job, it's even fashionable. Ramona Bishop, who is 29, married with no children and a homemaker who likes being one, is feeling picked on. "People always want to know why I'm not working. I tell them I have a job; I work at home. I like being my own boss. But they can't understand," she complains.

If the panelists believe women have unprecedented opportunities today, they are equally emphatic in giving men little credit for that. They perceive no great change in male thinking and claim that the men were only rubber-hosed into opening more jobs to them by laws against discrimination. "If the government hadn't required it to happen, it wouldn't have happened," declares Ann Standerfer.

So while it is easier to get a job now—even a job once labeled "men only"—women still have to struggle against ingrained male attitudes that no law can change. On the job, they have been patronized and resented. Coming home, some confront husbands who don't understand and don't help. "I fell like saying, 'Can't you see I'm running around like a

chicken with its head off?" But you can't see much from behind a newspaper," one working wife says.

The women in their 30s and beyond tended to approach their first jobs shadowed by a lack of self-confidence
and feelings of guilt. These attitudes, they say, are the resi-
due of their upbringing in a society that insisted women be-
longed at home and were suited mainly for making babies,
beds and breakfast. There is the sting of resentment in their
recollections.

"The message I got was that if I wanted a life of my
own, I must be a very selfish person," says Tica McCollom, a
research assistant who is married and has two children. "You
were expected to be a martyr, a thing that gave and gave and
asked nothing in return. For the first years I was married, I
felt incompetent and lucky to stay home, because Lord knows
what would happen if I ever got loose and had a job with real
responsibility."

Despite all the obstacles, however, the panelists sense
change in the air. One reason: Younger women today don't
carry the burden of past conditioning and are more inclined
to fight with men for equality. Declares Cynthia Giguere:
"I'm looking forward to getting my M.B.A. and going out to
challenge them all."

The older women applaud this. Ray Nell Busch, a 52-
year-old homemaker who has worked before, says: "When my
last child went out the front door to school, I went out the
back to work—but I felt so conflicted. I had the complete
support of my husband; it was my problem." Her daughters,
now in their 20s, don't share it, she says approvingly. One just
got a job with a tree-spraying company, fought for acceptance with male coworkers, and now does a man's job for
equal pay.

Midori Abe, 48, who never ventured into the work-
place because she felt she was unqualified, says with pride:
"My eldest daughter thinks she can do anything. She left herself options; she didn't get married right out of school, she
didn't stay in some secretarial slot. Now she's selling computers."

The panelists also are encouraged by individual men
who are giving way under the growing pressure to recognize

women as equals. Progress comes inch by painful inch and must be measured by little things—a husband doing the dishes without being asked, a respected male coworker offering a sincere compliment. But it is progress nonetheless, and over the years the inches grow into miles.

In medical school in the mid-1960s, Dr. Hildegard Messenbaugh, now a psychiatrist, was one of only three women in a class of 75. "The discrimination was incredible," she recalls. "We didn't even get pillows to sleep on. Guys would slam doors in your face; it was as if the rules of social intercourse had been suspended."

When she got married in school, she lost her scholarship—even though she was in the top 1% of the class. When she decided to have a baby in residency, she got no extra time off, giving birth on a Saturday and going back to work the next Wednesday. "They were afraid I couldn't handle the work, and the pressure on me to drop out was tremendous," she recalls.

But the influx of women into medicine has brought "a tremendous change" in the way they are treated and viewed by male colleagues. Discrimination such as Dr. Messenbaugh endured would be almost unheard of today, she adds.

Sherry Byerly, a 33-year-old divorced mother of two, has seen similar changes evolve in police work. Since she got a job as a police officer in suburban Lakewood, Colo., about five years ago, female officers have gradually won the department's trust. At first, they weren't allowed to cover beats alone in patrol cars; now she and other women work the same hours as the men and drive solo.

Most heartening to her has been a change in individual male attitudes toward women officers. "A few men accept us totally," notes Officer Byerly, who recently was told by one male colleague that he would rather have her as backup (second officer at the scene of a crime) than many of the men. "That was such a big step for me," she says with emotion.

But many working women say they still have to walk softly on the job, particularly if they're doing "man's work." Too many men, they feel, are still hostile to female excellence because the men are insecure and dread being shown up. Declares one panelist: "When a woman competes with men, they feel threatened. And because women feel they have to overachieve to really prove themselves, this makes the threat even greater to men who just don't have what it takes."

Dr. Messenbaugh recalls one point during her residency when she finally achieved male acceptance as a sort of "mother confessor." When she was named chief resident, however, this goodwill suddenly congealed into hostility. "They said, 'We didn't know you were competing against us,'" she recalls. Sherry Byerly notes that when she and another female officer led the force in arrests one month, "there wasn't a man in the place who was really thrilled about that."

Natalie Glass, a child-care worker who previously drove a cab, felt patronized and resented by male drivers. "The other drivers thought I got better trips and bigger tips because I was a woman." says the attractive 28-year-old. "They would have liked it better if I wasn't on the street. But I earned that money the way any driver does; I worked hard."

Wary and still a little fearful of male hostility, the women most affected confess that they try to evade it rather than elicit it by being too direct and forceful. Marla Harper, a divorced mother of three, is co-owner of a successful business that sells and installs kitchen cabinets and countertops, but she still finds it "extremely difficult" to criticize the proposals of architects and contractors she deals with.

Sherry Byerly manipulates coworkers and wishes she didn't feel she had to. Policemen still doubt that policewomen can handle the physical side of the job, and so Officer Byerly plays on this doubt to win their support and acceptance—even though she privately believes she's better than they are at avoiding trouble in the first place ("no one insults my female ego by telling me I'm afraid to fight"). She adds: "It's a fact that I'm not a man's physical equal. So I use that, I let them know I need them. You have to feed their egos."

She has had less luck in gaining the acceptance of their wives. At parties, she and other female cops talk shop outside with the men while the wives huddle inside. "There's a real schism there," she says regretfully. "I know they have to have more upstairs than to sit around talking about pregnancies they had 10 years ago. It's just that they don't know how to cope with women working with their husbands in what can often be an emotionally intimate situation."

Working women face additional strains at home. Those who have worked out specific agreements with their husbands seem to handle them best; Ann Standerfer, the bank personnel officer, and her husband split household chores 50-50. Hildegard Messenbaugh, the psychiatrist, worked everything out with her surgeon-husband when they had their first child, and he has pulled his share without complaint ever since. ("Gee, can you clone him?" another woman asks).

But some marriages shatter. Ann Schum, the secretary, separated from her husband when he failed to help at home after she went to work to augment family income. "I'm still carrying everything on my back except a man along with it," she says. "I'd become very resentful, very angry with him." Marla Harper says that when she went to work, "it was never with my ex-husband's support, but with a smirking kind of reservation."

Tension also rises when a husband is slow to see that work has made his wife a more independent, confident person. "I spent the first seven years of my marriage spoiling him rotten because I'd been conditioned into believing that's what I enjoyed doing," says Tica McCollom, the research assistant. When she went to work and discovered she had more ability than she thought, she grew angry because her husband didn't help enough at home and because she thought that he patronized her. "The most infuriating thing in the world is to have a man act surprised that you've got something between your ears," she says.

At the same time, she made unreasonable demands on him. They both wound up in counseling. "We've had a lot of adjusting to do," she says. "It was rough on me to discover that I had brains, but it was even rougher on him." The relationship is smoother now, and Tica McCollom believes that her job has helped draw her husband closer to their children. This delights her. "The other day I was watching him playing on the lawn with the kids, rolling around under the sprinkler like a big idiot," she says fondly, "and I thought, 'Hey, that's terrific. That's exactly what I had in mind when I got married.' "

For mothers without husbands, however, just stepping out the door each morning can be painful. Sherry Byerly feels it when she must leave her handicapped son when he is running a fever, or when her small daughter asks, "Mom, can you come to our shcool play today?"—and she knows she can't.

But all the working mothers, married or not, have learned that households don't have to be disrupted or unhappy when Mom goes to work.

Ann Schum, who must have her four children during the day, gathers them around her once a week for a family meeting at which they share feelings, settle disputes and arrange plans. "It's a time for men to listen as well as talk," she says, adding that the meetings bind her family ever closer together. Tica McCollom and her husband each take one of their two kids out to dinner and listen hard to that child.

And the women are raising their small daughters to be far less fearful and far more self-confident than they themselves were; the world that they will enter will be an entirely different one. Sherry Byerly encouraged her youngster when she became the only girl on a local baseball team. And when Tica McCollom's eight-year-old speaks of marriage, her mother says: "Hey, take your time. Think about what you want to be. You want to be an astrophysicist? Be one. Do whatever you want, whatever you do well."

Off Into Turbulent Skies

Feb. 6, 1973, was an historic day in American aviation. As Frontier Airlines flight 12 was winging to St. Louis from Denver, the flight engineer was Emily Howell Warner, the first woman to sit in the cockpit of a regularly scheduled U.S. airline. Mrs. Warner received carnations, and the press flocked to interview her.

Three days later, Mrs. Warner made her second working flight, also on the Denver-St. Louis route, and it was a different story. No flowers, no reporters. The pilot, Mrs. Warner recalls, uttered a total of eight frosty words to her during the journey: "Don't touch anything in the cockpit" and "Good night."

Five and a half years later, there were only 50 women among the approximately 37,000 airline pilots, copilots and engineers on certified U.S. carriers—and about 30 of the 50 women were engineers, who sit in the cockpit and operate certain controls, but don't actually fly the plane.

Controversy over the presence of women in the cockpit actually has grown. Many male pilots, perhaps predictably, haven't welcomed the change. Some airline passengers, of both sexes, voice some apprehension. Robert E. Bohan Jr., a retired U.S. Air Force colonel who is against having female pilots on passenger airlines, is pressing to make carriers disclose routinely the names of pilots on all flights. His rationale is that passengers, if they recognize a pilot's name as feminine and object, would have the option of switching flights. The Federal Aviation Administration has said that all pilots are tested adequately for stamina, strength and emotional stability. The FAA said it doesn't see any need for posting pilots' names.

But progress is being made, and the future looks more promising. Most of the 50 women serving in the cockpits of U.S. airlines have been hired since 1976. And the Future Airline Pilots of America, a private firm that provides career counseling and information in the field, estimates that by 1990 there will be at least 2,000 female pilots on certified airlines.

Major airlines are actively searching for qualified female candidates. (For a long while, they weren't hiring new pilots of either sex; the 1973 Arab oil embargo and the consequent leveling-off of air traffic, in effect, brought about a hiring freeze at many lines.)

The new drive to hire women isn't entirely voluntary. For example, as the result of a 1976 federal decree in an Equal Employment Opportunity Commission discrimination case against United Airlines, that carrier must give special attention to qualified females (and minority-group members) in hiring its next 1,200 pilots. If 10% of 100 qualified applicants for 20 pilots' jobs are women, United has to fill 20% of the jobs with women, for example.

Airline officials note that both men and women must meet the same stringent criteria when qualifying for a pilot's job, including intimate knowledge of such things as the aircraft, electronics and the hydraulic system.

But that seems lost on some members of the flying public. Bonnie Tiburzi Krantz, a flight engineer with American Airlines, recalls how a woman passenger pointed at her and disgustedly asked the pilot, "What is that?" And Terry London Rinehart, a flight engineer with Eastern Airlines, tells how a male passenger, flying with a woman pilot on Western, was so nervous that he asked for a priest.

Why the concern about women in the cockpit? Some of the conflicting attitudes were on view during a recent Braniff International flight from New York to Dallas, with Stephanie Wallach, 32, as copilot. A graduate of Wells College in Aurora, N.Y., she took flying lessons at Westchester County Airport and got a pilot's job with Braniff in 1975.

"The passengers have been great, and the response has been very good," she says. But when Braniff passenger Mary Hofmann, 62, found out that the copilot was female, she said that if she had known earlier, "I would have taken a different plane." Mrs. Hofmann said she dislikes the idea of women at the controls because "women are more emotional."

Most passengers, however, had either a positive attitude or were indifferent ot Miss Wallach's role on their flight. Among the indifferent was John Sessoms, a Texas bricklayer. "I don't care if it's an ape (flying) as long as the plane goes where it's supposed to," he said.

The comparison may be unflattering for Stephanie Wallach, but the indifference to her physical characteristics is welcome. She is five feet, six inches tall and weighs 114 pounds. And she doesn't think height and weight have anything to do with the stamina needed to fly a plane. "I think any healthy human being could do it," she says. "How strong could a 59-year-old guy who doesn't exercise be?"

Miss Wallach says that her male co-workers generally have supported her, but she acknowledges some instances of prejudice. One such instance, she says, was a rumor circulating around Braniff about her behavior while coming in for a landing during stormy weather. According to the rumor, Miss Wallach started to cry and told the pilot to take over and land the plane. Miss Wallach vehemently denies the rumor, but she is philosophical about such stories. "The guys who want to believe it will anyway," she says. "You have to learn to desensitize yourself."

Richard Goduti, who flew as the pilot with Miss Wallach to Dallas, isn't concerned about the sex of his cockpit colleagues. "I come to work to make a day's pay," he says, "and I don't care whom I work with." He says he is "glad to have women in the cockpit," and adds, "It's nice to have some feminine attributes around."

Nevertheless, some male pilots aren't entirely comfortable working with women. "I have mixed emotions about female pilots," says David A. Anderson, a pilot with United Airlines. "There's the male-ego aspect—we think we're unique, I suppose. And pilots on maternity leave sounds kind of funny." Other male pilots say that they don't have major objections to working with women but note that females in the cockpit tend to inhibit colorful language and dirty jokes.

There are also mixed emotions among flight attendants about women in the cockpit. Among the proponents of female pilots is Richard Waters, a flight attendant with Trans World Airlines. TWA currently doesn't have any female pilots (it hadn't fired any new pilots for some years), but Mr.

Waters says that he is looking forward to being aboard a female-piloted flight. "It's good to have a real mixture," he says.

Female flight attendants generally agree. Some stewardesses resent being subservient to other women, but many say they don't care about the pilot's sex. Others say they're glad that women are advancing.

The airlines using female pilots say reactions generally have been good. Texas International, with six women in the cockpit, says it has received letters from women happy to see new opportunities opening up for their sex. Western Airlines, with six female pilots, says it has received only three letters on the subject, two of them positive, and the third from a man who worried that the woman pilot wasn't strong enough to fly the plane.

Many female pilots, although not active feminists, credit the women's movement with helping them. Until the movement began, some say, they never thought an airline pilot's job would be open to them.

Although the female pilots are pleased at their advancement, some say they aren't trying to look and act like men. Most female pilots, for example, say their uniform is too masculine. That isn't surprising, because some airlines have simply refitted the traditional male pilot's outfit to conform to a female figure. At Braniff, Miss Wallach wears a jacket, tie, trousers and hat like those worn by her male counterparts. But she isn't always recognized as a pilot. When she climbs aboard a bus to the airport, she often is sized up by passengers as a bus-company employe. People ask her where to put their bags and when the bus leaves.

Hassled Women

The 40-year-old bank executive faced a business problem for which no graduate course in management had prepared her. No sooner had she settled into her new job as the first woman vice president of a Midwestern bank than the trouble started.

"I was hit from all directions at once with several important bank clients offering me their business on the condition that I go out with them," she recalls, asking that her name not be used. "I was responsible for keeping and building up these large accounts. If they pulled out, my career was finished."

At first she made light of the offers. Then she ignored them. When these tactics failed to stop the persistent phone calls at home and the suggestive remarks at business meetings, she lashed out. "I sat down with each client and told them that I make it a firm rule to keep business separate from my social life," she says. "I told them that they could take their business to another loan officer if they wanted to."

The stratagem worked. Though taken aback, the clients seemed to accept her terms. Not one took his business elsewhere. Still, the experience left her shaken. "Nobody ever talks about sexual harassment on the job," she says. "But when it happens to you that first time, it's frightening."

These days, the wall of silence surrounding the issue of sexual harassment is gradually crumbling. Across the country, small pockets of working women are boldly speaking out and seeking protection against unwanted sexual advances by bosses or clients. The incidents they describe are sometimes as blatant as a proposition coupled with the promise of advancement if accepted and the threat of dismissal if rejected. Or, the harassment may take the form of a physical overture disguised as a friendly pat, squeeze or pinch.

Men, too, can be the unwilling objects of such advances, but it happens less frequently. Eli Ginzberg, professor of economics at Columbia University's Graduate School of Business, explains: "Since men are in most of the positions of power, (sexual harassment) most often goes the other way."

Some women, of course, welcome these unexpected attentions and turn them to their advantage. Corporate and Hollywood lore is spiced with stories of the "casting couch" launching women on to stardom or a successful career. But many women react instead with fear, humiliation or anger. "To every women who has had it happen, the initial feeling is that there is something wrong with me," says Karen De-Crow,former president of the National Organization for Women. "Slowly people are becoming aware that it is a problem that is happening to other people."

No one knows for sure just how many women encounter harassment at work. Many women say it hasn't touched their careers. Others say they've faced it repeatedly. Working Women United, a women's group, conducted an informal survey of 155 working women and found that of those interviewed, 70 had experienced some form of sexual harassment in the office. An overwhelming 92% of those surveyed felt that it was a serious problem.

Unlike unwanted sexual advances by co-workers that can be brushed off with a crisp "Bug off, creep," attentions from bosses or important clients involve an element of coercion and require delicate handling. "It isn't a relationship where people have equal power or equal say," says a 30-year-old Pittsburgh health worker who was the object of amorous advances by a previous boss. "Implicit is the threat that a refusal will hurt your career or salary."

In Jan Crawford's case, the threat was explicit. She was a secretary in a California real-estate firm and was working hard to get ahead. The hard work was rewarded, and she was promoted to property-managing duties. Things went well, she says, until her immediate boss, a 45-year-old married man, asked her for a date. She was polite, but she refused. Later, at a business lunch, he told her: "You'll be sorry."

"It really shocked me because he said it in very quiet tones," she recalls. Two months later when she was fired for "inefficiency." her boss reminded her: "I told you that you'd be sorry."

"I was really devastated," Miss Crawford says. "For years I was frightened to pour myself into a job again. It was so easy to lose everything."

Psychological damage can manifest itself in other ways. After being promoted to the post of administrative assistant at one of the laboratories of a prestigious Eastern university, a 44-year-old mother of five discovered that the job included fending off one of her supervisors, a married professor who pawed her repeatedly. Rather than risk dismissal by telling him off, the woman, who is the sole support of her family, kept quiet. ("I was taught not to hurt other people and to be polite." she says ruefully.) Finally she complained to another supervisor. "He told me that any mature woman should be able to handle it," she recalls.

So she avoided the professor whenever possible. She began to dress dowdily. She took to walking down stairs rather than risk meeting him in an elevator. She asked for a transfer to another department—with no success. The pressures finally took their toll. She developed severe neck pains. Nine months after her promotion and in terrible pain. she quit her job. Shortly thereafter, the neck pains ceased.

Despite the apparent extent of the problem, sexual harassment isn't an issue that many corporations treat seriously. "With any other business problem, they would have had people hard at work researching and planning," says Margaret Henning, co-director of Simmons' graduate management program. "But as far as we can tell, nobody is doing anything." Businesswomen concur, noting that employe counselors tend to chalk up charges of misbehavior in high places to back-office gossip. Co-workers, while outwardly sympathetic, often harbor suspicions that the woman encouraged such actions.

Some women admit that they may unconsciously invite improper advances. A former analyst for Arthur D. Little Inc. recalls one incident that led her to examine her own behavior. While on a business trip to New York, she and four vice presidents of a client firm went out for a business dinner. Returning to her hotel, she found that all four men had telephoned her for a late-night date. "I couldn't stand what was happening to me," she says after a year of psychological counseling. "Clearly my behavior was way out of line."

Women's groups argue that anyone should feel free to rebuff advances without fear of reprisal. To win their point, women are thrashing out the issue in court, within their unions and among themselves. The legal arena is the toughest to crack. Unlike a more demonstrable job complaint such as low pay, sexual harassment is difficult to prove in court. "I'm afraid that the judges' reluctance to recognize this as sex discrimination stems from their fears that it could become a cause of action to blackmail men," Linda Singer, a Washington, D.C., attorney says.

By pressing their unions to set down guidelines on harassment, some women hope to forestall incidents before they occur. Besides creating the morals complaint bureau, the Screen Actors Guild in Los Angeles has written into its contract a prohibition against conducting job interviews outside the office. "We are more than ever finding out that the casting couch still exists," Kathleen Nolan, Guild president, says. She notes that the bureau receives complaints from both men and women.

As the issue of sexual harassment increasingly comes out into the open, women are turning to one another for mutual support and are sharing tactics to defend themselves against future incidents. Some single women have taken to wearing wedding rings, or to inventing fictional boyfriends, husbands and children to signal their unavailability. One woman active in fighting harassment observes that typically a harassed woman thinks that her experience is unique. Only after women begin talking to each other about the problem do they become aware of a common opening gambit used by executives on the prowl: "It starts very subtly when your boss calls you in for a business discussion and then shifts the topic around to his wife," she says.

Indeed, working women subjected to sexual harassment aren't the only ones hurt by it. Lin Farley, a leader in the campaign against harassment, once received a letter from a corporate president's wife. The letter described the wife's feelings upon discovering that her husband was forcing his attentions on an employe. "Please excuse me for not signing my name," she wrote. "But I feel highly insulted by my husband's actions, just as much as the woman who feels humiliated by the sexual harassment."

No "Banker's Hours"

"Your secretary came outside to inspect the no-parking signs we put up at the drive-in teller," the police lieutenant told Martin Hartmann, an assistant branch manager for Chicago's Continental Bank.

"Hey, that was no secretary," objected Mr. Hartmann. "That was my boss."

His boss is Challis M. Lowe, a 33-year-old black woman who earns more than $30,000 a year running the bank's first branch office, which opened in September 1976 and is located in a skyscraper lobby at the north end of Chicago's financial district. Well aware that Mrs. Lowe is in charge, her staff of 40 bankers, tellers and clerks have dubbed the branch "Challis's Palace." But outsiders, unaccustomed to dealing with a woman executive, sometimes mistake her for a secretary.

That's an error that, as the years go by, there is less and less excuse for: More women than ever before are working in executive positions. Antidiscrimination laws, pressure from women's groups and changing social values have encouraged companies to open up management ranks. And in company after company, the results are beginning to become evident—particularly in the banking industry.

However, in banking and elsewhere, the vast majority of women managers still are concentrated in entry-level, supervisory or management-training jobs; vice presidential posts in major companies have been achieved by only a relative handful of women. So while the female middle-manager may no longer be her company's only woman executive, she remains a relative newcomer who often is viewed with a mixture of sexist attitudes and cautious acceptance. And the hurdles that she must overcome may be greater than those faced by the few women in senior management, who already have achieved a large degree of success.

In middle management, "there's the greatest pressure

to compete. You've got a glut of people and only a few of them will make it to the top," observes Francine Gordon, assistant professor of organizational behavior at Stanford University's school of business. "A woman in that position is more threatening to men," she says.

Some experts believe that female middle-managers encounter difficulties because their upbringing and training haven't prepared them for a lifetime of work, much less a management career. Women tend to have narrow horizons that don't go beyond "limited and discreet time intervals," such as marriage and a family, whereas "a man expects to work all his life," notes Margaret Fenn, associate professor at the University of Washington's Graduate School of Business Administration.

Such are the strains of management, that some women executives suffer considerable guilt about being considered bad mothers because they work long hours. For example, Kay K. Mazuy, senior vice president of Shawmut Corp., a Boston bank-holding company, gets upset when schoolteachers or pediatricians want to discuss her two children in the middle of the afternoon. She feels they are really giving her "little jabs that say, 'if you were being a good mother you would be at home.'"

Female executives report that the predominantly male business world puts them at a disadvantage in another way. They complain that they are often isolated from informal social contacts by being excluded from lunches, drinking sessions or weekend golf with fellow executives. Such contacts form traditional "old-boy networks" that provide critical advice about how to get things done and who is important to know for advancement in a company.

For the same reason, women in management say they have trouble finding a corporate sponsor, a senior executive who will encourage them and bring them along as his career advances. The protege system is one way that men have typically moved up the corporate ladder. But if a man sponsors a woman, Prof. Gordon says, "people are likely to ask, 'what's going on between them?'"

The small number of female executives also means that they are expected to perform better on the job than men.

"We're still in the super Bionic Woman stage," observes Janet Jones, chairman of Management Woman Inc., a New York executive-search concern for women. Fortune 500 companies constantly ask her to find someone who is guaranteed to be successful, she says. "There's no margin for error," she adds.

The special burdens of being an isolated female, plus the normal tensions of middle management, often combine to place tremendous emotional stress on women executives. Consequently, physicians report, women executives are starting to fall prey to such traditionally male stress-related diseases as heart attacks, ulcers and high blood pressure.

Statistical evidence of the trend hasn't shown up yet. But as more women move into management-level jobs, "I think we will see an increase in coronary heart disease" among younger and younger women, says Dr. Ray Rosenman, associate director of San Francisco's Brunn Institute for Cardiovascular Disease.

The pressures and frustrations of being a woman middle-manager are clearly apparent in Challis Lowe's career. But there also is much satisfaction, and her experience suggests that some aspects of corporate life may get easier as the ranks of female executives swell.

At first glance, Challis Lowe doesn't appear to fit the part she plays: an ambitious, hard-driving executive determined to reach a high management position. She is a thin, seemingly shy person who speaks in a soft voice. Her carefully tailored suits and large, thick glasses give her the appearance of a schoolteacher.

In fact, her early ambition was to be a high-school math teacher, and she substituted in an elementary school after the birth of her first daughter, Daphne, in 1966. But after her second daughter was born two years later, she acted against the wishes of her husband, John, and decided to seek a fulltime business career. She wasn't looking for fulfillment or power, she says, so much as "peace of mind from getting out of the house during the day."

She did counseling for an employment agency for two years, and there she heard about opportunities for women in banking. So in 1971 she became a customer representative for

Continental Illinois National Bank & Trust Co.'s personal banking division, which services individual customers, rather than business and commercial accounts.

After a few years of opening accounts and counseling, Mrs. Lowe began to wonder if she would ever go higher in the bank. She was dubious because there was only one female officer in her section of personal banking. And when she asked her supervisor about a promotion, he suggested that she transfer to another area of the bank.

She ignored his suggestion and, instead, took a personnel department test, which indicated she had management talent. As a result, her work was watched more closely, and in mid-1974, at the age of 28, Mrs. Lowe was made assistant sales manager and, later that year, an officer. Early in 1975 she became sales manager.

Mrs. Lowe was Continental Bank's first black woman officer. Now the bank employs about 160 women executives—up from only 30 in 1973—seven of whom are black. Altogether, the bank has 1,300 persons in management.

As sales manager, Mrs. Lowe was in charge of half of the bank's family banking center, which handles all types of customer services. The promotion put her in charge of 30 bankers, most of whom were men. Uncomfortable about the situation, a few of the male veterans complained to her boss. One older woman opted for early retirement rather than take orders from the new manager. To this day, Mrs. Lowe says she doesn't know whether they resented her because she was black, female or under 30—or all three.

Sometimes, customers also were skeptical of her authority, refusing to talk to her and insisting that they be allowed "to see an officer." One elderly man was finally persuaded to confer with her, and was so pleased with the results that he told her, "You can be my secretary any time." Mrs. Lowe coolly replied, "I don't think you can afford me."

When Continental Bank decided to launch its first branch four blocks from the main officer, Mrs. Lowe was tapped to manage the branch. (At the time, Illinois law prohibited branch banking except for an additional office offering personal and limited commercial banking services within 1,500 feet of a bank's headquarters.) She took over her new

job in February 1976, months before the lobby office opened,
to direct the construction, design and equipping of the facility. In the process, Mrs. Lowe learned some lessons about
being a woman middle-manager. For the first time, she had to
deal with men in other bank departments, few of whom knew
her or had worked with a female executive before. This explains why, she says, "they tended to put my priorities on the
back burner. I found I had to prove myself with many of
them."

One bank official stalled on her request for some signs,
because, she thinks, he resented taking orders from a woman.
Undaunted, she called the official's boss and made arrangements directly with him.

Getting what she wants for her branch also requires
Mrs. Lowe to work closely with the three men and one
woman who are her fellow executives in personal banking. All
of these executives have profit responsibilities and all compete for staff and budget allocations from their boss, vice
president Lawrence A. Eldridge.

Two or three times every day, Mrs. Lowe leaves her
thickly carpeted, glassed-in office on the branch's mezzanine
level for meetings or a working lunch at the main office with
the other managers. At these meetings she sometimes finds
herself fighting to protect her turf. One dispute concerned
dinner plates that the bank gives away as premiums. She
argued with her colleagues that she shouldn't have to absorb
the marketing expenses when customers with accounts at the
main bank pick up free plates at her branch.

But the competition among the personal banking executives is more often friendly and low-keyed, and Mrs. Lowe
deliberately tries to encourage bonhomie. Whether it's a marketing strategy conference or an occasional drink after work,
Mrs. Lowe prepares diligently; for example, she keeps posted
on the latest sports scores, even though she hates sports. It's
vital for a woman "to work at becoming part of a company's
informal social network," she observes.

Her quick adaptation to office politics and her smooth
operation of the new office (its deposit volume was quickly
running four months ahead of schedule) won praise and,
more recently, a promotion to second vice president. Her

staff's morale is high, customers are pleased, "and we're getting good business there," says John H. Perkins, Continental Bank's president. "It's got to be because she's running the place well."

Challis Lowe pays a price for her success, however. A self-described perfectionist, she spends 12 hours a day at work and leaves for home after 7 p.m. with an attache case full of papers. For two years, she also took a special masters-of-business-administration program at Northwestern University, which she attended one day a week. At the same time, she attended a school study group one evening a week. Mrs. Lowe received her degree from Northwestern in June 1978, but then she promptly got just as busy as before by enrolling in a special training program in commercial lending at the bank.

Work and school are so time-consuming that she has little opportunity to relax in her apartment, which is in a middle-class, racially mixed neighborhood on Chicago's south side. "I don't do a lot of unwinding, except when I'm sleeping," she says. Before she went back to school, she would unwind by baking bread, kneading the dough "to a pulp, she jokes.

Her lack of leisure pursuits and the tensions of her job give Mrs. Lowe stomach upsets and an occasional flare-up of colitis, a stress-related inflammation of the colon. Her husband blames the colitis on her tendency to let pressures "build up to the point where she has to have an (emotional) explosion." After one promotion, he remembers, she tossed and turned a great deal in her sleep, and she was irritable at home for six months.

Another source of tension is Mrs. Lowe's guilt about being constantly away from her daughters, aged nine and 12. She often doesn't see them from one day to the next, especially when her school study group meets until late at night. "As a woman, I feel I should spend more time with them," she says. (Mrs. Lowe is the only female officer at Continental Bank with young children.)

John Lowe admits that he resents his wife's extended absences. Mrs. Lowe's career commitment "has shifted a lot of responsibility to me that I probably wouldn't have accepted normally," he says with a sigh. Mr. Lowe is a former television advertising salesman who returned to school full-time in an MBA program; thus Mrs. Lowe became the family's sole breadwinner. He takes the girls to their doctors' appointments and attends their school conferences.

Despite her guilt feelings, Challis Lowe wouldn't think of giving up her management job because, she says, it gives her a deep sense of accomplishment. Her "personal drive," she says, wasn't being "fulfilled" by staying at home.

Her drive is fueled by ambition. With a note of determination in her voice, she declares that her sights "aren't limited to becoming a second vice president." Her race and sex may help more than hinder her further advancement at Continental Bank.

But conflicting loyalties between work and home make Mrs. Lowe unsure that she would like to become president of Continental Bank—even if she could. "The road to the top is filled with more and more commitment to the job and less and less time with your family," she says her voice growing softer and less steady. Laughing nervously, she adds, "If I spent any more hours away from home, I might not have a family."

Going It Alone

Back in 1962, Liz Gude was living the kind of charmed life that most American girls dream of. She was married to a well-educated French teacher and was the mother of three toddlers. With the help of her father-in-law, she and her husband designed and built a comfortable Cape Cod home in the plush Boston suburb of Marshfield, Mass. She spent her days painting the rooms, tending to her vegetable garden, cooking and cleaning. "I was a suburban housewife back then with a vengeance," she says.

All that ended less than a year later, however, when she and her husband separated. Suddenly, she had to sell the house, care for three children alone and rebuild her life. Her most-immediate concern was finding a way to feed her family. Though she had a college degree, her years as a homemaker had left her ill-equipped to enter the job market, and for over year she worked as a waitress.

Today, she and her three teen-agers rent a ramshackle house on a run-down street in the university town of Cambridge, Mass. They make do on a hand-to-mouth budget that provides few extras and almost no savings. But Liz Gude, a slender, vivacious 44-year-old, has acquired a master's degree and has worked her way up to an $18,000-a-year job as a high-school guidance counselor. Sometime soon, she hopes to return to school to begin work on a doctorate in clinical psychology. Her ultimate goal: to combine work in psychology in a neighborhood clinic, a small private practice and college teaching.

After the divorce, Mrs. Gude says, "what happened to me was that I had to find out who I was and what I could do to support my family. That has been the search." And so it is with many female breadwinners who work, not to relieve boredom or to earn pin money, but to support families. Partly because nearly half these women don't have high-school diplomas, the majority subsist on welfare, alimony, child support and other such income, a Labor Department survey found, while those who do work unsually have to settle for low-paying factory and clerical jobs. About a third of them live below the poverty level, and more than a fourth are black.

Probably among the worst off are so-called displaced homemakers. Suddenly divorced or widowed, these women can't collect Social Security because they are too young, and they don't qualify for most federal aid because their children are too old. Nor can they usually find jobs; few of these women have readily marketable skills.

Such women "are at a standstill," says Deborah Shapiro, president of Parnell Personnel Consultants Inc., a Needham Heights, Mass., job-counseling firm. "Suddenly, they discover they have to support a family, and they're trying desperately to hold onto a house, so it's a mad scramble for money," she says. Their first ventures into the job market, she adds, are "like jumping into cold water. They feel, 'Who wants a 45-year-old woman who hasn't worked for years?' "

Even female breadwinners who do have job skills have long faced on-the-job discrimination that only now is beginning to ease. In making hiring and promotion decisions, employers have traditionally favored male employes who, they reasoned, had families to support. Only within the past few years has the business community come to recognize the high percentage of female employes who head households and thus have to work.

"Corporations looking for key talent preferred the married man with children," says Wendy Rue, executive director of the National Association for Female Executives Inc., a New York trade group. Now, however, she says companies looking for women "put breadwinners on the top of the list, because they, too, are responsible for their families' financial security."

But finding a job is only half the battle. Like all single parents, female breadwinners must do double-duty, sandwiching child-rearing in between demanding days at the office. And they must do it alone. For Liz Gude and thousands like her, there is no spouse at home waiting with dinner ready at the end of a long day. There is no one to help ferry children to and from music lessons or school parties. There is no one to care for the children when out-of-town business trips or evening meetings impinge on precious free time.

Though the transition from full-time homemaker to full-time wage earner was difficult for Liz Gude, she was more fortunate than most. For one thing, she had a college degree, one of a slim 6.6% of the female family heads who do. Even at that, her B.A. in art history from Smith College hadn't prepared her to file or type, much less pursue a profession. "We were being prepared to be accomplished wives of successful husbands," she says ruefully.

At first, her education served her well. She married Bill Scoble, her college sweetheart, right after graduation in 1956, and spent six years following him to Paris, Concord, N.H., and Marshfield. The couple's three children—Sarah, Anna and Clay—left her with little time to think about a career of her own.

But the marriage was crumbling fast and when she and her husband parted, in 1962, she was left with no income. Though both child support and alimony were provided for in the separation agreement, her husband was between jobs and the payments didn't begin for several months. (He still pays child support, but after the divorce, he exercised his legal option to discontinue alimony payments.) Her father-in-law agreed to keep up payments on the house until she sold it. When the divorce came through two years later, she sold her household possessions and sailed with the children to Paris, where she got a $4,800-a-year job assisting the director of an academic-year-abroad program. ("I was running away," she now admits.) She returned two years later to Boston, rented a $90-a-month apartment in suburban Newton and took a $6,000-a-year secretarial job at Harvard University.

About this time she began seeing a psychiatrist, a once-a-week process that continued on and off for five years. As a result of her therapy, Mrs. Gude (who has reverted to her maiden name but retains the title "Mrs.") decided to move to Cambridge, a community with a larger proportion of single parents, and to plunge headlong into a career.

She had always been peripherally interested in education, and with the help of strong recommendations from family friends, she found a $9,000-a-year job as Massachusetts' assistant director of educational television, developing classroom programs for teachers. "It was a huge step up for me because I was making the break from secretary to professional," she says.

But once in the job, she discovered that her avenues for advancement were blocked. When her boss left, she served as acting director for months. Then a man from outside was brought in to fill the position permanently. She didn't press the issue; she sensed that state officials weren't inclined to promote women to top posts at that time. "Women may go up the ladder so far, and that's where they stop," she says. "To move into the power brackets, they have to work twice as hard." A spokesman for the state commissioner of education says Mrs. Gude's assessment of the situation was "probably right, given the atmosphere at that time," but he won't comment on the specific incident.

Weary of working in the bureaucracy and anxious to move into another area of education, Mrs. Gude quit soon afterward to become sales director of a small educational publishing firm. She spent two years there selling textbooks and materials to school systems throughout the state. The heavy travel schedule that accompanied this job meant that more than ever she had to juggle her work responsibilities with those at home. She was on the road an average of twice a week and had to attend numerous out-of-town conferences during the spring book-selling season. Before accepting the job, she had arranged with her employer to attend only the day conferences; the men in her department handled overnight trips. "Sometimes I'd be up at 5 a.m. and back at 7 p.m.," she says "It was hard on my children, but it was a simple fact of life."

In 1969, she began attending Boston State College—"the cheapest place I could find"—to earn a master's degree in high-school counseling. Course work was squeezed in over five years after long days at the office and during summer vacations. While she was getting her degree, she was hired as an elementary-school health teacher in the Boston suburb of Brookline, and in 1975 she was promoted to the job of guidance counselor at the high school there.

The dual role of mother and breadwinner has forced Liz Gude to make a lot of hard choices. Job demands have cut into the time that she can devote to her children. One day a few years ago, for example, she opted to attend a professional conference rather than an activty day at one of her children's schools. "I had made a commitment to the conference, and I wanted to go—it would help me professionally," she says. "I had to decide which was more important." Because she makes a real effort to get to shcool activities in which her children play a part, she says they aren't "devastated" when she misses other events. "They regret it, but they understand," she says. In fact, having a single parent seems to have given the children independence and a sense of responsibility uncommon for their ages. "My mother never waited on us, so I know how to run a household myself," Sarah, the oldest of the three, says. The children function as adults so much of the time, Mrs. Gude says, that occasionally they have to remind her that they are still teen-agers.

Most of her employers have been understanding about her occasional need to leave work to care for her children. And sometimes she has improvised: When she worked at Harvard, she says she sometimes took a sick child to work, where he or she rested on a pillow under her desk. Her boss didn't complain as long as the work was done. Roger Aubrey, who as director of guidance and health education for the Brookline schools is one of her supervisors, says that Mrs. Gude's schedule at home hasn't hindered her performance on the job. "It's the old saw about going to a busy person to get things done," he says. "I see Liz here working at 6 o'clock at night."

Yet she has had to shelve some of her professional aspirations and to postpone others because of family commitments. She has turned down jobs, for example, because they would have left her even less time to spend with her children. One teaching offer in Brockton, for instance, would have meant a long commute, beginning before the children got up in the morning, and she rejected it. "It's really important for me to see my kids off to school," she says. And for many years it wasn't feasible to try to earn a doctorate, because she would have had to work summers and every night after her regular office hours for three or four years.

Later, Liz Gude got the job she wanted. But she doesn't have the kind of money she needs, and the lack of it has been her chief problem. Her income, including child-support payments, often doesn't cover extras or emergencies, such as a sudden, big dental bill. "It's those 'extras' that throw us for a loop for months," she says.

When the children were younger, child care was a major expense. During the school year, she spent at least $25 a week to hire high-school girls to babysit after school until she got home. During school vacations,she had to pay for eight, rather than four hours of help each day. Hiring full-time, live-in help was fiancially out of the question, she says, and the search for reliable babysitters was a constant worry.

From time to time, she has turned to her family for financial help. She took a $3,000 fund her father-in-law had set up for the children's college education, $600 from her own father and $2,000 from her savings to send her children to a private middle school. "It's important that school be a good place for them, because I'm not around as often as I'd like," she says.

The private-school expense, of course, has left little money for college. Mrs. Gude says all three of her children have faced the money crunch squarely and realize that they alone will have to finance college tuition costs. "We had a family conference, and they know how much I am going to help and how much they will have to put up themselves," she says.

Mrs. Gude says 19-year-old Sarah, for example, financed the entire $3,500 cost of tuition and incidentals for her first year at Lesley College in Cambridge through grants, loans and work. Now a sophomore major in journalism at the University of Massachusetts in Boston, Sarah spends only $500 for tuition and saves money by living at home. Anna, now 17 and a high-school senior, hopes to attend the University of Massachusetts at Amherst, where tuition runs $800 a year. Mrs. Gude says she and her former husband each plan to contribute $100 a month toward Anna's prospective costs of $2,000 a year for room and board—about what it would cost to have her at home. The third child, Clay, now is 16, and "it's a little early" to plan how to meet his educational expenses, Mrs. Gude says.

Another big educational bill still looming before Liz Gude is that for her own coursework for a doctorate. She feels that she can begin in the fall of 1979 or 1980, "because my kids are old enough so that I can put the time—time that I had to spend with them—into studying. I won't have that evening or weekend demand." As for the money, she figures that the first year alone will cost about $4,500. So in addition to holding down her full-time job—as she will continue to do after returning to school—she has been working as a part-time educational consultant for the past three years. The extra $600 to $1,000 a year that that work has brought in has been put into a "special account for myself" to help finance the first year of doctoral study, she says.

Though she hasn't ruled out remarriage, she says that over the years, she has met only three men she considered possible mates. One, a doctor, tried without success to relocate in Boston from Washington, D.C., where he worked. Eventually the relationship died. "I'm not a jet-setter," she says. "With three kids and no money and a job to hold down, I can't move for the sake of some guy."

Right now, her life mostly revolves around work, although, she says, "I have lots of friends." She is at her desk by 7:30 a.m., and often works late so that she doesn't have to bring it home. Her days are spent counseling anywhere from two to 10 teen-agers, teaching a psychology course, attending staff meetings and handling paper work.

She says she hasn't any regrets about her divorce. Even though she has missed sharing child-rearing with a husband, she sees an advantage in being forced to do things for herself. "I'm so happy about that," she says. "I'll miss my kids when they go, but I won't be sitting around in surburbia wondering what to with myself."

Back Into the Rat Race

Twenty years ago, most young women had limited, lifelong ambitions, and Carol Cravens wasn't any different.

"You bought the whole package," she remembers. "You believed a woman wasn't fulfilled unless she had a family and a home in the suburbs." So when she completed college in 1960, seven months pregnant with her first son, Mrs. Cravens knew she wasn't "going to ever do anything with the degree later. I always knew I would just have a family."

Such attitudes seem quaintly outdated today, now that the 44-year-old suburban mother of four works full-time as a junior-college counselor. Yet the road from depressed, bored housewife to aggressive career woman never has been an easy one. Along the way, Mrs. Cravens confronted such difficulties as an identity crisis, graduate schooling, juggled household tasks and a changed marital relationship.

Moreover, this rocky road can be even harder for a woman with high ambitions but few credentials. For Sandy Biggest, a mother who got the yen for a responsible paying job but had only a high school education, the road has been at the same time both easy and tough: easy, because her husband provides enough financial security that she really doesn't have to work at all, and tough, because she refused to settle for just any job. At one point two years ago, she said she wouldn't take anything less than a position selling sophisticated business machines at a minimum salary of $15,000 a year.

"I'd be working right now," she conceded at the time, "if I wasn't so fussy about the kind of work I'd take. I'm not looking for a job because we need the money, so why shouldn't I be choosy?"

Easy or tough, the road back to the paid labor force is a well-traveled one these days, as more and more middle-aged women are returning to work after 15 or 20 years as mothers and homemakers. In 1960, about 43% of U.S. women aged 35 to 44 held or were actively looking for jobs, according to the Labor Department. By 1976, the proportion had risen to 58%. That's why the sagas of Carol Cravens of Homewood, Ill., and Sandy Biggest of Lemont, Ill., are illuminating. Their heartache and growth, stumbling and self-discovery, are reenacted every day in countless households throughout the land.

By age 23, Mrs. Cravens was a college dropout who already had worked as a personnel clerk and as an Eastern Airlines stewardess. Then Carol got married, and she and her husband, Jack, returned to college to get their degrees in physical education. They supported themselves by working as physical-education instructors for the Chicago Park District. Mrs. Cravens, an athletic-looking woman with a ruddy complexion and short, light red hair, refereed basketball and taught dance and swimming. An exuberant, energetic person, she never lacked the stamina to take on another athletic assignment.

Then, all thoughts of working vanished after the birth of her son, John, in 1960. "My main concern was to raise the children. I never thought of doing anything else," she says. "No one ever told me raising children would be a part-time job, rather than a lifelong one."

Three other boys arrived in rapid succession: Mark in 1961, Jeffrey in 1963 and Scott in 1967. Jack Cravens became a traveling salesman for Gate City Steel Co., and the family moved from Chicago Heights to Appleton, Wis., where they lived until 1974. Then they moved to Homewood, a suburb just south of Chicago.

Like her mother and grandmother before her, Carol Cravens threw all of her energies into being the perfect wife and mother. "I made drapes, quilts, robes, even matching shirts for the boys and my husband. I canned fruit, hung wallpaper and baked coffee cakes." She played bridge and golf with other housewives. She gave fancy parties for her husband's colleagues, and proudly called herself Mrs. John Cravens.

But in the early 1970s, things changed. With Scott, the youngest, past the toddler stage, the usually ebullient woman began to feel depressed, and she couldn't understand why. Her life was full, her sons were healthy, the family owned a lovely home and yet, somehow, "There was something lack-ing," she recalls. "I would sit down and watch 'Lassie' on TV and almost cry." She had forgotten what adult books and mu-sic were like and felt intellectually inferior to Jack. "You don't know who you are or what you're doing any more," she says.

Mrs. Cravens brooded for five months before taking what was for her a bold step: She left Scott with a babysitter and drove 25 miles to the University of Wisconsin at Oshkosh —never before had she driven that far alone. When the uni-versity's courses proved too expensive, Mrs. Carvens began to teach baton-twirling and exercise two hours a week for the Appleton Park District. She also lost 11 pounds and landed a major role in a community theater production of "Cabaret." She was beginning to feel like a new woman.

By the time the family moved into a new brick, split-level house in Homewood, Mrs. Cravens knew that she want-ed a full-time career and that to do so, she needed a graduate degree. "I didn't just want a job that would lead nowhere. I wanted to make some money, and I wanted to grow."

She took a course in "Sociology of Women" at Gover-nors State University in nearby Park Forest. The course strengthened her self-confidence and made her angry about her previous passiveness. "I wasted 15 years of my life, doing things for others," she asserts, her sparkling, hazel-brown eyes flashing with resentment.

Her husband, a tall, beefy fellow with some traditional ideas about a woman's role, felt threatened by Carol's new ambitions. He conceded that her return to work would help finance their sons' college education. "But he didn't want me to go the career route," she says. "It was an ego thing. He was afraid I might make as much money as he did. We had quite a few arguments."

Despite her husband's misgivings, Mrs. Cravens began full-time graduate school at Governors State in spring 1975, when she was 41 years old. She completed her masters degree in community college counseling in December 1977. Because her classes lasted from 4 p.m. to 10 p.m. her sons had to pre-pare supper and clean up afterwards—tasks that they didn't take to very readily. She gave the boys cooking lessons on

weekends. On weekdays, she says, "I would leave notes saying, 'John and Mark, you cook. Jeff, you clean up. Scott, you
take out the dog.' If I found the pans were still in the sink
when I came home, I would put them on a tray and bring
them up to my son's (bedroom) desk."

On other occasions, the boys would "forget" to wash
their dirty clothes. "If they forgot, they didn't have clean un-
derwear the next day. That happened a few times," she remembers, crinkling her face with a hearty laugh.

Carol Cravens applied the same no-nonsense determination to her search for a job. While completing an independent project for school in November 1977, she visited several
local community colleges and discovered that she liked the
counseling center at Thornton Community College.

"I kept sticking my nose in the rooms there so much
that finally a guy said, 'Maybe you would like to work here.' I
said, 'Oh, yes. I used to be in personnel,' " The approach paid
off. The following Monday, she began working 20 hours a
week as a part-time career counselor for $2.50 an hour. The
part-time job was the proverbial foot in the door; she landed
a $14,000-a-year, full-time position at Thornton in May 1978.

The transition from school to full-time work proved
more difficult than the switch from homemaker to graduate
student. Mrs. Cravens hadn't worked in an office in 20 years,
and electric typewriters mystified her. "I didn't want anyone
to know that I couldn't set margins," she remarks with a wry
grin. "I figured it out myself so they wouldn't know I was an-
tiquated." (Actually, there was little basis for her apprehension, because most of her 10 colleagues are in their 30s and
40s.)

Mrs. Cravens also had to learn about office etiquette
and office politics. "When I was at home, I would take my
time talking on the phone," she recalls. "At work, I have to
get to the point a lot quicker." She has started trying to remember people's names better, a skill that she previously
lacked. "I feel everyone I meet now might be of some help to
me in the future." And as part of her program to advance in
her field, she reads books on office politics and studies who
does and doesn't get ahead in her office.

Tardiness was another problem. As a housewife, Mrs.

Cravens rarely had to be anywhere at a certain hour; she never wore a watch and habitually was about 10 minutes late. Initially, she arrived 15 minutes late for work so often that her boss, the dean of counseling, wanted to know why she couldn't arrive by 8:30 a.m. She blamed her children, who leave for school at 8 a.m. "Then I decided that wasn't the professional thing to say. Your children should be taken care of before you make your decision to enter a career. Your job has to come first." To solve her problem, she had her work hours changed to 9 a.m. to 5 p.m.

Becoming a career woman has led Mrs. Cravens to make other personal adjustments, too. She threw out her gigantic purse, in which she used to lug "Bandaids, hairbrushes, a flashlight, lots of hankies, an extra pair of socks and asthma pills for one son." She believes that it's more professional to carry a small handbag, "and to leave the kids' pictures at home."

As the paychecks build up, Mrs. Cravens is gradually updating her wardrobe to fit her new career image. "I looked in my closet, and all I found were short dresses, lots of slacks and sports clothes," she says. "I'm buying nice, good clothes: wools, matching sweaters and a couple of suits. I wanted to get things that put me into the business world."

Her full-time schedule leaves her little time for her jogging, and so she runs during her lunch hour. She rarely golfs, cooks, bakes or gardens these days, and she cleans house only on Saturdays, aided by her husband and the boys. No longer can she dash to the grocery store on the spur of the moment—a task that "used to be my 'biggie' of the day," she remembers.

Despite job hassles and personal changes, Carol Cravens thoroughly enjoys junior-college counseling. "Some days I come home bubbling like an 18-year-old," she says. She advises returning adult students, many of them former housewives, and she finds it easy to sympathize with the women's fears and uncertainties. "They come into my office, often freshly divorced, and don't know what to do with themselves. The first thing I say is, 'Learn to wipe your own nose, and you're on your way.'

"Unfortunately, we never learned that. We were

taught to depend on men. Yet we have to learn to make our-selves happy."

It's a lesson that Mrs. Cravens understands well. Grad-uate school and success on the job have changed her relation-ship with Jack. "I feel more equal to my husband than before. We can converse more intelligently." But more importantly, she adds, leaning forward to emphasize her words, "I don't feel like I have to depend on him like I used to. If I want to, I can make it without him." She wants to travel to Europe, learn new skills, perhaps start her own career-counseling business. "I feel I can do anything," she exults. "Nothing can stop me any more."

Sandy Biggest, the financially secure housewife in Le-mont, Ill., hasn't reached the point where she could make such a statement. Two things are stopping her from finding the kind of job she wants: her own choosiness and her lack of qualifications.

That Mrs. Biggest is financially secure seems clear enough. She and her husband, Ed, like to fly, and they own a two-seater airplane. The Biggests, both 35 years old, also have two cars and live with their two children, aged 11 and 16, in a fully-paid-for six-room house in Lemont, a pleasant suburb of Chicago. Ed is a well-paid mechanic for Amoco Chemical Co. And although the couple currently hasn't any outside income, Ed put in many seven-day weeks and Sandy also worked in the early days of their marriage. So they have ample reason to consider themselves well-fixed financially.

Such financial security puts Sandy Biggest in a far dif-ferent situation from that of many working women. Many wives have to work because their earnings provide the sole support for their families. Others seek to help make ends meet despite modest budgets. Still others work so that their families can afford worthy "extras" such as a home of their own or college education for their children. Sandy's reason for wanting to work, while quite different, isn't unimportant: She desires the self-fulfillment of doing something on her own.

Sandy Biggest "may well be typical of the woman who feels financially secure" but still wants to work, says Eileen M. Schaeffler, Chicago regional director of the Labor Department's Women's Bureau. She continues: "In the absence of economic necessity, she has the freedom to think of other factors—to expect the same pay and responsibilities as men she compares herself to. She doesn't have to make the compromises that others do."

Female job-seekers who are financially secure are indeed more fussy than men, says Gus Lambros, vice president of Future Personnel Services Inc., a Chicago employment agency. Men, he contends, are reared with the idea that they eventually will have a career and will have to make money for a family. They generally will go anywhere to land a job. Women, on the other hand, sometimes will refuse jobs if they have to walk several blocks to work, if office decorations aren't nice or if the money isn't quite right, he says.

And Sandy Biggest herself can attest to that. About two years ago, she turned down three offers of jobs selling insurance plans because of either insufficient or uncertain salary terms. Shortly thereafter, she called six business-machine companies but failed even to get an interview, either for lack of education or experience.

But she figured that the process of looking for a job is in itself beneficial, because it gave her a better idea of the kind of person the companies were seeking. And for a long while, she figured that getting an interview might be all that she needed to fulfill her job expectations. "You can go to 1,000 companies, and if you can finagle just one interview, you can get the job, especially in sales, where personality is so important," she said.

This approach illustrates what one women's job counselor believes is a common problem among housewives seeking to return to the job fold: naivete about business.

"These women generally aren't aware of the rules of the game in careers," says Diane Manhoff, director of job development and referral at Flexible Careers, a Chicago-based, nonprofit organization that helps women get jobs. "Their orientation hasn't been toward the future. They have a certain naivete about what it's like to get into and move ahead in business."

And, for a while at least, this may well have been one of Sandy's key problems, even though she wasn't totally without business experience. Shortly after graduating from high school, she chose to get married rather than go to college. Then, like many young wives, she worked: for a department store, in cosmetics sales; as a waitress, and as a hostess in a restaurant. But as her children were born and needed a mother's attentions, she first switched to part-time work and then quit working altogether.

Six years ago, with the children aged 10 and five and well on their way to a measure of independence, Sandy started full-time work as a bookkeeper for a door manufacturer. The job lasted until part of her division was eliminated.

What followed was a lengthy period of housework, which she found boring, and of desultory attempts to find another job—a job offering a certain status. She was dissatisfied with staying home because she didn't have enough to do to keep her busy, and because she felt strongly that she had the ability to go out and accomplish something on her own. "But I decided that if I was going to work, it would have to be something a little bit out of the ordinary," she said. "I don't care for the environment where you go in and do the same thing every day with the same people." In addition, even though she had her husband's encouragement in hunting for a job, she laid down some other conditions: flexible office hours and not too much traveling.

At that time, Sandy's previous office work and her "sales experience" were enough to convince her that she should go into a more-sophisticated area of sales. She pictured herself, perhaps 10 years later, "in management in some area."

At the same time, however, she was willing to concede that her search for such a job would be difficult. "If I'm rejected repeatedly," she said, "then I'll try getting the credentials they're looking for. Just because I'm a housewife, it doesn't mean I'm dead meat."

Then, after a six-month stint as an accounting clerk at De Cicco Overhead Doors Inc., a Lombard, Ill., installer of garage doors, Sandy decided to try getting the credentials. She has started taking courses at the Joliet (Ill.) Junior College, and she hopes to get an associate degree in accounting. After that, of course, she'll take another swing at the job market.

Protecting the Unborn

"You're empty; you're not the woman you used to be"
—Betty Moler.

"In January I said I'd never do it. But by May I felt they really meant business. . . . I felt backed up against a wall"—Barbara Cantwell.

Willow Island, W.Va., is "a wide place in the road," says one man who knows the place. It's a bleak spot in a depressed region, and one of the few local employers offering jobs at decent pay is the American Cyanamid Co. plant.

All of which had more than a little to do with the decision of Mrs. Moler and Mrs. Cantwell to have themselves sterilized. "I wish I had never done it," says Mrs. Cantwell, a 31-year-old divorcee who is supporting her two sons. "But I was scared." Scared, that is, of losing her job in the pigments division of the American Cyanamid plant, where a potential health hazard caused the company to restrict certain jobs to men or to women not capable of child-bearing. A disconcerting result was the decision of Mrs. Cantwell and four other women workers to be sterilized.

Their situation, and similar events involving women workers at Allied Chemical Corp., have dramatized an occupational-health problem confronting corporations that deal with hazardous substances: the possibility of damaging the unborn child.

The issue is emotional and replete with disputes over women's rights. Is the specter of fetal damage being used to deny jobs to women? Some women, their unions, and the government's Occupational Safety and Health Administration, say yes. Some working women think it's unnecessary to impose strict safeguards because they don't intend to have any children or to add to the families that they already have. The companies involved say their primary motive is the safety of their workers.

Difficult questions are raised. Must all female workers

of childbearing age be protected, or only those who plan to become mothers? May companies—which could face costly legal and insurance problems if work-place exposures cause fetal damage—protect themselves by inquiring about a worker's intentions to bear children or by denying women certain jobs? What about hazards to male reproductive capacity? Must employers adopt special safeguards for the unborn as well as for workers themselves? Should industry be required to undertake the expensive task of eliminating toxic hazards from the work place?

Complicating everything is a lack of consensus among scientists about the laboratory and field research already conducted on the matter. Policy makers aren't able to agree on how much animal research should be applied to humans. For example, scientific discord abounds over what level of sperm count from men constitutes sterility as opposed to low fertility.

Another problem arises from the fact that many industrial physicians don't know much about obstetrics, and many obstetricians don't know much about occupational hazards. However, the American College of Obstetricians and Gynecologists, aided by a federal grant, has issued guidelines to aid physicians in advising pregnant women whether they should work and on what types of jobs. In general, the guidelines say pregnant women can work if their pregnancy is normal and if the women aren't exposed to obvious hazards. But they stress that the physicians should study each case carefully.

Exposure to lead is getting the most attention. Lead "is perhaps the most well-publicized cause of reproductive problems in exposed women workers," a study of women's health problems on the job said. Lead can cause miscarriages and stillbirths and can cross the placenta of pregnant women and enter the blood of the fetus. It also can cause anemia and damage the brain, nerves and kidneys in male as well as female workers. So late in 1978 the Labor Department adopted a standard to limit exposure to lead. In general, the standard requires employers to maintain the rate of pay of a worker transferred to a low-lead-exposure level, for up to 18 months, until the worker's body has excreted the lead and blood tests show a reduction in blood lead levels.

But lead is only one of the dangers to the unborn child. Vinyl chloride, first identified as a cancer-causing agent, now is suspected of causing increased miscarriages and stillbirths among women whose husbands worked with the substance. Mercury, which in its organic form damaged the nervous systems of Japanese infants whose mothers ate mercury-contaminated fish, often contaminates dental offices, where many young women work; it poses a potential threat to their future offspring, researchers fear. And government scientists worry that anesthetic gases used in hospital operating rooms can increase the incidence of spontaneous abortions not only among exposed women workers but also among wives of exposed male workers, and can produce congenital malformations among their children. A California study has found that 29.7% of pregnant nurses working in operating rooms had spontaneous miscarriages, compared with 8.8% among pregnant general-duty nurses.

Illustrating the alarming possibilities was an episode at an Allied Chemical Co. plant in Danville, Ill., in 1977. Concern over fetal damage from a substance called Fluorocarbon 22 prompted Allied to lay off five women packagers. Two of the women got sterilized, to reclaim their jobs. Then it was decided that Fluorocarbon 22 actually wasn't a teratogen, or harmful to a fetus; the surgery had been needless.

Women are steadily moving into jobs where they once were found rarely, as in production work at chemical companies. The number of women working for U.S. chemical firms now exceeds 260,000. Firms working with toxic substances have been under pressure from government and labor unions to adapt their policies accordingly.

"As late as 1970, industry operated under the assumption (that) we could deny employment to individuals incompatible with the work," says Warren Ferguson, director of occupational safety at Allied Chemical. "Now laws dictate we must use women, the handicapped and others in shift work . . . which presents a series of new challenges."

The laws are dictating, and so are the insurance companies. Corporations and their insurance carriers are worried about potential liability for a company if a malformed fetus is linked to exposure to toxins in the work place (no such case seems to have emerged so far).

As these possibilities have dawned, in the past few years, companies have rushed to set policies on the subject. Olin Corp. vetoed the placement of women in ammunition plants where benzene is used as a solvent, and at installations where carbon disulfide is used in cellophane manufacture.

"The exposures would be too high for fetal safety," says Dr. Richard O'Connell, Olin's director of health affairs.

Allied Chemical has prohibited the use of carbon tetrachloride and chloroform—both considered to be fetal toxins—as solvents in laboratories where women work. Various big companies have stated flatly that they reserve the right to restrict women from holding plant jobs that might present hazards for pregnant women.

The companies seem uncertain about what substances are teratogenic, and at what concentrations. For example, Cyanamid made a search of the medical literature in 1977 and turned up a list of 30 substances it said might affect fetal development.

The list included lead, mercury, phosgene, vinyl chloride and carbon tetrachloride—a wide range of substances. However, Cyanamid's medical director, Dr. Robert Clyne, says that further review by the company led it to narrow the list to five toxins before implementing a policy of excluding women from some jobs. "But I still wouldn't let my daughter work with those 25," he says of the substances removed from the list.

All of this has generated resentment and suspicion among the women involved, and in their labor unions. The women at Cyanamid's Willow Island plant say they originally were told that "hundreds" of chemicals might be hazardous for them. By autumn the list was reduced to lead, used in the pigments division (where nine of the 23 women in production jobs worked).

"I smelled harassment when the problem was suddenly narrowed to the area where women worked," says Mrs. Cantwell.

Betty Moler says the pigments jobs pay about $225 a week, plus substantially more accured through night shifts, weekend work and so on. The company says it offered to keep the women at their old pay rates for 90 days, transferring them to "utility," or janitorial, work, paying about $175 a week with no extras, or to jobs in two other departments where they might hope to accumulate seniority and return to their former wage levels.

The women weren't mollified. Nor was their union, the Oil, Chemical and Atomic Workers Union, which says it intends to file lawsuits charging Cyanamid with sex discrimination in employment practices at the Willow Island plant.

Also concerned is OSHA, the U.S. government agency that monitors such matters. "We're concerned with exclusionary job practices," says John Froines, director of the division of toxic substances at OSHA, who contends that industry "has traditionally been unwilling to institute engineering controls"—that is, protective apparatus in plants to shield all workers from exposure to toxins. "The problem is to control the toxic substance, not the worker," says Mr. Froines. "The issue has become a social and economic one."

Cyanamid denies discrimination. "In the past we placed women anywhere in the plant where there were entry-level positions," says Glenn Mercer, superintendent of industrial relations for the company. "There was no policy until 1978 to restrict their placement, due to work-place health conditions." Mr. Mercer says the plant has been increasing the number of women employes.

Cyanamid and other companies say "engineering controls" sufficient to protect against all hazards are too expensive. "The difficulty and cost of implementing good industrial hygiene shouldn't be used as a blanket excuse to exclude women," asserts Petty Gehring, Dow Chemical Co.'s director of health and environmental services. "But if the cost is going to rise exponentially to reach a certain low level for uniquely fetal toxins, then it's justified to take women out of the work place."

Cyanamid's Dr. Clyne states flatly, "There's no practical, feasible level to protect the fetus primarily. We'd bankrupt American industry."

Dr. Kenneth Bridbord of the National Institute for Occupational Safety and Health says, however, "It's inappro-

priate for companies to paint the issue as being just one involving women." Mr. Froines of OSHA says, "There's no scientific basis to lead to work-place exclusion of either sex."

Indeed, toxicologists note that a damaged fetus may
result from a damaged sperm as well as a damaged egg. Dr.
Bridbord says many companies are failing to make the scientific distinction between a teratogen, which damages the fetus, and a mutagen, an agent that causes basic genetic
changes in male or female reproductive cells.

If a substance is a mutagen (as lead is, for instance) it
would seem that both sexes should be protected in the work
place. Situations involving male workers also have dire insurance potential. For instance, both Dow and Shell Chemical
Co. discovered two years ago that the pesticide dibromochlo-
ropropane, or DBCP, produced at some of their plants, was
lowering the sperm counts of male workers.

A $10 million suit on the workers' behalf still is pend-
ing in the courts. Aetna Life & Casualty Co. was the insurer
for both Dow and Shell. When the relevant policies came up
for renewal, Shell elected to self-insure. Dow's product liability was renewed, at a new figure that an Aetna spokesman
won't disclose.

However, the spokesman says the DBCP incident was
"a consideration in the renewal cost. . . . Once an accident
occurs, we're hooked and liable. The pricing of today's policy
is done against potential future losses. And the cost of a human mistake can be high."

The International Chemical Workers Union has been
arguing with Cyanamid about a case with implications for
both sexes. Nine women of childbearing age were transferred
from a Pearl River, N.Y., plant of the Lederle Laboratories
division because the plant was making two cancer drugs said
to be dangerous to pregnant women.

Stanley W. Eller, industrial hygienist for the ICW, has
filed a charge of imminent danger with OSHA on behalf of
the men still working with the drugs. The drugs, he says,
have as much potential for damaging sperm as for harming
the women.

"The same information they used to move out the
women they're citing as indicating no alarm for men, al-

though the hazard is stated in the Physician's Desk Reference," he says. The PDR, a standard medical reference book, indeed does mention hazards for men.

Among the women at Cyanamid's Willow Island plant, confusion and despondency are the chief reactions. Mrs. Cantwell, sterilized at the age of 31, says she once had hoped to remarry and have more children. "Instead, I now have to think about adopting children," she says.

Mary Carpenter, a 34-year-old widow and mother of two who also had been in the pigments division of the plant, rejected sterilization as a solution to her problem, after consultation with her second husband.

"I considered it, because I'm still paying off medical expenses from my first husband's death," she says. "But my husband said he didn't want me sterile, so I took the lower paying janitorial job. I still hope to get my old one in pigments back."

One chemical company hygienist suggests that "companies have to start making it easier for women to report pregnancies by assuring them that their jobs aren't at risk." However, the critical time of fetal development, when a toxin may do the most damage, is during the first three months, when a woman may not necessarily know that she is pregnant.

Chemical companies say the whole question is complicated by employes' rights to medical privacy, and the concurrent obligation to protect their unborn children. "We don't ask women if they're fertile, or to notify us if they're pregnant," says Edwin M. Halkyard, vice president for corporate relations at Allied. "When the two Danville plant women each called up on their own and asked if they could return to work if they showed proof of sterility, how could we say no?"

Exposure to lead is getting the most attention. Lead "is perhaps the most well-publicized cause of reproductive problems in exposed women workers," a study of women's health problems on the job said. Lead can cause miscarriages and stillbirths and can cross the placenta of pregnant women and enter the blood of the fetus. It also can cause anemia and damage the brain, nerves and kidneys in male as well as female workers.

But lead is only one of the dangers to the unborn child. Vinyl chloride, first identified as a cancer-causing agent, now is suspected of causing increased miscarriages and stillbirths among women whose husbands worked with the substance. Mercury, which in its organic form damaged the nervous systems of Japanese infants whose mothers ate mercury-contaminated fish, often contaminates dental offices, where many young women work; it poses a potential threat to their future offspring, researchers fear. And government scientists fear that anesthetic gases used in hospital operating rooms can increase the incidence of spontaneous abortions not only among exposed women workers but also among wives of exposed male workers, and can produce congenital malformations among their children. A California study has found that 29.7% of pregnant nurses working in operating rooms had spontaneous miscarriages, compared with 8.8% among pregnant general-duty nurses.

Until chemicals commonly used in the workplace are better tested, "we are going to be faced with a number of cases of fetal wastage and congenital abnormalities," warned Dr. John Finklea, former director of the National Institue for Occupational Safety and Health. He forecast that employers who expose workers to such hazards are going to face "liability involving substantial sums" as well as "great financial uncertainty."

Corporate managements quickly became aware of such problems quite early in the discussions about possible government standards. Dr. H. C. Scharnweber, corporate medical director of Dow Chemical Co., saw employers caught in a legal crossfire. If they permit exposure to occupational dangers, they face lawsuits "on behalf of every unsuccessful pregnancy." If they bar women workers from hazardous jobs, they face sex-discrimination charges by workers of their unions.

As a result, many employers took a cautious approach. They barred female workers from jobs requiring exposure to substances that could cause birth defects. Some physicians suggested that if exceptions are made, the female workers should be alerted to the hazard and asked to acknowledge it in writing.

At Dow Chemical, Dr. Scharnweber said, "no employe, male or female, will knowingly be exposed to hazardous levels" of material known to cause cancer or genetic mutations in humans. And, he added, "we will not place women capable of reproduction in any work situation" involving exposure to materials that can harm the fetus.

Portia Hamlar, a Chrysler Corp. attorney, argued that it is reasonable to require women working in hazardous areas to notify the employer if they are pregnant or capable of bearing children. Otherwise, she suggested, "the employer would invade the female employe's right to privacy of requiring periodic examinations to determine the existence of pregnancy among employes."

Some other companies favored banning pregnant women from hazardous jobs altogether, but unions and women's groups weren't prepared to accept that approach. There shouldn't be one set of health standards for men and another for women, they insisted. And because of evidence about dangers to male workers, "protection of the reproductive functions should be assured in both men and women," the United Auto Workers declared.

Carolyn Bell, an industrial hygienist for the United Rubber Workers, feared that without federal standards, workers would face a crazy quilt of employer rules. She worried that companies, in effect, would tell women that " 'if you are pregnant, you can have light exposure; if you are more than two months pregnant, medium exposure; and if you are on the pill, you can receive heavy exposure.' " She concluded, "That's ridiculous."

Section V

Fighting Back

Much of the progress made by working women in recent years has been facilitated by antidiscrimination legislation and favorable court decisions. That simple statement, however, tends to mask the complex and ever-changing state of the law as one court ruling follows another, year after year. The first chapter of this section discusses just one aspect of the mass of legal attack and counterattack—the running argument over what constitutes, legally, an intent to discriminate. Although this chapter, The Law's Complications, is narrowly focused, it lays bare some important matters. It shows that the law is a developing, changing concept—and that the change need not necessarily be in the direction of facilitating successful civil-rights complaints. It shows how legalistic the apparently simple notion of job discrimination can become. And it shows the frequently close connection between women's-rights and minority-rights cases.

The second chapter, Ma Bell's Daughters, gives an idea of how well a formal antidiscrimination agreement can work. In January 1973, American Telephone & Telegraph Co. signed, under federal prodding, a far-reaching civil-rights accord. Both because of the landmark nature of the agreement and the fact that the Bell System employs more American women than any other company, the situation at AT&T provides a sort of test of the usefulness of affirmative-action accords. In many ways, a really firm answer still hasn't emerged. Although the company's official policy is very enlightened, women employes say, inevitably not all of its employes down the line are. And although women have made great advances at AT&T, they still have a long way to go.

Women workers who feel that they have been treated unfairly can fight back in ways other than rushing into court, of course. In many cities, for example, secretaries are balking at doing various personal services—like making coffee and running errands—for their bosses. These women have organized into groups that have staged media events to call attention to office practices that they find objectionable. And these groups are widely viewed as the opening wedge for unionization efforts.

The fourth chapter of this section, entitled Antibias Inc., tells you how women and minority-group members can get help from job-counseling firms on what to do to progress in a career. Such specialized counseling has become a rapidly expanding business. The consultants assist companies, too, by helping recruit women and minorities and by teaching managers how to avoid discrimination lawsuits.

And the final chapter reports on the difficulties that have hampered the new women's banks. Conceived as a way of helping women who have faced credit discrimination, the banks were founded with high hopes. But so far, at least, these hopes have been frustrated, partly because regular established banks have acted to become more accommodating to women.

The Law's Complications

Fletcher Farrington, a Savannah, Ga., civil-rights lawyer, says he's advising clients with job-discrimination complaints "a lot differently today" than a year or two ago.

Among other things, he says, he is discouraging many clients from filing suits, cautioning them that "a lawsuit is the least-efficient way of doing what you want to do." Instead, he suggests that they try to reach an accommodation with their employer, rely on union grievance procedures or, in some cases, consider forming new labor unions.

The reason, he explains, is that recent Supreme Court decisions have been making it harder for minorities or women to prove that an employer has engaged in job discrimination in violation of the 1964 Civil Rights Act.

That law has been an indispensible tool for minorities and women in opening up employment opportunities. The Constitution's requirement of equal protection of the law for all persons can be invoked against public employers, and minority job applicants have, on occasion, successfully used an 1866 civil-rights law that bars race discrimination in the making and enforcement of private contracts. But there wasn't any all-encompassing ban on job discrimination on account of race, color, religion, sex or national origin prior to the 1964 act.

Like Mr. Farrington, some lawyers who defend companies have noticed the same trend in recent Supreme Court interpretations of that act. R. Lawrence Ashe Jr., an Atlanta attorney, says there's "no question—the law definitely is moving back more toward the middle of the road from the employer's point of view."

Actually, the change they detect is a subtle one. And not all lawyers agree that the court has retreated from the strong enforcement position it took in one particular case in 1971. That was its first major decision interpreting the job-bias provisions, known as Title VII, of the Civil Rights Act.

Confusion isn't surprising, as members of the court themselves have disagreed on whether they are abiding by the 1971 precedent.

The 1971 case was brought by a man named Griggs and 12 of this fellow black workers against Duke Power Co. The group challenged the company's requirement that employes have a high-school diploma or pass generalized intelligence tests before being hired or transferred to better jobs.

Chief Justice Warren Burger, writing for a unanimous court, held that "good intent or absence of discriminatory intent does not redeem employment procedures or testing mechanisms that operate as 'built-in headwinds' for minority groups and are unrelated to measuring job capability." Once a plaintiff has shown that an employment practice has a discriminatory impact, the court said, the burden is on the employer to show that any given requirement has a "manifest relationship" to the jobs in question and represents a "business necessity."

The tone of that decision, says an attorney with the Equal Employment Opportunity Commission, conveyed "an unstated instruction for the lower courts to continue to enforce Title VII vigorously." Since 1971, the Griggs case has been the primary foundation on which equal employment enforcement developed. The court's statement that intent didn't matter helped plaintiffs to win lots of cases.

However, in the past couple of years, the court has issued some decisions that raise questions about just how broadly the Griggs philosophy is to be applied. While the court repeatedly cites the 1971 case with apparent approval, it has found several situations lately where its principles didn't apply.

Remarking that the implications of Griggs were "enormous," David Rose, who heads the Justice Department's equal employment effort, believes that the court is now "cutting down on the outer reaches of those implications."

The first hint of trouble for the plaintiffs came in 1976, not in a Title VII case but in one brought under the Constitution's equal-protection guarantee. The case involved tests given to police training applicants in Washington, D.C.; Title

VII wasn't involved because the dispute arose before the Civil Rights Act was extended to public employes in 1972.

The court held, seven to two, that the constitutional standard for judging claims of discrimination was different from that applied under Title VII and that a plaintiff must prove discriminatory purpose, as well as disproportionate impact, to support a charge of constitutional violation. Justice William Brennan, joined by Justice Thurgood Marshall, dissented, warning that the decision "has the potential of significantly weakening statutory safeguards against discrimination in employment."

Justice Brennan was "only too prophetic," says a Washington civil-rights lawyer. Indeed, exactly six months later the court stunned civil-rights forces with a decision that employers could exclude pregnancy from company disability income plans without violating Title VII's ban on sex discrimination. The majority found, in a case involving General Electric Co., that the plaintiffs hadn't shown that the policy affecting pregnant women had the effect of discrimination based on sex.

Though the question of intent didn't seem directly involved in the GE case, Justice William Rehnquist, writing for the majority, brought it up; he indicated that he believed it was an open question whether one provision of Title VII required proof of intent to discriminate. His comment prompted a mini-debate in opinions by his fellow Justices as to whether the court was being consistent with the spirit of the Griggs decision.

The next blow for the civil-rights forces came in May 1977, when the court ruled, in a case involving the trucking industry, that a seniority system that perpetuated past discrimination was legal unless there was proof that it was set up for the purpose of discriminating. The court held that the Griggs rationale would have applied if it weren't for a specific exception for "bona fide" seniority systems that Congress had written into Title VII.

While thus preserving the Griggs doctrine, the high court was viewing it far less broadly than the lower courts, which had consistently found that seniority systems that locked minorities into less desirable jobs couldn't be "bona fide." They had inferred intent to discriminate.

Another recent decision calling into question the court's enthusiasm for the Griggs principles came in January 1978 in a case involving South Carolina teachers. The Justice Department, joined by the National Education Association, had challenged that state's use of the National Teachers' Examination to certify teachers for jobs and determine their pay levels. A far higher percentage of black applicants than white failed the test, and the Educational Testing Service, which designed the test, advised against its use for pay purposes and said it shouldn't be the sole criterion for certification.

Nevertheless, a federal court in South Carolina upheld the use of the test and the Supreme Court, without hearing oral argument or offering an explanation, summarily affirmed that decision. Justice Byron White dissented sharply, contending that the lower court had ignored the Griggs ruling and misread the decision in the Washington police case in which he had written the majority opinion. Justice White argued that a study used by the state to determine the validity of the teacher test had demonstrated only that "the test measured the familiarity of the candidate with the content of certain teacher-training courses."

An NAACP Legal Defense Fund Attorney, Barry Goldstein, who is more sanguine than many civil-rights lawyers about the court's recent job-bias rulings, says he simply doesn't understand the decision in the South Carolina teachers case. He acknowledges that "we're going to see a lot of defendants who are going to be arguing that this indicates a more moderate enforcement of the testing standards," but he says that recently issued EEOC guidelines on testing procedures help to mitigate any bad effects.

Mr. Ashe, the Atlanta attorney who represents employers, says he thinks the ruling "indicates that a reasonable standard of (test) validation will be applied by the Supreme Court." He notes that after the Griggs decision many employers simply gave up on testing because they felt they couldn't validate any test to the satisfaction of the EEOC and the courts.

There is at least one exception to the Supreme Court's

recent refusal to extend the implications of the Griggs ruling. In June 1977, the court held that minimum height and weight requirements for Alabama prison guards amounted to illegal sex discrimination because the requirements eliminated a disproportionate number of women and weren't shown to have a "manifest relation" to the job.

Nevertheless, the ambiguous trend has continued with the court holding in June 1978 that an employer can't be found guilty of discrimination simply because he failed to adopt procedures that would result in the maximum hiring of minorities. The court also said an employer may use, in his defense against bias charges, statistics that show a high percentage of minorities in his work force. Yet it warned that "a racially balanced work force cannot immunize an employer" from bias charges.

In that case, which involved General Refractories Co.'s Furnco Construction Corp. unit, the court avoided directly confronting the issue of intent. The majority declared that the blacks weren't charging "disparate impact" of a policy, as in the Griggs testing case, but rather "disparate treatment" of individuals, which an employer may rebut simply by showing he had a "legitimate, nondiscriminatory" reason for his actions. Justices Brennan and Marshall dissented in part, saying the court should have left the plaintiffs free to argue disparate impact as well.

Such a puzzling trend of cases isn't unusual, notes A. E. Dick Howard, a University of Virginia law professor who is writing a book on the Burger court. In general, where the Burger court has limited previous rulings in the race area, he says, "it is very much case-by-case. They prefer not to confront directly or overrule precedent."

Largely because of the confusion it has allowed to develop, the court is regularly being presented with fresh opportunities to clarify its position on the kind of proof needed to establish discrimination under Title VII. Presumably, it will do so one of these days. Certainly employers would like to see some clarifications. "Employers generally want to comply with the law; the difficulty is to try to figure out what the law is so you can go about complying," says Jay Siegel, a Hartford, Conn., attorney who complains that the intent issue is getting "dimmer and dimmer."

Ma Bell's Daughters

American Telephone & Telegraph Co., under heavy federal pressure, signed in January 1973 what has been hailed as the most far-reaching corporate civil-rights agreement ever negotiated.

The Bell System, among other things, agreed to give 26,000 women and racial-minority employes immediate wage increases amounting to $36 million in the first 12 months alone. Another $15 million was handed out to satisfy past claims of job discrimination. And the huge company's hiring and promotion practices were almost completely overhauled to put thousands of women and minority employes on career tracks that could eventually lead to better jobs or even management positions.

The agreement, furthermore, broke down job sex stereotypes to put women into higher-paying technical and outdoor jobs that formerly were almost completely a male domain. It also provided that a sizable percentage of hitherto "female" jobs, such as telephone operators and secretaries, would be filled by men.

At the signing of this consent decree, officials of the Equal Employment Opportunity Commission and the Labor Department, who had negotiated the agreement, were exultant. They saw a pattern developed that could be copied by other industries. Even AT&T expressed satisfaction that after more than two years of struggle, an agreement finally had been reached "clearing the air" and arriving at "a more precise understanding of what the law requires."

But how was the agreement actually worked out? Is it the Magna Carta of women's and minority rights it was supposed to be? In some ways, the jury is still out after all these years.

As might be expected, thousands of women who now are taking home bigger paychecks and are doing more responsible work are pleased.

"I love it," says Coleen Titus, one-time telephone operator who now installs and repairs telephones—a job that sometimes sends her scrambling up telephone poles—for Chesapeake & Potomac Telephone Co., a Bell subsidiary in Washington, D.C. Wearing her usual work clothes of jeans and a red plaid flannel shirt over a turtleneck sweater, the tall, slim blonde adds, "I like being outside, being active and the freedom of being on my own." It's very different from the sedentary, closely supervised operator's job she began in 1971 after graduating from high school.

The money is better, too. When Miss Titus was hired, the starting salary for operators was $92.50 a week. By early 1978, it was up to $155 with a maximum of $231 after four years. But she's on a different track now, with higher potentials: installers start at $179.50 and make $329.50 after five years.

Diane Thompson, a 28-year-old black woman, says it was only after the decree was signed that she began to think about career goals. Signed on eight years ago in the business-services department of New York Telephone Co. for $7,500 a year, she how has a $26,000-a-year second-level management job as a personnel staff supervisor.

But you don't turn a company the size of the Bell System around overnight. Says Raquel White, an engineering staff specialist at AT&T headquarters, "Company policy is fantastic. It's motherhood, apple pie, the flag. But that policy is implemented by people, and some of them carry around a lot of baggage from the past." Dee Alpert, employment compliance coordinator for the National Organization for Women, puts it more bluntly. "Sexism is still an integral part of the company," she says.

If one visualizes the Bell System as it sees itself—a vast pyramid with 10 different management levels and the chairman all alone on the 10th level—only four women have reached even the sixth level. They are: Virginia Dwyer, an assistant treasurer at AT&T; Grace Fippinger, a vice president of New York Telephone Co.; Jean Handley, a vice president of Southern New England Telephone Co., and Jo Fasciona, vice president for operator services of Pacific Telephone & Telegraph Co. And none has yet scaled the heights of the seventh level, that of an AT&T parent-company vice presidency. And this in a company employing more women than any other in the U.S.—402,997 at last count, about half of the company's work force.

To be sure, 1,330 women are in third-level management and above—jobs paying $30,000 and up; this is nearly four times as many as in 1972. And the number of minority-group members in these jobs almost quadrupled in the same period. But the fact is that white men still hold nearly 92% of Bell's upper-level executive positions.

Although women's progress has been too slow for some critics, it has been much too fast for another huge group in the company—the three unions representing most of its employes. Within a month after the agreement was signed, the unions were in court contending that AT&T's affirmative-action program conflicted with portions of their contracts regarding seniority and promotions. But the unions' appeal was turned down by two federal courts, and the Supreme Court declined to hear the case.

To put women and minority employes in better jobs, something called "affirmative-action override" was used more than 13,000 times from 1975 through 1977. The override, which in the name of affirmative action permits someone with less seniority to get a promotion, riles the unions the most. Charles Behney, a technician at Chesapeake & Potomac, complains, "For the past year and a half, I have lost $35 a week." He says he was passed over for a promotion that went to a woman with less seniority.

To administer and monitor all this job reshuffling, AT&T has had to set up a miniature Equal Employment Opportunity Commission within its own bureaucracy—although the internal agency is not so miniature, with a staff of 750 people at an annual salary cost of about $15 million.

Even this surveillance hasn't been enough to keep the big company completely within the EEOC guidelines. In 1974 and again in 1975, AT&T signed additional consent decrees calling for added compensation for women and minority employes. Moreover, the 1975 decree conceded that the company hadn't fully lived up to the terms of the 1973 agreement. And the end still is not in sight. Eleanor Holmes Norton, head of the EEOC, says. "The government's own compliance-monitoring mechanism appears to need improvement."

There are other challenges to AT&T. A number of private suits have been filed claiming that Bell companies still discriminate. One suit, filed by a white man and claiming reverse discrimination, was settled out of court. A suit filed in 1977 by women who are engineering layout clerks at Michigan Bell Telephone Co. claimed that men doing essentially the same job but with a different title made up to $72.50 more a week than women.

Not all the job frictions are man vs. woman situations. As part of the 1973 decreee, AT&T set up a management-assessment program for women college graduates hired into low-level management jobs between 1965 and 1971. Unlike men hired at the same time, most of the women weren't eligible for participation in a program that selected candidates for promotion. About 43% of the women who spent three days in an assessment center were recommended and put on a list for promotion.

The "recommended women," as they were called in the company, have done well, but not without arousing resentment among women who arrived at their present jobs without such programs. "Why shouldn't I be included? All I have is the law protecting old people," complains a woman in middle management at New York Telephone who started as a business-office representative in 1951.

To make the complex system work, employes were divided into 10 categories by gender, race or ethnic group. Ultimate goals in 14 job categories were set in agreement with the government, but no date was set for achieving them. Because in 1972, the U.S. labor force contained 38% women, the AT&T formula provided that some of its jobs should be 38% staffed by women. For other jobs, which were believed to be less attractive to women, the percentages were set somewhat lower, after negotiation with the EEOC. Intermediate targets, also government approved, were devised for each of about 300 work locations. Only Bell Labs and Western Electric Co., AT&T's manufacturing subsidiary, were excluded from the agreement.

Because of the way the targets were devised, it isn't

surprising that most Bell companies are meeting close to
100% of them. ("They have to or the personnel vice president
gets fired," says one operating company official only half-jok-
ingly.) But in some cases it will take decades to reach the
ultimate goals. Ironically, one result of the consent decree has
been to reduce the number of women employes by 12,728
from the 1972 figure. "There are fewer women now because
we're doing what we're supposed to be doing" and putting
men in the lower-level jobs that were once exclusively female,
says Donald Liebers, director of human-resources administration for AT&T.

Right now, AT&T has 7,833 men in telephone-opera-
tor jobs; nearly 7% of all operators are men, compared with
1.3% at the end of 1972. On the other hand, only 1,788 women
hold skilled outside technical jobs, such as cable splicer. Although this total is up sharply from just 38 at the end of 1972,
women still hold less than 3% of such outdoor jobs, far below
the 19% target under the program.

One problem has been that the accident rate for
women is three times that of men. Moreover, women have six
times as many accidents climbing telephone poles. Most accidents have been minor—scrapes, bruises and sprained ankles
—but one woman was killed when she fell off a pole in Kan-
sas. A major factor in the higher accident rate for women has
been the lack of equipment specifically designed for them. So
some equipment has been redesigned. For example, the angle
of the "climbers" attached to women's boots has been read-
justed because women tend to be smaller. In addition, pole-
climbing training has been expanded.

Other hurdles have had to be overcome. For example,
Ann Smith, a 32-year-old construction foreman at South-
western Bell Telephone Co., recalls that when she first became an outside plant technician (formerly called a lineman)
in April 1974, her greatest worry was that she wouldn't be
able to master a childhood fear of falling. The job required
climbing telephone poles, and she says she had nightmares
for the first year and a half. But she later became proficient
enough to teach pole-climbing—and so at ease about climbing that she and her husband, whom she met when they both
were outside plant technicians, were married on top of a tele-

phone pole. (The justice of the peace stayed on the ground.)

Still another hurdle was the fact that many women felt overly defensive about their lack of knowledge of specialized tools. One female installer recalls the first time a colleague asked for a no-bounce hammer (a shot-filled device useful in hammering objects in a confined space). She didn't know what it was. And women who never have played baseball have had to learn to toss things to someone on a telephone pole.

Then there were the gibes and ostracism inflicted on women who took formerly all-male jobs. A woman engineer, the only one in her department, ate lunch alone for a year and a half. Her mealtime isolation ended only when another woman joined the department.

And Phillis Barker, a $20,000-a-year account representative for Illinois Bell, says many of her customers "can't hide their surprise at seeing a young black woman." More important, she says blacks and women still can go only so far. "My background is different," she says. "When you get to the level of top management, personal associations count a lot. I'm not going to live in that neighborhood. I'm not going to know those people, and I'm not going to be on the board of that private school because my kids go there. Very few women and very few blacks have those associations."

Men, too, have found themselves in positions calling for some personal adjustment. Gerald Medrano was hired as a service-order writer for Illinois Bell Telephone Co. after he told an interviewer he knew how to type. It wasn't exactly what the 25-year-old ex-Marine had in mind when he applied for a job, but because he was unemployed, he took what was available. He says he gets a lot of kidding from his friends.

Despite its internal conflicts, the AT&T program is still regarded by government officials as a personnel landmark. The EEOC frequently refers other corporations to Bell companies for advice in setting up their own affirmative-action programs. The Bell agreement, in fact, has served as a model for similar agreements by United Airlines, National Broadcasting Co. and Readers Digest Association, in which those companies made settlements of more than $1 million each to women and minority employes who had complained of job discrimination.

AT&T also has launched many innovative programs to encourage employes to take nontraditional jobs and programs to help them adjust to the change. Illinois Bell, for example, frequently sets aside a day to give women a chance to see what's involved in technical jobs—to handle the tools, go down a manhole or climb a pole. The Bell System has been more successful in putting women into semiskilled inside craft jobs than in other parts of its program. At present more than 35% of these jobs are filled by women, close to the ultimate goal of 38%.

The future of all this is uncertain, of course. However, when the consent decree expired in January 1979, government civil-rights attorneys said AT&T had "substantially complied" with the 1973 agreement and recommended against any extension of the decree. The government offered statistical evidence of what it termed "substantial progress" by the company in reducing job discrimination. For example, the report said, women currently hold 28.5% of all management jobs in the Bell System, up from 22.4% in 1973, the report said. On top management jobs, women have risen to 6.9% from 2.1% in 1973, and in craft jobs they are up to 9.5% from 2.8%, the report added. Blacks and Hispanics also have made significant gains.

But whatever happens in the future, the phone company has been permanently changed. Says Phyllis Wallace, a professor at the Alfred P. Sloan School of Management at MIT and author of a monograph on the AT&T case, "Women and minorities are now in positions where they will keep putting pressure on the company. They will file charges or threaten to file. You can't go backwards."

Secretaries' Revolt

Executives these days better think twice before asking their secretaries to make coffee.

The secretary may regard the chore as demeaning. In addition, she may be seething anyway because she feels underpaid, overworked and cheated out of a chance for promotion.

In having to make coffee, she has a lot of company, of course. A survey by Chicago's Dartnell Institute for Business Research a couple of years ago found that about 78% of middle- and top-level secretaries—those paid more than the national average—still had to serve coffee to their bosses. The poll also found that 65% were forced to do "office housekeeping" and that 64% prepared personal correspondence. And often bosses also requested help with personal chores ranging from visits to the bank, shopping, running other errands and typing things for the family.

The tasks were accepted more readily by the highest-paid secretaries. But even at the top level, only 28% of the secretaries considered all these chores legitimate, and only 49% deemed some of them legitimate. Among middle-level secretaries, only 10% viewed all these tasks as proper, and 26% termed none of them acceptable.

Moreover, this lack of enthusiasm for the personal duties was expressed even though most secretaries conceded that they spent less than 5% of their working time doing them. Apparently, what the secretaries mainly objected to concerns a matter of principle. And because of this matter of principle, the executive who asks for his morning cup of coffee risks suddenly being confronted by his secretary and her angry co-workers demanding action on their grievances. If they don't get it, they might well bring in reinforcements, with protest signs and television cameras in tow.

In short, secretaries and other female office workers are turning militant and getting organized. They are a large group—about one-third of all working women hold an office clerical job—but one long ignored by unions, which until recently considered them too difficult and costly to organize.

However, a loose confederation of office-worker groups has sprung up in many major U.S. cities; the groups represent thousands of dissatisfied women at banks, insurance companies, law firms, publishing companies, brokerage houses and universities. Seeking stronger enforcement of antidiscrimination laws, these groups use leaflets, pickets, lawsuits and colorful, well-publicized protests to get their points across.

Boston, New York, Cleveland and Chicago workers have staged "pettiest office procedure" contests to call attention to office chores that they consider unreasonable. In Cleveland, the embarrassed winner was Kelly, McCann & Livingstone, a big law firm where one senior partner's secretary complained that she had to keep him supplied with fresh, sliced carrots every day. (The secretary who submitted the entry has since resigned, but her replacement "doesn't mind" the task, according to senior partner Donald B. McCann.)

Office-worker groups are making significant gains, too. In Chicago, Women Employed, or WE, has won more than $1.1 million in back-pay and salary-increase awards from several large corporations. In Cleveland, pressure by Women Working is forcing the city government to hire and promote more women and minorities. After marching and filing charges, San Francisco's Women Organized for Employment won a ban on separate job listings for men and women by employment agencies and newspaper classified advertisements. And in Boston, some major publishing houses have bowed to demands by a group called "Nine to Five" and have instituted job descriptions and posting of job openings for their workers.

While many employers dismiss the activists as publicity-seeking gadflies, others see the fledgling office-workers movement as the opening wedge in a drive to unionize secretaries and other clerical employes. The Teamsters, Amalgamated Clothing Workers and United Auto Workers already are organizing the offices of private industry, their efforts spurred not only by the popularity of office-worker groups but also by the feminist movement, increased mechanization of office work and expansion of white-collar employment. Their stepped-up activities almost certainly will mean higher labor costs for employers.

Some unions, in fact, are using the new office-worker groups as organizing tools. The 600,000-member Service Employes International union formed Local 925 in Boston at the request of "Nine to Five." The office-worker group's ties remain close; it answers the union local's phone when the staffer is out. In its first sizable election, in the spring of 1977, the new local signed up about 175 clerks, typists and editorial assistants at Allyn & Bacon Inc.,; the company thus became Boston's first large publishing house to be organized. Similarly, contacts with New York's Women Office Workers helped the Distributive Workers of America union win representation elections for clerks at a hospital and a museum.

The office-workers movement also is gaining political clout. Early in 1977, the organizations helped block a Ford administration attempt to weaken federal affirmative-action rules. Later, they won praise from a more-sympathetic Carter administration.

"These groups are very effective in acting as a conscience of the government. . . . They find out about potential violations of the statutes in ways we might not," commented Donald Elisberg, then the Assistant Secretary of Labor responsible for enforcing equal-opportunity requirements for federal contractors.

What the office-worker movement is all about can be better gauged by examining Women Employed, the oldest and largest of the groups. Begun in early 1973 by Chicago community organizers and feminist activists, it grew to 825 paid members by 1978. They are mostly women in their late twenties who work as secretaries, clerks and technical and semi-professional employes for about 100 different businesses in Chicago's downtown Loop.

Ironically, Women Employed's seven full-time staff members could justifiably criticize their own employer's working conditions. The tiny, three-room headquarters is jammed with desks, typewriters, towering piles of paper and jangling phones. The seven women each earn between $7,500 and $13,500 a year and average 60-hour work-weeks. without overtime pay. Like other office-worker groups, WE is short of funds. It operates on a $100,000 annual budget, derived from membership dues, foundation grants and sales of baked goods, crafts and cookbooks.

WE's tactics in combating discriminatory job practices range from individual counseling to class-action lawsuits. But its main function is to solicit complaints from disgruntled office workers and then file charges with state or federal agencies. These efforts, WE claims, have forced 40 Chicago concerns—including Kraft Inc., CNA Financial Corp. and Continental Illinois National Bank & Trust Co.—to award back pay or revise affirmative-action plans.

The experience of Harris Trust & Savings Bank, one of WE's early corporate targets, tells much about how the group operates. Through surveys and interviews with employes of the Harris Bankcorp Inc. subsidiary, WE gathered allegations of pay disparities, inadequate promotion opportunities and sex-segregated training programs. Then, about two dozen WE members went to discuss the charges with John L. Stephens, Harris senior vice president for employe relations.

What happened next is disputed. According to Kathleen Blunt, WE associate director, the session ended abruptly when Mr. Stephens angrily shouted, "We don't have any (affirmative-action) problems here!" Mr. Stephens, however, denies blowing up. Instead, he says, the women were hostile, used obscenities and made "nonnegotiable" demands, leaving with the threat to "cause you trouble."

Trouble was what the bank got. First, WE filed sex-bias charges with the Treasury Department, which enforces equal-employment laws in the banking industry. When Treasury didn't act, WE officials complained about a "whitewash" before a U.S. Senate committee. The result: The Labor Department revived the investigation and eventually issued a complaint against Harris.

Harris denied the government's charges and requested a hearing on the matter. Even so, WE has kept up the pressure. It later sent 25 placard-carrying women marching into the bank's lobby. Television lights glared as they demanded to see Mr. Stephens to give him a "Dubious Achievement

Certificate" for doing "the least for equal opportunity this year."

The mass media are one of Women Employed's most potent weapons, and it often manipulates them to good advantage. Iris Rivera, a secretary, was fired when she refused to brew coffee for lawyers in the Illinois appellate defender's office. The next day, 50 WE supporters showed up at her office during lunch. Amid the whir and click of cameras, they facetiously showed how to get coffee from a machine and how to brew a potful. They left a bag of soggy grounds for her boss. (Mrs. Rivera was later reinstated, and she doesn't have to make coffee anymore.)

Not all WE members seek or want such publicity, however. "Any time there is an article about Women Employed in the paper, the vice president of my area starts to nitpick (about work)," complains Jean Hoffenkamp, a WE official who asks that her insurance-company employer not be identified. "If you name my company, I will be fired." Day Creamer, WE executive director, charges that other bosses harass group members by throwing away leaflets or sending "spies" to WE meetings.

For their part, some employers find the prospect of unfavorable press coverage ample reason to avoid contact with the office-worker group. "Nobody is going to tell me how to run this company," asserts Roger S. Olsen, senior vice president and manager of the Continental Insurance Cos. Chicago office. "I don't want to have 10 to 15 women come up here, bring the news media along, pin me against the wall and throw darts."

Sometimes, WE has learned, damaging publicity, government investigations and leaflets don't bring results. One such failure occurred when office workers being laid off by CNA Financial asked WE to help them win reinstatement. (Earlier, a WE antidiscrimination campaign against Continental Casualty Co., a CNA unit, had resulted in the federal government ordering payment of nearly $1 million in back wages and salary increases to women and minority employes.) "I said to the women, 'Look, companies are dictators. The only way people can fight this thing is to organize,' " recalls Miss Blunt, the WE associate director. She helped the women set up an organizing committee, but the effort collapsed when the committee failed to get a majority of coworkers to sign union-authorization cards.

During the CNA drive, no local unions responded to Women Employed's request for expertise and financial assistance; as a result, WE leaders were left at least temporarily dubious about organized labor's interest in office workers. Nevertheless, they say, WE members are increasingly aware of the need for collective bargaining to guarantee newly-won gains in pay and promotions.

AFl-CIO Professional Employes Department director Jack Golodner looks at such moves and concludes that soon, office-worker groups everywhere will "turn around and say, 'Hey, we're a union. And there's nothing bad about being a union.' " That realization, he predicts, will bring about more formal union ties and accelerate organizing drives in America's offices.

Antibias Inc.

Antidiscrimination has become a booming industry.

Dozens of specialized companies are prospering by helping corporations find minority-group and female executives, as well as by training managers to steer clear of discrimination lawsuits. These consulting firms also are conducting workshops for women and minority-group members who want to get ahead.

Some of these companies that started with one or two people only a few years ago have grown to million-dollar-a-year businesses. "We're billing in a week what we used to bill in a year," says G. Todd Jagerson, a former B52 bomber pilot who eight years ago started EEO Services, a New York consulting concern specializing in compliance with the Equal Employment Opportunity laws.

At the same time, however, even insiders concede that the boom has attracted fly-by-night operators. "Many consultants have slapped together an act, and much of the work in the field is too shallow to produce long-term basic change," says Margaret Hennig, a partner in Hennig-Jardim Associates, Boston consultants in EEO-related work. And some critics also contend that the services are often willing tools of corporations that want window-dressing. "Lots of companies buy our program just so they can tell their government EEO compliance officer that they're doing it," says one annoyed—but willing—consultant.

The specialized firms are growing because companies increasingly have trouble with antidiscrimination laws, which in recent years have sharply increased the penalties for discrimination in employment on the basis of race, color, religion, sex, national origin, age and physical handicaps. In addition, large government contractors and subcontractors now must conduct "affirmative-action" programs to hire and promote more women and minority employes. Some class-action lawsuits against companies accused of discrimination have resulted in multimillion-dollar judgments.

Many companies find it best to hire outside help. "We tried some things internally, and they just weren't that successful; the in-company group didn't have much more experience than the rest of management," says William N. Enes, senior vice president of Hoffmann-La Roche Inc., the Swiss-controlled pharmaceutical concern in Nutley, N.J.

Hoffmann-LaRoche initially hired Boyle-Kirkman Associates, New York, to conduct a one-day awareness seminar for managers to analyze prejudice against women and minorities. Although Mr. Enes has some doubts about how much this accomplished, he says a two-day Boyle-Kirkman program that helped women employes set goals and advance in the company "has definitely produced substantive results. My own secretary took it," he adds, "and she has since moved into an administrative job. The course played a major role in this."

Among other things, Boyle-Kirkman "women's workshops" show employes how to investigate opportunities within their companies and establish personal development plans. Participants also practice arguing for their ideas, then watch their performance on videotape. Sometimes, Boyle-Kirkman even asks women to "do a three-minute brag about their accomplishments," says Barbara Boyle Sullivan, president of the consulting concern. "Women have been brought up to be very modest and humble," she contends. The brief exercise helps make them "comfortable talking about themselves and their achievements," an important aid in getting ahead, she says.

Many corporations also turn to specialized recruiters, especially in fields where qualified women and minority members are scarce. For instance, Management Woman Inc., New York, says it has placed three women plant managers. Also, on one occasion, the company was assigned to find a woman attorney specializing in international taxation. "We ourselves thought the chances weren't very good," says Anne P. Hyde, president of the four-year-old concern. But in seven weeks, Management Woman identified 225 female tax lawyers, including more than 30 with international tax experience, and filled the job, Miss Hyde says. The company keeps on file 9,000 resumes on women and relies on a "network of contacts among professional women" to help fill jobs, Janet E. Jones, chairman, says.

Other specialized companies prosper by helping corporations defend themselves against lawsuits over alleged discrimination. Psychological Services Inc., Los Angeles, says that close to half of its business involves legal defense work. Among other services, the concern helps companies document the contention that their employment tests and other selection procedures aren't discriminatory, often by showing that a test does in fact involve skills directly related to the job. Another company, Information Science Inc., Montvale, N.J., offers a computer software system that, among other things, prepares the voluminous EEO compliance reports that many companies must submit to the government. It also pinpoints where a company must hire or promote more women and minority members to comply with the law.

However, many specialized concerns that help corporations do more for women and minorities also help them justify doing less. Information Science says it has helped some companies justify stretching out deadlines in meeting EEO goals—often by demonstrating with "hard data" that the shorter deadlines just aren't feasible, says Edward James, the company's director of EEO services.

EEO training programs of various sorts are booming. Leopold & Associates, Chicago, has sold to numerous major corporations a course using filmed vignettes to illustrate EEO compliance problems that managers face—or create for themselves. In one episode, a woman with six years of seniority complains that she is earning $18 a week less than a recently hired male doing the same work. The boss blithely explains that the man is worth more in the job because he can sometimes be called upon to lift heavy cartons. The course then shows how such reasoning is no longer a legal defense for paying women less than men and can lead to lawsuits.

Leopold sells the course, including films and participant manuals, for $3,650 plus $10 per participant or rents it for $500 a week plus $10 per participant. The company says that all managers and supervisors at New York's Chase Manhattan Bank recently took the course and that the course has been used by the state of Tennessee, among other government bodies. Similarly, EEO Services in New York says that 780,000 supervisors and managers have taken its four-hour Equal Employment Opportunity law basic-compliance course, which spells out what the law requires in a matter-of-fact way. The company also counsels corporations. It often suggests tough tactics, such as cutting bonuses of executives lagging in EEO compliance. "We tell companies, 'You better start treating your people the way the government is treating you—hold them accountable,'" Mr. Jagerson says. The concern says it has worked for 320 of the 500 largest industrial companies in the U.S.

Boyle-Kirkman also stresses consulting as well as training. When a box-manufacturing company said it couldn't attract women or minority-group members for its factory jobs, Boyle-Kirkman suggested adding a simple line to the next help-wanted advertisement: "We welcome women and minorities." The ad attracted 600 applicants, including 200 women and 150 minority members, the consulting concern's Mrs. Sullivan says.

She also cites a case in which a client company, by revising an offensive approach in job interviews and taking similar steps, increased its staff of female sales representatives to 101 from 44. Promoting a woman to a sales manager's job reduced a pervasive fear that selling in this company was a dead-end for women, Mrs. Sullivan adds. This move was one reason, she says, that turnover among the company's saleswomen plunged to 15% a year from 45% in the past.

However, Mrs. Sullivan says Boyle-Kirkman's "biggest product" is a three-day course for managers on such topics as avoiding sexist and illegal job-interview questions. For instance, a question like, "Who will take care of the kids when you're traveling?" can lead to trouble because it isn't job-related and wouldn't be directed at a man, Mrs. Sullivan says. A safer approach is to say: "The job involves travel. Will this cause you any problems.?

Employes as well as employers sometimes pay for special help. Jeanine Montas, a Haitian-born former bank supervisor in New York, paid $280 for eight counseling sessions at

Garely, Franck & Marshall, also of New York, and she says the experience changed her career. She says it made her more effective in her bank job and persuaded her to open her own employment agency. "I always had a dormant desire to strike out on my own, but I had always thought it was beyond my reach," she says. "They showed me how to do it."

Feminist Flop?

The time seemed ripe in the early 1970s for the formation of women's banks. Despite the increasing impact of women on the economy, financial institutions still were discriminating against them in lending and in managerial advancement in the institutions themselves.

So some people thought that the best way to guarantee equal treatment for women would be to set up banks expressly for them, just as special banks have been organized to help blacks and Hispanics. To qualify for a government program designed to aid women's banks, the institutions had to have more than half of their stock owned by women, a majority of female directors and a "significant" percentage of women in senior management positions. By the end of 1976, three such banks had opened in California and another in New York City. Hopes were high.

So far, however, the overall record of the eight women's banks currently in existence isn't encouraging. They have lost more money than other independent banks formed around the same time, some have been forced to recapitalize and others have had dizzying turnover in staff and top management. The reasons are varied; they range from the failure of women depositors to support the banks to inexperienced or poor management. There also has been much internal bickering, partly stemming from feminist sentiments.

Although the newer women's banks seem to have learned from their predecessors' mistakes, it's still too early to call even the newer ones unqualified successes. "There aren't any shining stars among women's banks," concedes Lynda Fluent, president of First Women's Bank of California, based in Los Angeles.

Ironically, the very conditions that gave rise to women's banks also led to credit reforms that have blunted one of their major reasons for opening. The banks are set up under the Treasury Department's Minority Bank Deposit

Program, which seeks to persuade government agencies and large corporations to deposit funds in minority-controlled financial institutions.

Women's banks were organized, in part, to give female applicants for loans a better break than they were getting from existing banks. But by the time three years ago that First Women's Bank in New York—the first of its kind in the country—had opened, Congress had amended the Equal Credit Opportunity Act to prohibit discrimination based on sex or marital status. A recent report to Congress from a dozen regulatory agencies indicates that most financial institutions are complying with the law.

Moreover, bankers cracked open the vaults a bit more for another reason. More women were entering the labor force and thus increasing their financial clout. "In the last five years, it has become very obvious to everyone, including bankers, that women are a tremendous untapped market," says Madeline McWhinney, a former president of New York City's First Women's Bank. Now, "there just isn't the same need for women's banks."

In California, 12 independent banks were opened in 1976. The three women's banks lost an average of $523,000 in their first two years of operations. Seven of the remaining nine new banks at least broke even after their first year of operation and the next year showed an average profit of $239,000. First Women's Bank of New York had lost $2.2 million by the end of 1977. The only other independent bank chartered in New York in 1975 had a loss of $204,000 during its first full year of operations, but showed a $54,000 profit in 1977.

The women's banks have suffered from more than just poor timing. Few of the banks' founders had any commercial-banking experience. Many were political activists pursuing the cause of female equality while disregarding practical business considerations. Finding qualified officers was an even bigger hurdle. Although women make up 66% of the banking industry's work force, only 26% hold some sort of managment position. The few women in higher-level jobs usually work in large banks and have had little experience running small, independent institutions.

First Women's Bank of New York, for example, hired as its first president Mrs. McWhinney, who had been an officer of the Federal Reserve Bank of New York. She resigned a year later after the First Women's Bank had lost $1.7 million. "The directors and I had very different ideas about how a bank should be run," Mrs. McWhinney says. "Several of them tried to get their feet into management."

When they couldn't find qualified women, some banks resorted to hiring male chief executives. First Women's Bank of California named as president a Los Angeles banker, Rowan Henry, then spent considerable time trying to explain why. "Everytime Rowan gave a speech, you could tell people were thinking, 'See, they couldn't find a woman to run a women's bank,' " says Gladys Fogel, bank chairman. "And it was harder for a man to get involved with women's needs," she adds. Later, the bank hired Lynda Fluent as president.

Executive-suite turmoil has especially wracked Western Women's Bank in San Francisco. Shortly after the bank opened, Patricia Connolly assumed the title of president as well as chairman and Richard Barber, a banker, was hired as managing officer. The two officers battled continuously because of differences in policy and personality, insiders say.

Mrs. Connolly and her husband, John, wanted the bank to spend more on advertising and to try to attract corporate depositors. Mr. Barber says that the bank has enough visibility and that publicity has hurt more than helped. As for attracting large depositors, Mr. Barber adds, "I say hallelujah if we can get anyone to walk in the front door."

After a year of bitter fighting, Mrs. Connolly resigned from the bank and sold her stock to her husband. At an acrimonious shareholder meeting in April 1978, Mr. Connolly succeeded in putting three of his nominees on the 13-person board. All three have since resigned, the bank says.

"We just haven't acted like business people," Mr. Barber says. "If we spent less time arguing among ourselves, we could spend more time getting the bank into the black." After the bank lost $383,000 of its initial $1.3 million capitalization in its first two years, California regulatory authorities forced it to recapitalize. To improve the bank's financial situation,

Mr. Barber has cut expenses by subleasing office space and paring the payroll.

Large offices, plush accoutrements and too much staff nearly crippled First Women's Bank in New York. Although the organizers fell $1 million short of their goal of an initial capitalization of $4 million, they spent $883,000 on leasehold improvements, furniture and other trappings for elaborate quarters near Park Avenue. At one point, the staff exceeded 50 people; now, it has been trimmed to 22. "The bank was far too fancy," says Lynn D. Salvage, a former vice president of Bankers Trust Co., who was named president of First Women's in January 1977. "We just couldn't handle it."
In addition, she says, a 24-hour automated teller often broke down, an outside computer firm made frequent mistakes and much-touted "no-return checks" were an administrative nightmare. The checks, which produced carbon copies immediately and thus helped the customer remember how many checks had been written, were filed by date of deposit rather than the depositor's name. Sometimes it took hours to find individual checks. The system has since been discontinued.

Even more damaging to First Women's and the other banks were the sizable number of bad loans. "Our bank was somewhat of a soft touch on loans for women," Miss Salvage says. In its first few years, the bank extended $4.4 million in consumer loans, mainly to women, compared to $3.6 million in commercial loans, which tend to be much more stable because they involve businesses with assets as collateral. An unusually large loan-loss reserve of $319,000 was required in just the first full year of operations, and Miss Salvage says a "significant" number of the consumer loans to women are in default. In 1977, the bank "borrowed" six officers from major New York banks to help straighten out the loan department.

Bad loans weren't limited to female borrowers, however. The largest single loan made by the Women's Bank in San Diego was $230,000 to the male organizers of a professional volleyball team. It was a high-risk loan for a small institution, and the gamble failed. The loan is in default.

Despite loans to women, the women's banks haven't been able to attract sizable deposits from women. "If we had the support of all the women in Los Angeles, we'd have so much we couldn't handle it all," says an official of First Women's Bank of California. She adds that many women seem reluctant to abandon the stability and convenience of a large bank for a new one, just because it is owned and run by women.

The very nature of women's banks may be working against quick financial success. "When you put 'women' in the name, it cuts out half the market," one financial analyst says. "It's like being in the juvenile-clothing business and selling only to baby girls."

That's the main reason that shareholders of the San Diego bank voted recently to change the institution's name to California Coastal Bank. "Banking is such a competitive business that you can't afford to lose any segment of the population from the outset," says Veryl Mortenson, the bank's chairman. "We did that by calling ourselves a women's bank." The name change has outraged some female shareholders, who are seeking to restore the original title.

The newest women's banks, in Denver, Washington, D.C., Richmond, Va., and Greenwich, Conn., are trying to learn from past mistakes. They all have women presidents, but have sought to mute feminist overtones. Both the Virginia and Connecticut banks have lost less than $100,000 each during their first full year of operation. The other two banks have been open only a few months.

In addition, at least eight female-owned-and-run savings and loan associations have opened or are about to open. Of those, only one is using "women" in its name. "The bad image of women's banks have made it more difficult for us to raise capital," the organizer of one of the S&Ls says.

Officials of the first four women's banks all are convinced that they have learned their lessons and that they eventually can make a go of it. The New York bank, for example, achieved a profit of more than $90,000 for the first 11 months of 1978, compared with a net loss of $526,791 in all 1977, Miss Salvage said during a lengthy and often-turbulent annual meeting late in December 1978. The improvement was due mainly to cost savings, higher yields on loans, improvements in the bank's loan portfolio and increased U.S.

government deposits. "We have had a dramatic turnaround," Miss Salvage said.

Nevertheless, the bank's 1977 annual report, issued in the fall of 1978, warned that the bank's ability to continue as a going concern "is dependent on its ability to obtain additional equity financing" as well as making a profit. Miss Salvage said the bank is trying to arrange a $3 million recapitalization, preferably through a private placement.

Although some observers consider women's banks unnecessary, proponents say women still need the special education and counseling that only female institutions can provide. "Women still fear financial institutions," says Kay Bergin, deputy commissioner of the Connecticut Banking Department. "They're afraid of being rejected, of appearing foolish by asking the wrong questions. In a women's bank, there's a feeling of sisterhood that says we're all in this together."

Section VI

Coping With Life

Whenever anyone criticizes working women, sooner or later the criticism tends to center on women who have small children but work anyway. Since many such working mothers leave their children at day-care centers, the quality of care that such centers offer, and their ultimate effect on the children attending them, stir considerable emotion. So in this section on Coping With Life—that is, life outside of the job itself—we begin with a discussion on the sharp division of opinion in this country about day-care centers and the job they do.

In addition, the huge movement of wives into the work force stirs fears that, for various reasons, many marriages will be torn apart. In Marriages Under Strain, you will read about that danger. You will find that the marriages most likely to be disrupted are those in which the husband's role as bread-winner and the wife's role as homemaker are sharply, traditionally defined. And you also will find that many marriages have been strengthened by the wife's employment.

Any strain on a marriage in which both partners work tends to be increased if both spouses aren't just holding routine jobs to earn money but rather are pursuing definite careers. In a chapter on Twin Careers, you will read about such conflicts. You also will get some expert advice on handling these problems from a psychologist who has helped many such couples.

Two dual-career problems of this kind are discussed in detail in the following two chapters. In Moving Experiences, you will read about the difficult problems posed by job transfers—problems that probably will become more common as more and more women enter management ranks. And the final chapter, Careers in Collision, probes into another problem that can trouble two-career couples—the real or potential conflicts of interest arising when spouses work in sensitive areas for competing companies.

Day Care: Boom and Bust?

Each weekday at 8 a.m., Ellen Galinsky, a teacher at Bank Street College of Education in New York, escorts her four-year-old daughter, Lara, to the day-care center at the college on Manhattan's Upper West Side. Then Mrs. Galinsky goes off to teach and do research. She returns in the afternoon to take Lara home.

"Lara has flourished in day care," Mrs. Galinsky says. After three years at the center, she reports her duaghter is "very adventuresome and in touch with other people's feelings. It's a wonderful way to raise a child."

In Los Angeles, however, day care for Ursula El-Tawansy was "a series of horror stories." After two years of unhappy experiences with baby sitters, day-care homes and day-care centers, Mrs. El-Tawansy quit her job as a successful real-estate broker to stay home and take care of her 2½-year-old daughter, Sabrina.

"I didn't want to sacrifice my baby for the job," she says. Mrs. El-Tawansy was unable to find "good substitute-mother care" in day-care homes; at a licensed day-care center, she felt as if she were treating her daughter "like merchandise—just dropping her off and picking her up."

Mrs. Galinsky and Mrs. El-Tawansy aren't unusual in that as parents, they hold sharply divergent views of the value of day care for their children. For that matter, the nation's leading experts in child development can't agree, either. Some worry that day care may be doing serious harm to America's children, damaging little psyches in ways that won't show up until the teen or adult years. Others say "good-quality" day care has, at worst, a neutral impact. Still other applaud day care as liberating for the mother and good for the child.

On one point, however, there isn't any dispute: Parents' use of day care in one form or another is not only here to stay, it is also likely to increase. "The clearest trend is that more women with young children are going to work," explains Richard Ruopp, director of the federally funded National Day Care Study. "Most women don't even have a choice; they must work to support their family. We can wish we were still on the gold standard, but it just isn't going to happen."

Today, nearly half of all mothers with children under 18 work, or more than double the rate of three decades ago. The increase has been sharper for mothers of children under six. Now, about 40% of these preschoolers' mothers have jobs, compared with 14% in 1950. The result: Five million American children under the age of 13 now spend 30 hours or more a week in the care of someone other than their parents or schoolteachers.

Surprisingly, however, in a society that values highly the welfare of its youth,little scientific research has been done on how this trend might affect those children. Jerome Kagan, professor of human development at Harvard University, says there are only six "good" studies of day care's impact in the first five years of a youngster's life, and they all concern "quality day care" at facilities set up for research purposes.

Prof. Kagan himself did such a study. He compared children between the ages of 3½ months and 29 months who attended a research day-care center in Boston with an identical group of children raised at home by their mothers. His finding: There wasn't any "difference in intellectual and social development" between the groups.

Still, the professor says, most child psychologists argue that it's usually better for a child to be raised by its biological mother: His research and that of others showing no adverse impact from good day care are "too fragile" to convince psychologists holding this view. And perhaps, he adds, existing testing methods might be too crude to detect differences caused by the two types of child care. "So logically, we can never say there are no harmful effects of day care. When the birth-control pill came out, it was supposed to be harmless, but we later found that it is harmful to some women."

If that sounds ominous, remember that Prof. Kagan is

talking about day-care centers, which only 21% of the country's day-care children attend. There aren't *any* major studies of the other ways in which children of working parents are cared for in the U.S.—by relatives in the relatives' homes (1.3 million children); by nonrelatives in "family" day-care homes (1.2 million); by relatives in the child's own home (938,000); or by unrelated baby sitters in the child's own home (620-,000).

For most working parents, of course, the question isn't whether day care is good or bad for children. Rather, their problem is finding an affordable place where a child can spend an enjoyable few hours or a day in safe surroundings under the watchful eye of an adult. "We see a tremendous amount of agonizing by women over what kind of child care they should put their kids into while they work," says Francis Roberts, president of Bank Street College of Education, which specializes in early-childhood education. "Actually, we've seen very few day-care arrangements that have hurt children."

Similar reassurances come from a government-funded study of some 57 private and public day-care centers in Atlanta, Detroit and Seattle. The study didn't seek to assess the quality of day care offered in the centers but rather to find out what federal regulations are needed for federally funded centers. Nonetheless, says Richard Ruopp, whose Cambridge, Mass., research firm, ABT Associates Inc., conducted the study for the government, researchers found "nothing approaching harm" in the day-care arrangements they observed.

However, a sharply different view of the quality of day care offered in the U.S. has emerged. Its leading proponent is Dr. Selma Fraiberg, a child psychiatrist at the University of Michigan, who after years of her own research has concluded that the availability of decent day care "is worse today" than before.

Indeed, her book, "Every Child's Birthright: In Defense of Mothering," sent shock waves through the child-care field. A sample of its contents: "I must make a blanket indictment of . . . (day-care centers) which provide anonymous sitters for small children," she writes. "I worry about babies and small children who are delivered like packages to neighbors, to strangers, to storage houses."

Dr. Fraiberg isn't against all day care. For instance, she says children between the ages of three and six can profit from half-day nursery-school-type programs involving small groups and qualified teachers. The problem, she maintains, is that children in most day-care centers are there nine to 11 hours a day—too long a time away from home—and suffer from a lack of educational programs and decently paid, qualified teachers.

As a result, during the years when a child must "learn trust and valuation of himself and others," these places instead "teach values for survival," she says. There are "large numbers of toddlers and small children" under five who show "excessive anxieties which can be attributed in some degree to this experience," she adds.

Those who run day-care centers for profit—a multi-million-dollar industry encompassing 60% of the country's 29,000 licensed day-care centers—strongly dispute such comments. "Our centers give safe, secure care as well as a developmentally rich experience," says Gerald Benowitz, president of Mini-Skools Ltd., a privately held California company that operates 82 day-care centers around the U.S.

The Mini-Skools centers are fairly typical of those run by most big chain operators. Aimed at children of middle-class parents, Mini-Skools centers charge from $36 a week for preschoolers up to $55 a week for infants. Younger children get more supervision than older ones; among infants, the ratio of staff to children is one-to-four, while among children between three and five years old, the ratio is one-to-15.

The staff isn't highly paid. State-certified Mini-Skools teachers make $7,500 a year, and assistants draw the minimum wage. But the centers themselves do well financially, Mini-Skools says, with average revenue of $300,000 annually.

This contrast between the modest pay of the teachers and the substantial revenues of the centers sparks another line of criticism. Some mothers wonder whether profit-oriented day-care chains aren't likely to be tempted to ignore the best interests of the children attending them. They wonder whether poorly paid teachers aren't often poorly qualified as well, whether an attempt to cut food costs doesn't also cut quality and whether a center that increases the number of children per teacher to maximize profits also isn't minimizing the time that the teacher can spend with each child.

Yet the atmosphere at centers run by big chains like Mini-Skools isn't unlike that found in a suburban public school's kindergarten. The eight-to-ten-hour days are structured, with periods set aside for play, rest, snacks and story-telling.

In this respect, the centers provide quite a contrast to some less-formal day-care arrangements. For instance, at one "family day-care home" in Los Angeles, where just one woman looks after 10 children ranging from infants to five-year-olds, a visitor finds the smaller children crying while the older ones play amid abandoned clothing and half-eaten cookies. One anguished working mother reports that whenever she picks up her two-year-old son there, he is "like a zombie—it's just too much for him to cope with."

Yet chats with children themselves suggest that even established day-care centers can't always replace time with Mom. At a Mini-Skools center in Orange County, Calif., for instance, five-year-old Scott Aaron says that most days, he would rather go to the center than stay home. But a four-year-old playmate, Louis Stephen, confesses, "When I go to this school I cry. I don't like it."

At the Colorado Springs, Colo., facility of Children's World Inc.—described by one expert as one of the best for-profit centers in the country—children have an indoor swimming pool and a program that offers gymnastics, music, art and various field trips. Yet Cody Hargrave, a six-year-old who has attended the center for three years, says that while it's fun to swim and jump on the trampoline, "I'd rather be with my parents." And one teacher there says privately that she will never let her children (when she has them) go to even a good day-care center like Children's World because "the parents really don't get to spend much time with their children—only an hour in the morning before the child comes here and an hour at night before the child goes to bed. I'll quit for a while and raise the child myself—no matter what the economic cost."

Of course, many working mothers don't feel they have the option to quit. And according to some experts, that isn't necessarily bad. In many cases, argues Francis Roberts of Bank Street College, it's less stressful for a mother to work than to stay at home all the time with a child. "The parent is more in control of her own life," he says. "The woman gains new respect. The child is happier."

Day care hasn't always been such a source of controversy. The first programs were started in the 1850s as welcome charity for the children of immigrant parents who worked long hours to make a living. During World War II, the government opened 3,100 centers to care for children of defense-plant workers; one private concern, a forerunner of the Kaiser industrial companies, cared for 1,000 children a day while their mothers turned out warships.

After the war, these centers closed, and the concept itself seemed to fade until early in the last decade, when the government began funding day-care as part of its Head Start education program for children of the poor. In the late 1960s and early 1970s, when the number of mothers in the labor force started increasing rapidly, many U.S. companies opened day-care centers—and closed them almost as quickly. Typical was the experience of American Telephone & Telegraph Co., which closed centers in Washington, D.C., and Columbus, Ohio, after finding that most employes didn't like bringing children along to work.

Now, the rush to day care is on again, led by parents in middle-class, two-income families. But they won't always like what they will find, concede those who regulate the industry. In New York City, for instance, over 1,200 day-care centers operate under what's considered the toughest day-care code in the country. Yet, says Edith G. Clute, chief of the city's Division of Day Care, surveillance by her 18-member staff is often "minimal," and as a result the 1,200 centers are "a mixed bag that ranges from the very good to the very bad." In the absence of a larger inspection staff, "our main thrust is to develop a parent constituency," Mrs. Clute says. "Our hope is that parents will understand what good child care is and try to enforce it."

Marriages Under Strain

Melody Gunn went back to teaching despite her husband's concern that she couldn't handle a job, care for their child and keep up the houswork, too. "I was afraid it would be too much for her and she'd get bitchy," recalls James Gunn, also a school teacher in Rockford, Ill.

What happened? "Our marriage is much better now than it was when I was at home," Mrs. Gunn says. Her husband agrees.

Jean Horton took a job as a church secretary in Jacksonville, Fla.,—also over her husband's objection. "She told me that life was passing her by," recalls Jerry Horton, an engineer with the U.S. Army Corps of Engineers. "But I thought we had all the life we needed in the family."

What happened? The Hortons are divorced, and the eight children live with their mother.

In both these families, a fast-growing social phenomeonon met head on with a venerable institution. That the collision produced such profoundly different results, however, comes as no surprise to many psychologists and marriage counselors. For better *and* for worse, they say, the rapid influx of wives like Melody Gunn and Jean Horton into the labor force is altering the nature of marriages across the country.

Most affected are so-called traditional marriages in which the husband's role as breadwinner and the wife's role as homemaker and mother are sharply defined. A wife who takes an outside job in such a situation can threaten her husband's ego, upset her in-laws and work herself into physical and emotional exhaustion. Divorce is often a solution to such problems, especially because the wife's income makes it easier for couples to break up.

But for a family able to cope with stresses, a working wife can bring fresh perspective to marriage. Her income can free the family from financial worries. And if her job is satisfying, her sense of well-being is often shared by husband and children alike. "It's a change as significant as the civil-rights movement," says Jack Mallory, an Atlanta marriage counselor.

The Labor Department reports that by March 1968, nearly 48% of all married women in the U.S. held jobs or were looking for work, up sharply from the 30% who were in the labor force in 1960. Much of that increase, according to social scientists, comes from mothers with young children who traditionally have been kept out of the labor force by household duties and social pressures. But persistently high inflation, coupled with the feminist movement's gains in opening better jobs for women, have led many young mothers to work for the first time or to resume interrupted careers.

Increased job opportunities for women are already changing when they marry. As young women are able to find better jobs after high school or college, they are able to delay marriage. That's important, because social scientists believe more-mature individuals are better able to choose lifelong mates. A delay in marriage brings a subsequent delay in having children, a change that child psychologists welcome because more-mature parents are better prepared to rear children. There are also fewer children per marriage—1.07 in 1977 compared with 1.27 at the start of the decade—and more couples who choose dual careers without children.

But there also has been a sharp rise in the divorce rate, which has nearly doubled in the past 10 years. (Census Bureau demographers say, however, that in the wake of that long surge, the divorce rate per 1,000 population has remained fairly constant for a couple of years, and that in divorce-prone California, the rate already has begun to decline.) The huge number of divorces—estimated at 1,097,000 in 1977—probably reflects, at least in part, the strains that working wives produce in marriages. What's more, "the fact that a woman has a job and has found that she's valuable to someone other than her husband makes it that much easier for her to get out of a bad marriage," explains a marriage counselor. "The fact that she's got a job also makes it easier on her husband's wallet," he adds.

"Without my job, I probably wouldn't have gotten a divorce," agrees Donna Hein, who has managed an Atlanta office for six years. In 1977, she got a divorce—her husband was a "workaholic" with little time for her or her children, she says—and today, she lives on her own monthly salary of $950 plus $350 a month in child-support payments.

Women who were married early in life and were tied to a home with small children often find that their first job opens up a whole new world. Some of these women are choosing to leave their marriages and pursue careers. Says an official of Parents Without Partners, an organization for divorced or widowed men and women: "A lot more women are just deciding to chuck it all and really start to live."

Most observers agree that any marriage in which the wife works is going to encounter some tensions, but the most susceptible are marriages that have produced children. "Children make it infinitely more complicated to work out the problems," says Dr. Ruth Moulton, assistant professor of clinical psychiatry at Columbia University.

"I'd like to spend more time with my husband, but with the situation we're in, I have to work and do the housework too," says Sharon Selleck, a 32-year-old commercial artist in Minneapolis. Mrs. Selleck and her husband Wayne both work full time; in addition, Mr. Selleck serves as the organist for a local church. They also have a five-year-old son.

That load—a job, housework and child care—"can really drain you," Mrs. Selleck says, "but you learn to cope with it." Adds her husband: "The combination of both of us working and having a five-year-old is what really does it."

Mr. Selleck says he's willing to do some things around th house, such as make beds and vacuum occasionally, "but I wouldn't pretend to say we divide the housework up evenly." Indeed, with his two jobs and Mrs. Selleck's child-care and housework chores, "we have to be careful that we don't get snippy with each other when we're tired in the evenings," he adds.

Experts say few husbands are willing to assume much of the housework load. "The husband may do some of the interesting or challenging things around the house, such as occasionally cooking or some house repairs," says Kristin Moore, a sociologist with the Urban Institute, a Washington-based research firm. "But women have to do the large amount of the housework, and it tends to be drudgery."

Adds Dr. Moulton of Columbia University: "A working woman is really expected, in her mind and in her husband's, to run the house." The upshot for the job-holding wife, she says, can be a work-week of 80 to 100 hours.

Attitudes like that can cause other problems, too. Many young men brought up in traditional families carry with them the notion that it somehow isn't masculine to have a wife who works. "It can be an uncomforable feeling for a man when his wife goes to work," says Harold Kellner, a New York psychologist. "Her working can rob him of his identity as the provider for the family."

For instance, Wayne Selleck in Minneapolis says it disturbs him that his wife must work in order for them to buy a house. "I guess I have some of this old-fashioned feeling that I ought to be the supporter," he says. "I feel a little inadequate sometimes." (Working wives are often aware of such sentiments. And as a result, suggests Alice Rossi, professor of sociology at the University of Massachusetts, wives pursuing careers become reluctant to earn more than their husbands or take a higher-status position. Instead, subconsciously fearful of upsetting their marriage, they sometimes restrict their own job progress, she says.)

Parents and in-laws also can create friction in a marriage, especialy if a child is involved. "Grandparents tend to say a working wife is neglecting the grandchildren, and the husband's parents might say she's not taking good care of their son," says Marjorie Bufkin, an Atlanta marriage counselor. "How serious a problem that is depends upon whether they live two blocks away or two states away."

There's also the problem of the jealous husband who resents his wife's getting dressed up every day and meeting men at her job. "For every husband who's proud of his wife and her career, there's another one who is jealous," says Dr. Moulton of Columbia. She adds that it is an illogical attitude, since the husband doesn't have any more control over his wife when she stays at home than he does when she's at work. Marriage counselors, however, say they are indeed aware of more on-the-job extra-marital affairs. "When a husband and wife are both dead tired at the end of the day, some of the romance tends to go out of the marriage," Mrs. Bufkin says. "Many times, they find they can regain that romance in an office affair."

While many couples encounter some or all of these problems, most manage to cope with the strains. And in many cases, managing the strain means the husband must abandon the traditional male role and pitch in more around the house.

"I probably couldn't manage to work and rear a child too without my husband's cooperation," says Gay Romack, a Phoenix, Ariz., real-estate broker. Mrs. Romack's job often takes her away from home at night, and when it does, her husband John, a contractor, baby-sits for the couple's three-year-old daughter. That's good, she says, because it gives her husband a more active role in raising the child. Adds Mr. Romack: "One of us has to do it, and I don't mind taking over whenever I'm needed.

Despite the help from her husband, however, Mrs. Romack says things do go undone; she has just learned not to let them bother her. "There are times like yesterday when we hadn't had any milk in the refrigerator in two days," she says. Once, that would have upset her—but no longer.

Husbands who support their wives' desire to work, meanwhile, often find that she becomes a better partner.

"Melody put a real strain on me when she wasn't working," recalls James Gunn, the Rockford, Ill., school-teacher. "When I came home at night, she would want to sit down and have a drink and talk, and all I wanted to do was rest."

That wasn't the only problem. Before Melody Gunn began teaching school herself, the family was "struggling" on his $16,000-a-year salary. "I figure we were spending about $200 a month more than I was making," Mr. Gunn says. "We were stuck at home, and we couldn't afford to spend any money on the house. We would have friends over for bridge, but it wasn't satisfying her desire to get out and it wasn't helping me work on the house," a task he enjoys. (Their home, for which they paid $27,000, needs an extra $10,000 worth of work.)

Once Mrs. Gunn took her $11,000-a-year job, however, their financial burden eased considerably. And "as soon as that problem was solved for us when Melody went to work, a lot of other problems tended to fall into place," Mr. Gunn adds. Now, the couple dines out regularly, Mr. Gunn has the supplies he needs for home repairs, and Mrs. Gunn "is much happier."

There are some less obvious benefits as well that men might gain through their working wives. For one thing, decision-making and problem-solving become a joint venture, lifting a burden off the husband's shoulders. Also, "with a working wife, a man can refuse a transfer, quit his job or just tell his boss to go to hell," says Kristin Moore, the Urban Institute sociologist. "A wife's job provides a lot of freedom if men are just willing to accept it."

Twin Careers

Both husband and wife planned careers in investment banking in New York, but banking firms didn't like the idea of hiring a person whose spouse might be working for a competitor. So she agreed to look for another type of financial job.

A young professor wanted to stay at Harvard, but his wife couldn't get a teaching post there. So he switched to a less prestigious university, but one where they both are guaranteed tenure.

Another woman, a Russian expert, sought to live in the Soviet Union for a couple of years to further her career. Her husband is a statistical consultant whose contracts and career would be unsettled by going there with her. They haven't yet solved their dilemma.

As these examples suggest, conflicts and potential conflicts between career-seeking marriage partners are becoming common and complex. Expert testimony to this effect—and some helpful hints for easing the conflicts—come from Patricia Light, chief psychologist in the office of career development at the Harvard Business School.

When Mrs. Light took on the job, she expected to deal chiefly with traditional student difficulties: personality problems, identity crises, overwork, depression. To her surprise, she found that one of the most-common calls for help came from young couples anxious over how they were going to handle separate careers.

"There's absolutely no question that the two-career couple is a direction in which we will continue to go, and probably at an accelerating pace," declares Mrs. Light, herself involved in a two-career marriage; her husband teaches at the Harvard School of Education, and they have two small children. Higher education levels, the feminist movement, efforts to limit population growth, and other factors all push the trend to dual-career marriages, Mrs. Light believes. And, she warns, business firms are sooner or later going to have to change many personnel policies if they want to compete for these bright young men and women.

In most families where both husband and wife work, they labor at more or less routine jobs and chiefly want to enlarge family income. In two-career marriages, however, money is rarely the major motivation; each partner, usually well educated, aims to advance steadily in the chosen business or profession and seeks psychological as well as financial satisfaction.

The dual-career problem has many facets, of course. One is the issue, still faced chiefly by women, of role conflicts. Despite women's liberation, Mrs. Light finds, society generally still expects a married career woman to continue to fulfill also the traditional roles of companion, housekeeper, mother and hostess.

"Things are beginning to change," Mrs. Light says, "but very slowly. The burden of proof still falls on the wife if the souffle for the dinner party falls or if the kids don't have clean clothes for school. Men are for the most part still shielded culturally from this sort of role strain. Typically, unless family needs reach crisis proportions, people just naturally expect the man to put the demands of work first."

Conflict arises in many other ways, too. How much competition will the partners feel with each other? If career opportunities clash, which career gives way? What is each partner prepared to do for the other's career?

Having children intensifies all the strains, of course; yet almost all the young couples whom Mrs. Light has counseled individually and in special group discussions had definitely decided to have children eventually. Most career wives, though, plan to have the children later, after their own careers have been firmly established. Then when they have the children, they figure, they can resume part-time or full-time work more easily.

Even then, though, trials abound: corporate discrimination against women who drop out to have babies, parental guilt feelings that the children will be neglected, arguments over which parent comes home to take the sick child to the doctor.

With problems so perplexing, just what help can Mrs. Light offer? The most important thing, she tells couples, is to try to think and talk about questions in advance. The woman, for example, should try to figure out whether she really will be able to juggle all the different roles, and find out just how her husband will help.

"Talking things over and trying to anticipate trouble spots isn't going to solve all the problems," Mrs. Light declares. "But then at least, they don't come up and hit you in the face with quite the same force." And, she adds, "there are few if any institutional devices that will help two-career couples make it work. Above all, they have to be very creative and flexible."

If one is offered a good opportunity in a city 200 miles from where the other is happily at work, perhaps they can live in between and commute daily in opposite directions. Quite a few couples, she finds, are willing to consider living apart in different cities during the week and just spending weekends together. "They argue that's not so different from the situation where one partner is always traveling and away from home anyhow," she says.

One partner may have to change his or her career goal. One wife, who's an expert on international finance, ought to be working in Europe or New York, but her engineer husband wants a career with a manufacturing firm in a small Midwestern city. So she began looking for a teaching job in universities near that city.

More couples, too, Mrs. Light says, "seem to have the idea that they can alternate cycles of opportunity—one partner's career being the prime concern for a few years, and then the other career getting priority." And when a corporation asks a young executive to transfer to another city, the wife's situation increasingly influences his decision. "It's no longer certain," Mrs. Light says. "that a young man with a career wife will automatically accept a transfer to a place that gives the wife a mediocre career opportunity."

Another of Mrs. Light's precepts is the need to be realistic in estimating how much can really be accomplished. She cites "Dottie's fantasy"—the case of a talented, hard-driving young woman clearly headed for the top of a major corporation. Yet Dottie also sees herself sitting on the sofa each night reading bedtime stories to two freshly-scrubbed kids.

"For her, time is elastic," Mrs. Light observes. "She thinks she can have everything, as long as she's willing to work harder and run faster." But that's extremely naive, Mrs. Light believes. To get to the top will require long days and lots of travel—and Dottie simply isn't going to have much time for children. "Two-career couples," Mrs. Light asserts, "must set priorities, make choices, accept tradeoffs."

Even more than for most people, time and energy are critically scarce resources for two-career couples, and their use must be carefully planned. Mrs. Light advises. "Spontaneity may be great," she says, "but two-career couples will find that planning ahead helps make things work—that allocating your time and energy carefully keeps you from chasing your tail." This means not only planning flexible work patterns but also planning relaxed time together and even time alone for each partner.

A two-career couple must be willing, too, to spend their money to save time and energy: to buy labor-saving appliances, to hire people to do household jobs, to employ a reliable and sympathetic person to take care of the children during working hours and to hire baby-sitters frequently to give themsleves ample diversion.

They must work out what each partner has to do for the children. Mrs. Light's husband, for example, is on full-time child-caring duty two weekday afternoons, and she's on duty the other three; they usually can trade if an office crisis develops for either one. Two-career couples with children must also develop a strong relationship with the children's caretaker. Mrs. Light says, so that the caretaker has a clear idea of how the parents want disciplinary and other child-rearing troubles handled.

And they must show creativity in working out relationships with their employers. One acquaintance starts work an hour later than her co-workers, having taken the children to school first. Her husband leaves work for 40 minutes each day at 3:15 to pick up the kids and take them to a babysitter.

Both husband and wife make up the lost time at the end of the day.

"This isn't the sort of demand you make when you go in for your first personnel interview," Mrs. Light admonishes. "You have to build your relationship with your employers first, so they become confident that you're going to get all your work done, even though you need special arrangements to do it."

Just as two-career couples have to learn to compromise and adjust, so will many companies, Mrs. Light believes. They will have to permit some employes to work unusual hours, refrain from penalizing an employe who turns down a transfer, guarantee that women who drop out to have babies can return to their old career levels, and perhaps provide new routes to top management that are easier for a man or woman in a dual-career marriage to follow.

"We're not going to see major change in business attitudes overnight," Mrs. Light concedes. "Many companies will insist that all this simply isn't their problem. But more companies are going to recognize that a very different group of young people is coming out of the colleges and universities today and that corporate policies must accommodate them to some extent. Otherwise, they're going to lose out on getting the services of some extremely talented young people."

Moving Experience

Doris Etelson, 48, a vice president of Howard Johnson Co., lives and works in the Boston area. Her husband, Robert, owns an air-freight company in Newark, N.J. He lives in Pomona, N.Y.

Every weekend, Mrs. Etelson drives or hops on a plane to visit Mr. Etelson in Pomona. Twice a week, her husband takes a plane to spend the night in Boston. Two days a week they are apart.

This is the arrangement that the Etelsons have been living with since Mrs. Etelson was named as the big food and motor-lodge company's first woman vice president. It is also the price that the Etelsons have to pay to maintain two successful careers.

They have been able to keep to this tiring, expensive schedule because their children are in their twenties and no longer at home, because Mr. Etelson has encouraged his wife's career, and because they are affluent. For many other, younger career women with children or with husbands settled in their own careers, a transfer often is impossible. The result, many women fear, is that talented female executives are likely to see their careers stagnate.

Although the transfer as a route to corporate advancement is showing signs of declining, the fact remains that for the highest-flying people in national companies, the transfer is a clear road to the top. But many companies concede that they are loath to suggest a transfer to a married woman because of the fear of provoking a domestic crisis.

The problem of the transfer affects relatively few women at present. But it clearly is a dilemma that more and more women are going to face as women hired in the early 1970s to meet affirmative-action goals gain the experience needed for promotion.

Women have a deep apprehension about moving, observes Janet Jones, chairman of Management Woman Inc., a

New York firm that places middle and upper-level women executives. Most, she claims, aim for promotions that don't involve moving, or they choose fields or companies less likely to require mobility. Even when asked, fewer women than men accept a move, she says. (However, there also is a clear trend for men with working wives to turn down transfers.)

Indeed, only 5% to 10% of the 100,000 employes who were transferred by the 600 largest U.S. companies in 1976 were women, estimates Merrill Lynch Relocation Management Inc., a subsidiary of the holding company for the big brokerage concern. Perhaps half of these women had children, many of them probably school-aged, Weston Edwards, chief executive of the relocation-consulting firm, estimates. Many of the women, he says, were divorced.

Mr. Edwards notes that employes most likely to be considered for transfer earn $20,000 a year or more. The Census Bureau says that by 1976 that level of earnings was reached by only 328,000 women, or 1.1% of the 29.8 million women working full time.

But even many of those women, whose earnings and training clearly qualify them for the promotion that involves a transfer, are blocked by their husbands' careers. An obvious reason many husbands are reluctant to follow their wives to new jobs is fear that their own careers will suffer or that they simply will be unable to get another job. Long-distance commuting is possible, but even then the problems are legion—especially if there are children at home.

Thus, the "critical issue" for working couples is how to make their "shared vision of equality" a reality, says William Chafe, associate professor of history at Duke University and a student of the American family. Certainly, he says, couples who want to have both dual careers and children will never make it to the top of their professions. "It's tough enough to do it in the first place, but it can never be done in this situation," he says. Prof. Chafe says childless couples will have an easier time of it, but not without sacrifices, such as weekend commuting if a transfer is crucial to a career. "That can't last indefinitely, and it could cause a split in the marriage," he adds.

Prof. Chafe believes that only a "dramatic change" in

business policy will ease the transfer dilemma for working couples. Such a change, he says, would include flexible working hours, corporate day-care centers, and opportunities for shared positions to accommodate working parents. "We're talking about a social revolution," he says.

A few couples, however, do combine long-distance commuting and children. An example is Sharon Kirkman Donegan, 36, vice president of Boyle/Kirkman Associates Inc., a New York management-consulting firm. In 1975 she married L. E. Donegan Jr., the president of Keydata Corp. of Boston and the father of a 13-year-old son, Matthew. She says that when they married "there was never a question" about giving up her New York job. But, she says, keeping a 10-room Boston town house and a New York apartment, flying home on weekends and providing for household help and part-time child care "costs all you make. The whole arrangement works because of an incredible amount of organization and planning, energy and stamina."

Some women complain that they never get the chance to try to work out the intricacies of a transfer because their companies simply refuse to transfer them in the belief that it would disrupt their families. Mrs. Kirkman Donegan believes that corporate managers subconsciously discriminate against women in choosing which employes to transfer. Managers, she says, "internalize and personalize" their decisions by relating them to how they would feel if their own wives were asked to move. "It's a subconscious, paternalistic attitude, a secret mental process," she says.

But Joan F. Showalter, a personnel vice president of CBS Inc., New York, disagrees. As women advance, they have the same "option for growth" as men, she says. "We're sophisticated here. There's no discrimination relative to personal considerations." And James M. Shipton, senior vice president of First Chicago Corp. and its subsidiary, First National Bank of Chicago, says, "I've never heard a manager say he wouldn't consider a woman because he wouldn't want his own wife to go."

To counter any hint of prejudice, General Motors Corp. has put promotions in each plant or division in the hands of a committee of line supervisors instead of one manager. "We still have our share of chauvinists," but now they "only have one vote each," says Gerald Kahler, director of human resources planning for GM. As a result, the number of women whom GM is asking to move "has increased dramatically," and if a husband and wife work for the company, both are considered for transfer together, Mr. Kahler says.

But at some companies, women are considered a "transfer risk." Because of the large investment involved in training and then transferring an employe, these companies want to guard against the possibility of a woman leaving to get married or to have children. "It's not that we mistrust them, it's that we don't know," says Owen Johnson, a personnel vice president at Continental Illinois National Bank & Trust Co. of Chicago. "The commitment she makes at 25 isn't what it might be in her 30s; it's iffy," he says.

Even so, says Mr. Johnson, Continental Illinois is "taking the risk" by training women for overseas jobs. If a married woman indicates she can take a transfer, she and her husband meet with supervisors to discuss any problems connected with a move.

The bank, like a growing number of other employers, will help in finding a new job for a husband in the case of his wife's transfer. But often a long-distance commute is the only answer. Take for example, American Airlines employe Adrianna Bovian, 31, who in the past 12 years has risen to manager of advertising and program development from a part-time clerk. For most of the past seven years she has worked in New York and has visited her husband in Ann Arbor, Mich., on weekends. Her husband, Roger, 37, owns a tennis club.

Mrs. Boylan concedes that weekend commuting "is a strain." She said, "There are times during the week when I am lonely, and at times my husband has said, 'I wish you'd come back.'"

But for the Etelsons, the commuting couple at the beginning of this chapter, living and working in different cities seems to have produced few anxieties. Mr. Etelson is enthusiastic about the arrangement. The one-hour plane flight to Boston, he says, is a lot less taxing than the 70-minute drive from his office to his home. More than that, he says, the arrangement has opened "a whole new vista" for both of them after years of suburban living. He says he enjoys Boston and has fun "doing local restaurants and visiting the shops." Nor, he says, is he troubled by having an executive for a wife. "I'm satisfied with my work," he says. "I built my company, and I'm proud of it. Whatever success she gets, she's entitled to."

Ironically, one person opposed to the Etelsons' living apart is Howard B. Johnson, chairman and president of the company. The commuting arrangement, he says, "is a risk" for Doris Etelson because it might put "stress on her happy home" or disrupt her discipline on the job. "I'm not happy with it, but if she's willing to make the sacrifice, I'm willing to take the chance. I may not like the idea, but I'm crazy about Doris," he says.

The Etelsons were married in 1950, and for the first years of their marriage, Mrs. Etelson operated a cafeteria in an industrial plant. She stopped working between 1958 and 1961 to care for her two young daughters. In 1961, she joined Howard Johnson as a food supervisor for seven restaurants. From the beginning, she says, she had the clearcut goal of going "as far as I could in management and to take it step by step." She became head supervisor for 25 restaurants in 1965, then area manager for seven restaurants in 1968, a "significant step" that "didn't come easily," she says.

She was nemed staff assistant to a divisional manager in 1970 and advanced to director of administration in 1972. At the same time, she was working toward her bachelor's degree in economics at an extension of the State University of New York. (She graduated in 1974 and later began work on her master's degree in business administration.)

Mrs. Etelson says she realized that her next move up would depend on her willingness to go where an executive job opened up. But because her husband had his business in New Jersey, she couldn't go just anywhere. "It was limiting me, and therefore my value to my company," she says.

She confronted the problem by applying for top corporate spots in New York, Wilmington, Del., and Boston. The jobs would have involved running many restaurants and required long, erratic hours. But Mr. Johnson refused to hear of Mrs. Etelson taking on such a job if she would have to make a long-distance commute. "It wouldn't have been a happy ending for her or for the company. I wasn't going to contribute to anything that would make her home life unhappy," he says.

But Mrs. Etelson persisted, and in 1977 Mr. Johnson relented and offered her the newly created post of vice president of service standards. The job involves finding ways of upgrading the quality of customer service at Howard Johnson restaurants.

Mrs. Etelson says that she simply couldn't have considered her arrangement if her children had been below high-school age, nor could she have accepted without her husband's cooperation. But, she says, "he knew I had devoted time and effort to my career. After all, I have supported him in his business."

Careers in Collision

When Susan T., a patent attorney for Baxter Travenol Laboratories Inc., decided to marry a patent lawyer for rival Abbott Laboratories, her boss acted "as if I had just kidnapped the Lindbergh baby," she recalls.

"He said that if any Baxter secrets leaked to Abbott, he would assume that I had passed them on," she adds. Upset by his distrust, Susan reluctantly quit the Deerfield, Ill., hospital-supply concern a few months later. She joined a private Chicago law firm and prefers anonymity to avoid further problems.

Her former boss says he never questioned Susan's integrity, but worried about sensitive information slipping out inadvertently at home. "I mean, if you had a choice between two patent attorneys of roughly equal competence, wouldn't you choose the one that didn't have that problem?" he asks.

Dual-career couples "are a corporate time bomb," and conflicts of interest represent part of that lit fuse, says Douglas T. Hall, chairman of the organizational-behavior department at Northwestern University's graduate school of management.

Formerly confined to blood relatives, clashes of personal and working relationships are occurring more these days between spouses—the result of more women working, especially as professionals and executives. Such conflicts arise when a man's employer has business or political dealings with his wife's organization or when she works for a competitor or vice versa.

Real or potential, the conflicts affect couples in banking, law, computers, accounting, advertising, management consulting and the media, as well as in politics. Typically, conflicts between working husbands and wives only get to be a problem when both work as professionals or executives in important areas, such as sales, research and development, finance, planning or personnel. Many companies say they couldn't care less about a spouse working on a competitor's assembly line or in a low-level clerical job.

A few employers already deal head-on with conflicts of interest between spouses. Major accounting firms, for example, require auditors and accountants to sign oaths annually that no relatives—including marriage partners—work for clients.

But the oath isn't a sure-fire preventive measure, concedes William B. Haase, personnel-division director in Arthur Young & Co.'s Chicago office. If, despite the oath, such a conflict did occur, the accountant would be moved to another client assignment and possibly, Mr. Haase adds, one person "would have to leave his or her employer."

Civil-rights experts say companies can develop specific policies for couples without fear of successful litigation as long as they enforce the regulations equitably. That's what the Blue Cross health-insurance plan in Columbus, Ga., did in drawing up a written ban on hiring or continued employment of anyone whose mate works for a competitor. (The policy doesn't extend to blood relatives, however.)

A secretary unsuccessfully challenged the Blue Cross rule after she was fired because neither she nor her husband, a salesman for Pilot Life Insurance Co., would resign. She lost her sex-discrimination suit in a federal appeals court. She contended that Blue Cross had failed to take any action against a male employe in a similar predicament. Blue Cross said it had been unaware of that situation; when it found out, it reminded the male employe of its rule, and his wife quit her job with a competitor.

But most concerns just muddle along. Personnel officers complain that they cannot avoid the conflicts issue in advance because federal antibias rules prevent them from inquiring about a job applicant's marital status. At some companies, if someone with a marital conflict of interest is hired, a supervisor may make a point of reviewing general guidelines about confidentiality and business dealings with relatives. Other companies simply ignore the situation; they say they respect their staffers' loyalty. Still others arrange transfers, seek resignations or find different suppliers when a person's job collides with that of a spouse.

In general, bosses feel awkward about policing employes' private lives. "I don't know how you go about legislating behavior at home," says Eugene Croisant, senior vice president and head of corporate personnel services for Chicago's Continental Illinois National Bank & Trust Co. "It isn't something that we or other organizations had to give serious consideration to before."

Conflicts of interest can create sticky moments for the couples as well as their employers. The employes find they must adjust their personal lives to keep work and marriage separate.

Not surprisingly, Forest City Enterprises, a Cleveland real-estate developer, stopped bidding on housing-rehabilitation contracts for the city after Ruth Miller, the vice chairman's wife, began a stint as Cleveland's director of community development. As added insurance, Mrs. Miller locked her briefcase when she walked into the house, and, she says, her husband, Sam, "didn't even know the combination."

Couples like the Millers also bar "shop talk" from the dinner table. But practically speaking, most such spouses are too committed to their careers to avoid sharing some details about work. "We talk, but not about specific clients for either of our firms," declares Blue Olson, a management consultant with Booz, Allen & Hamilton Inc. Her husband, Cliff, consults for Peat, Marwick, Mitchell & Co. in Chicago. She says she once offered to drop Cliff off for a client presentation on her way to work, "but he refused to even tell me where he was going."

Cliff Olson says that he and Blue do discuss work specifics sometimes and that such discussions help avoid uncomfortable confrontations with clients. For instance, because Blue told Cliff about one project she had done, he turned down a similar assignment from the same corporation four months later.

Conflicting allegiances can put severe strains on a marriage, says Northwestern's Prof. Hall, who has been studying two-career couples. "Any time two important parts of your life have to be kept separate, it takes a lot of emotional energy to maintain that boundary," he says.

Karol Emmerich, assistant treasurer of Dayton-Hudson Corp. of Minneapolis, recalls having tiffs with her husband when he was working as an investment analyst for Investors Diversified Services Inc., a mutual-fund concern with Dayton-Hudson stock in its portfolio. "At dinner he would ask, 'Are you going to have a good quarter?'" Not wishing to violate insider-trading rules, she would decline to answer. "He got real ticked off about it." she adds. "He kept saying, 'You don't trust me. You don't trust me.'"

One Chicago executive believes his marriage broke up partly because his wife resented his informing the company legal counsel about her employment as a recruiter with an executive-recruiting firm used by his company. His tip led the company to stop doing business with the recruiting firm she works for.

A spouse employed by a customer or a competitor can create personal problems on the job as well. One woman says co-workers tease her with a big show of covering their desks when her husband comes by the office. Because both Blue and Cliff Olson also do recruiting, her colleagues like to inquire. "How many people is Peat Marwick recruiting this year?" She tells them, "I don't know," whether she does or not, because she says she would feel uncomfortable telling them, "I do know and I would rather not say."

When Linda Mathews, then Hong Kong bureau chief for the Los Angeles Times, journeyed to China on an assignment, she took a separate room from her husband, Jay, the Washington Post's Hong Kong bureau chief. Phones and typewriters in the adjoining rooms prevented them from scooping each other, she says, even though "Jay slept over."

John McKibbin runs into difficulties entertaining customers with his wife along. He sells aluminum for Republic Foil, a Danbury, Conn., unit of National Steel Corp. His wife, Kay, is a metals-purchasing agent for Macton Corp., which makes revolving stages. She has agreed to refrain from buying from him, but there's a snag: Frequently, Kay joins John and a customer for dinner, where she could learn of a Republic price cut, a new product or other information her regular supplier wouldn't know about. The couple decided that "all business would be handled before cocktails and dinner," Mr. McKibbin says, but the arrangement "is diffficult to keep up," especially when a customer brings up the deal again during dinner.

In other instances, the appearance of a conflict of interest can seriously interfere with career plans. One pair of Harvard business-school students planned investment-banking careers. But the New York firms they talked to didn't like the idea of hiring someone whose spouse worked for a competitor. The husband and wife argued over whose career was more important. The woman finally decided to take a commercial-banking job, at a slightly lower salary.

A New Jersey Supreme Court ethics committee prohibits private attorneys from taking criminal cases if their spouses are prosecutors, but the committee has refused to extend the prohibition to brothers. The policy is "a hell of an infringement on my right to earn a living," asserts Stephen J. Moses, a Hackensack, N.J., lawyer who had to give up 15% of his practice after his wife became an assistant county prosecutor.

Digital Equipment Corp. rejected J. Shirley Henry for a Cleveland computer-sales job after finding out that her husband was a systems engineer in Cleveland for Datapoint Corp., a rival based in San Antonio. She then sold computers for Hewlett-Packard Co. Eventually, she believes, the corporate and personal pressures of her present situation will force her or her husband, James, to leave the computer field. "You can't do an entirely aggressive job in sales if you're balancing that against something else, like the fact that your husband works for a competitor," Mrs. Henry says.

Conflicts at lower levels pale by comparison to those that flare up when a marriage partner reaches upper management. Charlotte J. is a case in point. The $30,000-a-year New York airlines executive married a middle manager with another air carrier, and for four years neither airline objected. Then he was named regional vice president in Los Angeles, at $50,000 a year, and she asked for a transfer to a top financial and marketing-analysts position there. The company turned her down, arguing that she and her husband would be preparing regional budgets for their respective airlines.

"I know you are both more concerned about your careers than about industrial espionage," Charlotte says a senior executive told her, "but I am afraid of the appearance of a conflict of interest and the precedent it would set." He offered her a Dallas post instead. She refused and began looking for another job.

No matter how they may try to avoid marital conflicts of interest, many companies may end up simply having to trust employes' discretion. Sears, Roebuck & Co. has some uneasy moments when it discovered that an important personnel staffer handling executive-compensation data was the wife of a personnel man at another retailer. Even worse, the competitor was trying to woo away Sears executives. "It would have been interesting for them to know what (Sears) people were making," recalls Charles Bacon, Sears vice president for personnel and employe relations. But he says the company had "enough confidence" in the veteran worker that it never brought the matter up, and no leaks ensued.

Section VII

The Impact of Working Women

The influx of women into the work force is bringing many changes—changes in management practices, in labor unions and in marketing techniques. Even more broadly, it is spurring arguments about what this development might mean for society in general. Some people argue, for example, that the money earned by working women enables the rich to get richer. But in any event, life in cities and towns all across the country is being changed in many different ways.

At many companies, the changes go far beyond the obvious presence of many more female employes than in the past. Frequently, working hours are being made more flexible, particularly for the convenience of working mothers. In addition, other forms of alternative hours now are being permitted. And as a result of their wives' incomes, many husbands now feel able, perhaps for the first time, to change jobs in mid-career.

In many unions, too, female members are becoming more important. So some priorities in contract bargaining are being changed, and some unions are getting their first female officials. Aware of the decline in the proportion of union members in the total work force and aware of the growing numbers of women workers, labor unions are responding to the new situation.

Also responding to the change with alacrity are many marketers, who see the working woman—and the two-income family—as a growing, affluent market. In the chapter entitled A High-Class Market, you will read about some of the companies that either are offering new products or services geared to the working woman or are selling their traditional products with advertising geared to the working woman. The examples cited hardly exhaust the list; in the changing climate, additional businesses are being affected all the time. For instance, it is beginning to seem likely that the rapid growth of mail-order sales and the proliferation of mail-order companies are largely due to the large numbers of working women who have plenty of money but not enough time to go shopping. On the other hand, operators of indoor tennis facilities are finding it harder and harder to keep their courts full during the daytime; too many women who used to play tennis while the children were in school have gone to work.

The next chapter, The Rich Get Richer, begins by discussing the contention that the huge influx of women into the work force is tending to increase disparities of income among American families. It also delves into the various motives that draw into the labor force women from all economic levels of society. And it tells how resentments sometimes flare among working women who come from such varying backgrounds.

In the final section of this chapter, we'll visit Morton Grove, Ill., and see some of the ways in which life has changed in that Chicago suburb. It's a chapter that probably could have been written in much the same way about most of the suburbs in the country, and many other places as well.

Changing the Old Company

Any woman professional at Prudential Insurance Co. who sought a maternity leave used to get this reply: If a job opened up when she was ready to work again, then Prudential would be happy to give her an interview. "The understanding was that she'd start at ground zero again," recalls John R. Murray, the company's associate director of personnel research.

Like many employers, Prudential has scrapped that policy and now offers its women workers a six-month maternity leave. But potentially more significant to the young married women who are beginning to move into Prudential's management ranks are the insurer's studies on how to keep homebound new mothers working for the company.

In one of these experimental programs, a handful of female executives on maternity leave pick up special writing assignments—proposals for group-insurance contracts or real-estate purchases are examples—at the office and work on them at home. Mr. Murray says that the program not only keeps these women working but also is "economical, keeps us supplied with a mother lode of women managers and has legal advantages, too."

This experiment at Prudential is but one example of how working women—particularly working wives and mothers—are influencing the way managers manage these days. Once regarded as a cheap if unstable source of labor, women are now such a large factor in the work force—more than 41% of all U.S. workers—that a company that ignores their needs does so at its peril. "Managers are rethinking everything they ever thought about women and work," observes Helen McLane, vice president of Heidrick & Struggles Inc., a management-consulting and executive-search firm.

What new attitudes don't change, laws do. Forty states and the federal government prohibit sex discrimination in employment; 37 states and the federal government ban sex discrimination in pay. Although a large influx of young women into the labor force in recent years has held down the average wages of all women in comparison to men's earnings, a tour of nearly any office or plant today finds women holding jobs once performed only by men.

In many companies, these women already have brought revisions in labor contracts, training procedures and such basic management considerations as how to criticize, how to reward and how to fire. And more changes are coming.

Because so many married women are working now, experts say, both they and their husbands often find themselves with more money and less time to spend it than ever before. As a result, many two-income couples are starting to pressure employers for new benefits like more flexible working hours —while looking askance at traditional incentives like transfers and promotions.

"We're only at the resentment stages now," says Ralph E. Smith, a labor economist who studies the working-women trend for the nonprofit Urban Institute. "But as you have more families with two workers making decent livings, they're going to put pressure on their employers to reduce work time."

Even today, of course, the most-common way to reduce time on the job is to work part-time, and that is exactly what many Americans are doing: 20.4 million people, or one out of every five employed, work less than 35 hours a week. Most of them are women, and they typically work in sales and clerical jobs at retailers, fast-food chains, banks, insurance companies, hotels, hospitals and the like. In the past decade, the ranks of part-timers have expanded three times as fast as the number of full-timers. This growth seems clearly destined to continue. The number of employed women in the prime childbearing years of 20 to 34 will increase by more than one-third by 1985, the Labor Department estimates, and many of them will seek to shorten their work hours because of child-care duties.

Already, many manufacturing and light-assembly plants in suburban areas offer "mothers' hours," roughly from 9 a.m. to 2:30 p.m., to attract local women with school-age children. In 1972, Honeywell Inc.'s Micro Switch division in Marlborough, Mass., was one of the first plants with mothers' hours in the Boston area. Now many other electronics and computer-assembly companies have similar hours, Louise Hale, personnel manager at the Honeywell plant, says.

As employers have come to recognize the importance of part-time workers to their operations and as labor unions have gradually discarded their longstanding opposition to the concept, part-time workers have started to win more fringe benefits. More than half of all "permanent" part-time workers now receive on a pro rata basis such benefits as vacations, sick leaves, pensions and health and life insurance. In 1972, by contrast, most part-timers got only vacation time.

Moreover, growing demand for alternatives to the nine-to-five work day is producing some interesting variations in part-time jobs. The states of California and Wisconsin have pilot projects in job sharing, so called because it allows two workers to share one job, one salary and one set of benefits. A dozen other states offer their employes "flexitime," which doesn't shorten the work day but lets workers set their own starting and stopping time, and gives them more freedom to schedule personal business.

Private industry also is experimenting with these programs. According to a survey by the American Management Association, for instance, 13% of all private employers with more than 50 workers offer flexi-time. Perhaps typical is American Orthodontics Corp., a Sheboygan, Wis., dental-products marker that instituted flexi-time as a way to reduce turnover among its mostly female staff of machine operators. In addition to setting their own starting time, the employes also can take long lunch hours "if they have a child in a play at school, for example," says John Viglietti, company vice president. The result: "Nobody leaves because they're unhappy," he reports.

Though usually designed with women in mind, alternative work-week arrangements can benefit men, too. In 1977, David and Lauris Wagner together earned $16,000, he as a part-time hearings examiner for a Wisconsin state agency and she as a part-time nurse. Mr. Wagner figures that if he had worked full time, his salary alone would have totaled $16,000.

But more important than the money was the time he has been able to spend building an addition to the couple's Madison-area home and developing a private practice as an attorney. "Working wives offer their husbands the flexibility to do what they want with their lives," Mr. Wagner says.

Of course, the two-career couple that can't or won't opt for shorter hours is still the norm—and nevertheless a cause of concern for many employers. At Hartford Insurance Co., a "significant" number of such employes are turning down promotions and transfers if they involve more work, longer hours and added responsibility, says Susan Kintner, director of human resources.

"They're telling me, 'No thank you, not now. You can't pay us enough to make it worth our while,'" she adds. Hartford, however, no longer automatically dead-ends workers who reject a move. Explains Miss Kintner: "A productive employe is always worth asking again."

Working wives also are freeing men who have become unhappy in their jobs to make mid-life career changes. After managing a small chain of clothing stores in Austin, Texas, for 26 years, Morton Plotsky found the job "old hat—the incentive was gone." So he decided to become a real-estate agent—an abrupt transition that could have been financially painful if it weren't for the $12,000 a year his wife, Frances, earned as a program coordinator at the University of Texas.

Today, the Plotskys are better off—financially and emotionally—than ever before. "That's the nice part of the women's liberation movement," Mrs. Plotsky says. "It's really people liberation."

Ironically, however, some employers contend that one of their big problems these days is convincing women to take advantage of the opportunities equal-employment laws and new personnel policies offer them. In 1976, for instance, the United Auto Workers union bargained successfully to ease access to promotions and training programs for women and minority-group members. Today, however, auto makers like General Motors Corp. "sometimes drag women kicking and screaming" into training programs that can lead to better jobs, says Donald Pfeifer, GM's assistant director of labor relations.

"It's social conditioning—they never aspired to those jobs before," says Mr. Pfeifer, who notes that only 58 of the company's 68,000 skilled-trades workers are women. "It's hard to convince them to aspire now."

Of course, there are many women who do aspire to leave jobs they have come to perceive as lacking in status and pay. An example is Kathleen McAlister, who as a secretary for the City of Dallas chafed at the low pay ($800 a month), low status and dead-end nature of her job. So she went back to school, earned a degree and became a $1,200-a-month administrative assistant to the city council.

Today, Miss McAlister says, there isn't "any limit" to the job opportunities open to her. Many managers apparently agree. According to Charles Pistor, president of Republic National Bank of Dallas, so great is the demand for bright career women that "there's a hazard in losing them after you've trained them. There's a greater tendency for a woman to get outside alternative opportunities than for a man."

And while most personnel managers say it's unpopular to say so, the vice president of a Chicago bank admits he's leary of training young women for future management jobs because he fears that the career and family plans they express at age 25 will change by 30. (The fear isn't entirely groundless: The expected upturn in the birth rate is attributed to working women who postponed motherhood while in their 20s but who now, as they approach the end of their most fertile years, are deciding to have families.)

Having to consider babies, husbands and families is new for many managers, and it's forcing them to change their attitudes toward employes' personal lives. "Managers like to think that workers aren't involved in the real world," says Martha Williams, a professor at the University of Texas Graduate School of Social Work. And in the days where there was always a wife at home to care for sick children, oversee repairmen or take the car in for service, that kind of thinking was possible.

No longer. Managers are having to view their employes as "half a couple, with a half the couple's problems and responsibilities," says Cynthia Fuchs Epstein, co-director of Columbia University's Project for the Study of Sex Roles and Social Change. The results are often personnel arrangements unheard of a decade ago. Thus, when Lomas & Nettleton Financial Corp. in Dallas hired Pat Hoyt as its director of communications, it agreed to let her work in Houston, where she lived with her husband and children. Lomas & Nettleton was almost as accommodating to its male employes, Mrs. Hoyt says. One took off afternoons to help his daughter process her divorce and another took time to see his daughter through drug problems.

Much less easy for male bosses is the task of disciplining a female subordinate. Male managers are often "scared to death" to criticize women, fearing tears and tantrums, says Anne Harlan, an assistant professor at Harvard University's business school. And that's too bad, she adds, because without feedback, women don't know what they're doing wrong and aren't able to improve.

Worse, says Prof. Harlan, many male managers today are afraid to fire imcompetent women; instead, they just move them to other jobs. "She and I didn't communicate much, and I was afraid she would sue us if I fired her," admits an Oklahoma City oil-company executive. "So I had her transferred to another department."

Then too, many men and women still are uncomfortable with the sexual overtones of a close working relationship. One result, observes Prof. Harlan, is that older men are reluctant to become mentors to young women, and women are reluctant to have them offer. Thus the mentor—who was once essential to a young man's career, training him in his job and pulling him up the corporate ladder— is declining in importance, she says.

And Miss Kinter of Hartford Insurance says managers come to her "all the time" wondering what to do about employes whose spouses object to their taking business trips with members of the opposite sex. "I travel alone," says the personnel administrator of a Denver oil company and its first woman executive. "My boss is concerned how it might look otherwise."

At other companies, though, men are adapting to the

presence of women in formerly male-only jobs. At American Express Co., for instance, there are so many sales-women these days that regional sales meetings end with everyone dancing. Those meetings "used to be like a fraternity party," a company public-relations man says. "Now, they're like a prom."

New Birth in Labor

Not long ago, a Maryland postal worker won the vice presidency of her union local—a first for a woman—and she looked forward to handling members' grievances, the vice president's responsibility. But when she arrived at the union office, the local's president said, "Oh, I'm so glad they elected you vice president. Now, we can finally get the files straightened out."

Working women are wielding more clout in the U.S. labor movement these days, both at the local and national level, because union women are more numerous and activist than ever before. One of every five union members is a woman, and female unionists now total 4.3 million, up 1.1 million since 1956. In fact, women accounted for more than half the total growth in union membership between 1966 and 1976.

But as the Maryland incident suggests, union leaders' traditional attitudes fade slowly. Union women "have a very long way to go" before they share equal footing with men in organized labor, says Joyce Miller, president of the Coalition of Labor Union Women, a national lobbying group. Men still dominate top union posts.

Yet even that picture is changing rapidly. Since 1976 alone, a number of major unions with significant female membership have elected their first female vice president or added more women to their executive boards. Among them are: Amalgamated Meat Cutters and Butcher Workmen of North America, American Federation of State, County and Municipal Employes and the International Ladies' Garment Workers Union. "And when I go around the country to speak, more women are saying, 'I am a shop steward. I am president of my union local. I am on the bargaining committee. Or, I am an organizer,'" observes Cynthia McCaughan, the AFL-CIO's coordinator of women's activities, a post created in 1976.

The increasing numbers and visibility of women unionists are influencing organized labor's bargaining agenda and organizing strategies, which, in turn, affect the nation's employers. Female officers of locals and headquarters staffers are pressing for greater attention to bargaining issues that concern women. Unions have long opposed some of these issues, such as flexible working hours and fringe benefits for part-timers. Other issues of concern to women include: upgrading salaries of traditional "women's jobs," improved maternity benefits, more personal-leave time, equity in pensions and training programs to promote women out of dead-end clerical jobs.

Activists also are urging their unions to recruit women more aggressively, especially those in white-collar jobs, where organizing efforts often have failed. For example, the 600,000-member Service Employes International Union recently began a campaign to organize clerical and professional employes in government, hospitals, universities, banks and insurance companies. To assist the drive, the union now employs about 300 women among some 750 local and national organizers, compared with 70 out of 650 a decade ago, says John Geagin, the Service Employes' head organizer. (Overall, women make up nearly half the union membership, up from 28% in 1966.) Mr. Geagin adds, "We're responding to women members saying, 'It's time to build the union in a different way.'"

Actually, unions don't need much persuasion to accelerate organizing drives in rapidly expanding white-collar industries, which employ the overwhelming majority of working women. With U.S. manufacturing employment shrinking, the proportion of unionized workers in the total labor force is declining. Just one of five American workers holds a union card today; more than one out of four did in 1970. Some observers think the very future of the U.S. labor movement depends on its ability to woo more women into its ranks. "Women are a tremendous growth area for unions," says Edward Lawler III, a labor consultant and program director for the University of Michigan's Institute for Social Research.

The enrollment of more white-collar women in unions is one of several factors likely to strengthen women's power in organized labor. Another factor is that economists don't see any slowdown, at least through 1990, in the entrance of women into the job market. Many working women are no longer quitting to raise families. And corporate affirmative-action programs are enabling others to land skilled, blue-collar jobs previously held only by men. "As the work force changes and becomes more equal in its sex composition, unions' rules of the game will change to further reflect the needs of these (women) workers," predicts Martin Gerber, the United Auto Workers' organizing director.

A third factor is the emergence of the 7,000-member Coalition of Labor Union Women as an influential lobbying force. Initially ignored by the AFL-CIO's all-male hierarchy and beset by internal factionalism, the CLUW has recently begun to gain recognition for forging an alliance between unions and feminist organizations. Congressional observers say this alliance helped secure passage of legislation that bars employers from discriminating against pregnant women workers and covers hiring, promotion, seniority rights and fringe benefits worth millions of dollars.

CLUW's 85 board members, typically senior women labor officials, are pressuring their own unions to employ more women staffers and to step up their commitment to the proposed Equal Rights Amendment. Thus, some labor organizations agreed not to hold their conventions in states that haven't ratified the amendment and to withhold political contributions from candidates who oppose it. Because of CLUW, "no union leader stands up today without tipping his hat to women's rights. That's a big change," says Marge Albert, a Distributive Workers of America organizer and coalition board member.

In addition, the coalition is pushing hard for union and federal action on a new issue—equal pay for comparable work. Equal wages for men and women working at identical jobs aren't enough to end sex bias, union women contend. They say women should get equal pay for different jobs of "comparable worth"—jobs requiring equivalent skills, effort and responsibility.

Applied nationwide, the comparable-worth concept could have significant economic impact on employers. An analysis of 121 job classifications in the State of Washington found that women received about 20% lower pay than men for comparable work. The state personnel chief estimated that it would cost the state an additional $74 million to offer all state employes equal pay for jobs of equal value.

However, the growing clout of women unionists is most apparent not in CLUW, but in individual unions. Take the 600,000-member Communications Workers of America, for instance. Half of its members are women, but no one spoke of their interests until 1975, when Glenn Watts, CWA president, named Patsy Fryman as his assistant, the first woman in the post. While lacking an executive board vote, she notes, "I am able to put forth programs and policies for the board to act on." Miss Fryman adds, "Sometimes I'm successful, and sometimes I'm not."

At her urging, the CWA fought for and won paid pregnancy leaves in 1977 for the Bell System employes that it represents. In that year, Miss Fryman convinced the board to reserve its opposition to "flexitime"—flexible starting and quitting hours. As a result, CWA locals at Mountain States Telephone & Telegraph Co. and four other American Telephone & Telegraph Co. units have created pilot flexitime projects.

Women also are influencing union goals on the local level. As secretary-treasurer of the Bakery, Confectionery and Tobacco Workers' local 300 in Chicago, Marjorie Brantley has been the sole woman on the Nabisco Inc. national negotiating council for six years. In 1975, she persuaded the council to fight to end discriminatory wage rates, especially in the lowest-paying jobs. For example, female general helpers did essentially the same work as male floor helpers in Nabisco bakeries, but they earned 17 cents an hour less. Nabisco agreed to narrow the gap to 10 cents an hour.

Union officials say that as individual members, recently hired women tend to be more active than minority-group men. Unlike the latter, "women express the desire to get involved in the union on many levels," says Joe Romano, president of United Steelworkers Local 15271, which bargains for 1,300 employes at Danly Machine Corp.'s steel fabricating plant in Cicero, Ill. Since 1975, the number of female clerical and production workers has leaped to 140 from 13 at the plant, and many attend the local's meetings.

"Because of their participation, we have put women on every standing committee," Mr. Romano says. "This will make it easier for the women to make their needs known to us." Because of women's complaints, the local now is insisting on cleaner, larger women's restrooms.

Similarly, union organizers are finding that white-collar campaigns may succeed only with female employes' support—even when they are a minority of the bargaining unit. "If you haven't convinced the women to join a union, you're likely to lose the election," observes Robert W. McCaffrey, director of the Steelworkers' Office, Technical and Professional Department. The union learned this lesson the hard way; it lost a clerical election recently at Hibbing Taconite Co. in Hibbing, Minn. About 24 of the 60 employes were women. "I guess we just didn't convince them," Mr. McCaffrey says sadly.

Although more women are speaking up, joining bargaining committees and winning local offices, men still run the American labor movement. No woman has ever sat on the powerful, 35-member AFL-CIO Executive Council. Only four small unions have female presidents; one of those, the Screen Actors Guild's Kathleen Nolan, was initially elected by a write-in vote. About 80% of the Garment Workers' rank and file are women, but only two of 26 executive board members are. Based on their proportion of membership, "women get half the number of leadership positions they're entitled to in most unions," observes Anne H. Nelson, associate director of Cornell University's Institute for Education and Research on Women and Work in New York.

There are several explanations. For one thing, experts say, many female unionists hold traditional views and are satisfied with helper, rather than leader, roles. So they run for secretary of their local, but not president. And married union women often have family duties that leave them little time or interest for union activities. "That's me. When I get off work, I like to go home. . . . There's no place I'd rather be," says Paula Klestik, a 25-year-old Danly worker. "Anyhow, I was always taught that union meetings were a bunch of guys getting together in a tavern and getting wasted."

Moreover, union women occasionally prefer a man as their union representative. Yvonne Porter, a 35-year-old black woman who became a Steelworker staffer in Gary, Ind., in 1977, recalls how at one steel-plant credit union, women clerical employes objected to her "because I was new. They felt I couldn't write their contract." Mrs. Porter negotiated the contract anyhow. "I stand six feet, three inches," she declares, "and I stand my ground."

Other women won't relocate or take jobs requiring constant travel and late hours, although both are often necessary to advance in a union's hierarchy. This reluctance frustrates unions wanting to hire more women organizers and other professionals. So unions are recruiting on college campuses, promoting clerical workers at headquarters into professional jobs and teaching leadership skills to women. The municipal employes' union, for instance, is offering more leadership training for rank-and-file women largely because of demands by a women's caucus, the union's first, at its 1978 national convention.

Male resistance also has hindered labor-union women. Two CWA staffers have sex-bias suit spending against the union because, they contend, male supervisors denied them field promotions. In the wake of affirmative-action programs, many blue-collar men resent women landing skilled-trades jobs, sometimes at the expense of senior male colleagues. So these men typically refuse to vote for female union officers, Mr. Lawler of the University of Michigan notes.

In other cases, union officials simply believe that women's issues aren't important. A few years ago, a 175,000-member union passed a resolution condemning contract language that discriminated against women. A female staff member sent the union president a note offering to compile a checklist for locals to review their contracts. "Nothing happened," she remembers. "I never got an answer."

Jack Golodner, director of the AFL-CIO's Professional Employes Department, explains why such views persist. "The older generation of organized labor's leadership came into dominance when the work force was predominantly male and a large portion of women workers weren't looking at work as a way of fulfillment. You can't blame them for their attitudes about where unions' priorities should be." But now, Mr. Golodner adds, "We're beginning to get a new generation of younger leaders with different attitudes."

A High-Class Market

Mine Safety Appliances Co. is offering for sale a new hard hat. Betting that the number of women construction and trades workers will continue to rise, the Pittsburgh concern has shaved 28 cubic inches off its standard model in deference to the narrower female skull.

Like any new product, the scaled-down hard hat "is a gamble," acknowledges Mine Safety sales executive James Madden. "But I imagine that the way things are going today, it'll be helpful to women and make a profit."

No doubt. For the way things *are* going today is that more American women than ever—about 41 million of them —are at work, bringing home paychecks totaling an estimated $250 billion or more a year. And to a growing number of companies like Mine Safety, helping working women spend those dollars is shaping up to be one of the more lucrative, if often difficult, marketing challenges to come along in decades.

Already, for instance, there are firms that clean homes for working women, run their errands, or, in exchange for a few hundred dollars and several spare evenings, teach the ambitious among them how to climb the corporate ladder. More typical, however, are established concerns—purveyors of everything from automobiles to perfume—that by changing product design or advertising strategy seek to sell working women goods and services that they sometimes don't even know they're going to need. And Madison Avenue, which prides itself—indeed, thrives—on its exhaustive scrutiny of the consumer, has come up against a bit of demographic data that it can no longer ignore: In the U.S. today, there are more working women than full-time housewives.

"This market is a very hot prospect, and I want a piece of it," says Robert F. Young, president and publisher of Family Circle Inc., a New York Times Co. division whose namesake magazine long has held a large share of the housewife market. Now, through a new magazine appropriately titled *Women Who Work*, the publisher hopes to reach job-holding women—and all the liquor, auto and other advertisers who had eschewed Family Circle.

No one knows the precise size of the working-women market—only that it is big and growing. One hotel official, for instance, says women now make up more than 10% of all business people traveling. As a result, some hotels are trying hard to cater specifically to female executives. Chicago's Drake Hotel, for instance, has a policy of protecting lone women guests from male harassment in its bars. The Drake also says it won't automate its elevators because women feel safer with an operator along. In another example, some Hilton hotels offer special "Lady Hilton" rooms, where the decor and furnishings are "more feminine." And many hotels now provide such female amenities as skirt hangers, shower caps, special mirrors, wig and hat stands, needle-and-thread kits and special lingerie soaps.

Similarly, the auto industry is beginning to recognize the importance of the female market. J.D. Power & Associates, a marketing-research concern, says that by 1977 more than $8 billion worth of new cars were being purchased annually by women in their own names; over two-thirds of these female buyers worked full time. "Traditionally, women are considered to have little knowledge about automobiles and how to make the proper decision when selecting a model to buy," writes Dave Power, president of the firm. "However, our research shows this situation is changing rapidly."

Indeed, some in the advertising business contend there are still many manufacturers—particularly those who make household items and "feminine" products—who haven't yet grasped the money-making potential offered by the influx of women into the labor force. The lack of products and advertising campaigns aimed at working women is "appalling—it's a show of marketing stupidity," says Lois Geraci Ernst, who has set up her own agency. Advertising to Women Inc., to correct the situation.

Admittedly, some of the advertising stereotypes that many women find objectionable—such as that of the dizzy housewife who needs Mr. Clean to tell her how to run her home—are tending to fade a bit from the nation's TV screens. Although housewives in slice-of-life commercials still polish floors and scrub work shirts to enviable brightness, hubby is more often called upon to lend a hand. And working women, invariably outfitted in tailored suits, are turning up to pitch everything from airlines to fragrances.

The fact remains, however, that little scientific research has been done on the spending patterns of working women, or on how such patterns might differ from those of women who labor at home. But the few studies available severely test conventional wisdom. For instance, according to a survey by Associated Merchandising Corp., a large buying concern, managerial and professional women—who spend $4.6 billion a year on "work" clothes—don't much care for the mannish fashions designers and department stores try to sell them. Such a woman does want to appear businesslike, the survey reports, but "she doesn't want to abandon her femininity for the sake of a dress code."

Rena Bartos, senior vice president of J. Walter Thompson Co. says marketers' biggest problems come when they assume "that the character of working women is the same as the old cliched housewife." For according to studies she has collected, there are surprising differences. Working women, for instance, tend to buy and use *more* floor wax and rug shampoo than do women who stay at home. And when it comes to indigestion aids, women who have chosen to be homemakers consume proportionately more of these non-prescription products than do either women who have jobs or women who say they plan to get one.

Profitably exploiting these differences demands marketing savvy. "Just taking a women in a commercial and putting a briefcase in her hand doesn't mean you are communicating with the new working woman," Mrs. Bartos notes.

One of the more straightforward approaches to selling to working women is the campaign developed by J. Walter Thompson for Baby Fresh, a pre-moistened paper towel from Scott Paper Co. Armed with surveys showing that working wives tend to get more help around the house from husbands, and that men generally are buying household goods them-

selves these days, the agency devised an ad that depicts a
young father cleaning an infant with Baby Fresh.

Then there's Enjoli, a new perfume from Squibb
Corp.'s Charles of the Ritz group. Although its slogan is "The
Eight-Hour Perfume for the 24-Hour Woman," Enjoli isn't
radically different in composition or fragrance from many
other perfumes. What is different is the target.

"We're celebrating (the working woman's) multiplici-
ty," says Brenda Harburger, vice president of the Squibb
unit. "She need give up nothing for being a working woman
but, indeed, she's pretty exciting." In return for helping working women feel exciting. Enjoli's makers expect to gross between $10 million and $15 million in the product's first year.

In trying to sell to women nowadays, a key difficulty is
the number of different "submarkets" both within the female
population as a whole and within the working-women group.
While about half of U.S. women work, three out of five of
these women also are married and presumably keep up a
home. Their attitudes, furthermore, range from very traditional to ultra-feminist. And so ad copy with a "liberated"
tone may work well for one product but bomb with another.

Fully aware of the tricky problem of appealing to one
group without offending another, Boeing Co. and its ad agency, Cole & Weber, took great care in a campaign aimed at
selling commercial-airline tickets to women. The magazine ad
showed a businesswomen poring over paper work on a night
flight, and its caption read: "A woman's work is never done."
A major decision concerning the ad, according to Hal Newsom, executive vice president and creative director of Cole &
Weber, involved the selection of the woman who appeared in
the photograph. A fortyish model was picked after more than
50 candidates had been screened. "I think she conveys that
she is probably married, maybe has a couple of teen-agers,
darns socks, knows the right wine to order and laughs at
Monty Python." Mr. Newsom says. Boeing says it received
about 100 letters—all favorable—in response to the ad.

Although the diversity of the woman's market gives
advertising agencies headaches, it also offers marketing opportunities. In the fragrance category, for example, it has
spawned the introduction of a host of new products "posi-

tioned" to sell to one particular segment or another. Prince Matchabelli's Aviance commercials showed a housewife seductively stripping off rubber gloves and apron before welcoming her husband home from work. "In this commercial, we were talking to the housewife—the forgotten woman in fragrance ads," says its creator, Mrs. Ernst. By contrast, ads for Revlon's Charlie feature a breezy young woman in a pantsuit and aim at more up-to-date, urban career types. Both products are highly successful.

It's in the purchase of big-ticket durable goods, expensive services and everyday staples that the increasing number of working women is having the biggest impact, however. That's because many of these women—nearly 23 million—are married, combining their income with that of a husband to create a new unit with considerable economic clout, the two-income family.

"The phenomenon of the working wife has catapulted many families into the earnings class of $25,000 or more," says Fabian Linden, director of consumer research for the Conference Board. As a result, he explains, there is a booming market for "that whole world of goods and services that make for the 'good life.'"

In Detroit, for instance, some auto-industry observers credit the advent of the working wife with sustaining high levels of new-car sales even though automobile prices have been rising sharply in the past several years.

The reason: Not only have working wives' contribution to family discretionary income made cars more "affordable," but it also has created demand for a second or even a third family car that's often a sporty, option-laden model. "If wives hadn't returned to work and if they hadn't added discretionary income," observes one auto-company analyst, "cars would have tended to be more sedate, like the four-door family car."

Instead, auto makers say, working women—single as well as married—tend to buy smaller cars (they handle better) and then load them with such high-profit options as automatic transmissions, extra mirrors, power locks and windows, plush upholstery and two-tone paint jobs

Understandably, Detroit is reluctant to offend such

buyers. "We don't see women as a special market for pink cars or lace upholstery," insists Gorden MacKenzie, a Ford Motor Co. vice president. But at General Motors Corp.'s Oldsmobile division, marketing director James Bostic concedes that until a few years ago, auto-company advertising aimed at women was often "token."

One embarrassing example: an ad placed in Ms. Magazine for Oldsmobile's Starfire that trumpted, "It's a car only a man can appreciate." Today, with surveys showing that women are involved one way or the other in nearly half of all new-car purchase decisions, "we have an altered state of consciousness about selling to women," Mr. Bostic says.

So have other auto makers. At Ford, John R. Bowers, director of advertising and marketing, stresses that men still are the company's main target audience, but he adds: "We're conscious of the growing importance of women in car purchases, and this is reflected in the way we select media." For example, he says, Ford now advertises in such magazines as Cosmopolitan, Vogue, Redbook and Ms. "This wouldn't have been the case five years ago," he adds. Similarly, tire companies have begun using advertising campaigns directed specifically at women.

Appliance makers also are finding working wives to be a ready market for expensive time-saving devices once considered the toys of the rich. Currently, for instance, microwave-oven manufacturers sell over two million of the quick-cooking units annually at prices ranging from $350 to over $1,100 each. Yet by 1985, says William George, president of Litton Industries Inc.'s microwave-products division, the size of that market is expected to triple, mainly because of the growing spending power of working women.

The same trend has affected the food industry as well. Restaurants attribute much of their $50 billion annual volume to two-income families without the time or inclination to dine at home every evening.

For supermarkets, the impact is less clear-cut. Catering to working women requires later operating hours that push up costs. But according to Progressive Grocer, a trade publication, the extra overhead may be worthwhile. In a survey, the magzaine found working women are less inclined to take advantage of specials and cents-off coupons than are housewives, and in fact they spend more on individual food items than do their stay-at-home counterparts.

Insurance companies are another group to benefit from the increasing financial independence of women. Between 1971 and 1976, the face value of life-insurance contracts sold to women almost doubled to an average $12,000 per policy; the value of policies sold to men increased at only about half that rate over the same period.

Only recently, however, have life-insurance carriers stepped up efforts to tap this market. Typical is the approach now being taken by Equitable Life Assurance Society of the U.S., which has seen the value of its individual women's policies grow to 21% of all the company's insurance in force in 1977 from only 14% in 1970. Today, Equitable is hiring more female agents and developing advertising campaigns aimed at convincing working wives that if they die, their families would suffer a severe financial loss that only life insurance could replace.

Brokerage houses also are entering the picture. Besides advertising directly to women, firms such as E.F. Hutton & Co. and Merrill Lynch, Pierce, Fenner & Smith offer seminars in cities around the country to instruct women in investment planning. "A brokerage house can be like walking into a men's bar for a lot of women," says Ann Benson, investor-information specialist for Merrill Lynch. She explains that although women shareholders in U.S corporations have long outnumbered men, these accounts often were in name only. "Now, because women are earning their own money, they want to control it and participate more," she says.

Similarly, Lone Star Industries, a building-products manufacturer, has run ads in Vogue that are aimed at attracting female shareholders. The ads all have a fashion theme. The copy line on one: "Fashions come and go, but cement is never out."

Advertising dollars from companies that once sold almost exclusively to men have breathed life into some women's magazines and have prompted other publishers to rush out new publications to attract the interest of working women. "We're leavening the traditional women's ads for perfume and make-up with ads that used to appear solely in men's magazines," says Kate Rand Lloyd, editor-in-chief of Working Woman, which, after a painful start-up that included reorganization under the Bankruptcy Act, is enjoying an influx of liquor, auto and life-insurance ads.

Working Woman is getting plenty of competitors, however. Among the new magazines: Self, the first new magazine started by Conde Nast in 39 years; and New Dawn, a self-described "feminist-oriented Redbook" from North American Publishing Co. Perhaps typical of the new genre is Women Who Work, the Family Circle Inc. publication. "We're directing the magazine at the two-paycheck family where the woman is workking to earn money for a better house, car or . . . you fill in the blank," explains Mr. Young of the New York Times, Co. division.

The Rich Get Richer

Nancy Hammer, the 48-year-old wife of a prominent Pittsburgh executive, has gone back to work. She currently earns nearly $20,000 a year as director of public relations for Chatham College in Pittsburgh's fashionable East End.

Mrs. Hammer doesn't need the money. The income of her husband—Gulf Oil Corp. executive vice president Harold H. Hammer—is comfortably in six figures. Instead, she wants the sense of professional achievement and satisfaction that she feels only a full-time, well-paying job will provide.

Across town in the blue-collar suburbs, Judith Wynn, 30 years old, also has gone back to work. She wasn't seeking any sublime personal satisfactions when she took a $2.95-an-hour job as a sales clerk at Gee Bee, a local budget department store. Rather, she wanted to supplement the $12,000 her husband makes annually as a truck mechanic. The extra income helps her family "get by," Mrs. Wynn says; returning to work means she can buy new clothes and better food for her two children.

But while the Wynns are moderately better off because a wife went to work, consider how the Hammers have fared: With Mrs. Hammer earning more than three times as much as her cross-town counterpart, the gap has widened between the Hammer family's income of well over $100,000 and the Wynn family's income of about $18,000. Thus, some economists contend that along with the benefits of women's expanding role in the work force could come a widening of the economic differentials between America's "rich" couples and its poorer ones. Furthermore, future gains for sexual equality in the work place—through equalization of men's and women's pay—could have the unintended effect of increasing even more the economic disparities among American families. Explains Lester Thurow, an economist at the Massachusetts Institute of Technology: "If males who earn high incomes are married to women who could earn high incomes in a perfectly fair and liberated world, then women's liberation will make the distribution of income more unequal."

Also disturbing are the tensions arising between wives who work because of strict financial need and those who work because they want the status, satisfaction and adventure of carving out a niche in the labor market. It's increasingly common, for instance, to hear lower-income wives express resentment at the competition—social as well as economic—they face from middle- and upper-income women who, they feel, don't have to work. Many affluent wives, meanwhile, are quick to contend that their paychecks are indeed needed to afford a "middle-class" life style these days.

Of course, nobody is suggesting that such disparities among the ranks of working wives threaten to rip apart the social fabric or that wives should base a decision on whether or not to work solely on their husbands' income. Moreover, anybody upset by the Hammers' affluence might be more likely to complain about Mr. Hammer's income of well over $100,000 than about Mrs. Hammer's income of less than $20,000.

Besides, the widening of the income gap between the Hammers and the Wynns may not be quite so significant as the total numbers imply. For one thing, the Wynns gain far more than the Hammers in terms of percentages: Even if Mr. Hammer earned a flat $100,000 rather than considerably more, the $20,000 added by Mrs. Hammer's job increases their combined income by only 20%. In contrast, when Mrs. Wynn adds $6,000 to her husband's income of $12,000, she lifts the family total 50%. Even more important, all those figures ignore the tax bite, which is far sharper on high than low incomes. When Mrs. Hammer's income is added on top of her husband's, she presumably incurs federal income taxes at a rate exceeding 50%. She also must pay about 6% in Social Security taxes, and, if she lives in a high-tax state such as New York, another 14% in state income taxes. What Mrs. Hammer has left after taxes is surprisingly little; she is practically a volunteer worker.

So although the influx of prosperous wives into the work force does "tend to make the extremes further apart" between "have" and "have-not" families, says Commerce

Secretary Juanita Kreps, that development still isn't likely to bring major changes in overall family-income distribution. In fact, statistical studies have shown repeatedly that the distribution of income among all families hasn't changed significantly over the past two decades.

Mrs. Kreps, herself a noted labor economist, makes another important point. She says that although any rise in economic inequality would disturb Americans who believe "that extremes of wealth and poverty aren't legitimate," such disparities alone "wouldn't argue in any way against encouraging women to work." Moreover, some conservatives contend that there is something to be said for inequality of income; they argue that the long-running atttempt to equalize incomes in this country has discouraged capital investments and thus, ironically, has impeded creation of jobs for lower-income people.

Whatever the merits of such arguments, it is clear that several decades ago there was a strong statistical link between a wife's decision to work and her family's financial need. In 1951, for instance, figures show that wives whose husbands earned under $3,000 annually were three times as likely to be in the paid labor force as were wives whose husbands made over $7,000—a salary then considered "middle income."

Over the past few years, however, well-to-do women have been returning to the labor force at a much faster rate than other wives. According to University of Wisconsin economist Sheldon Danziger, labor-force participation by wives whose husbands earned more than $30,000 jumped 38% between 1967 and 1974, while participation by wives whose husbands earned $2,000 to $6,000 increased only 11%.

The extent of this trend's impact can be seen in the characteristics of the "income elite"—U.S. families whose total annual income of $22,200 or more puts them in the top 20% of all families in earnings. According to a recent Conference Board analysis, in 54% of these families, the wife worked; in 1965, by contrast, only 44% of families in the top category had working wives. The implication is clear: A goodly number of today's top-income families get that way only because wives go to work.

But viewed from a different perspective, the swelling ranks of working wives also has begun to widen slightly the gap in purchasing power between "have" families and those less fortunate. For not only do more wives of husbands who earn over $20,000 work themselves; these women also tend to get better paying jobs than do the wives of lower-income men. Even in the depths of the 1974 recession, working wives whose husbands earned between $20,000 and $30,000 were commanding an average $1,000 a year more than wives whose husbands made $6,000 to $10,000.

Against this background, it's instructive to compare the attitudes and motives of prosperous working wives with those of women from lower-income families. "A career is a state of mind," explains Mrs. Hammer, the Pittsburgh executive's wife who opted for full-time work after growing tired of the "volunteerism" of the Junior League. Even though she doesn't feel any financial pinch, Mrs. Hammer insists on bringing home a respectable income. "You're paid for what you're worth," she says, "I would hate to settle for less."

This desire for a job that is well-paying is expressed by many well-to-do women. Listen to Midge Sheldon, a Maine resident who formerly worked as a speech therapist at a Pittsburgh hospital while her husband held an executive position. "It is important that working women be paid their worth," Mrs. Sheldon says. "It isn't relevant that they don't need it. They may not financially, but they do psychically. If the government doesn't take it all away, she can give it away or buy with her own money crazy things for which she doesn't have to give any explanations or apologies. In this society, a person's competence is too often judged by what they earn. And that's just the way it is."

Besides, Mrs. Sheldon adds, "Wives of high-salaried men are usually brighter and better-educated than wives of low-salaried workers. They represent some of our best efforts at high-level education. Are we going to have them sit at home because we don't think they should be paid to work? What a waste of talent, education-money and national resources!"

Of course, such reasons for desiring for a well-paying career job would seem remote to a woman like Doris Filius, who toils all night cleaning a Pittsburgh office building. Mrs. Filius, 53, was divorced three years ago. She receives less than $1,000 annually in child support, and she and her three children who are still at home must make ends meet on her income of less than $10,000. "We manage," she says.

Working all night and caring for her children during the day, Mrs. Filius says she's "lucky" to get four or five hours of sleep in any 24-hour period. She doesn't understand why women would work if they didn't have to. "I would like nothing better than to have a man say, 'Quit . . . stay home,' " she says wearily.

As head of a household, Mrs. Filius is a member of the most underprivileged group of working wives. But at least she's white. Black and Hispanic women in the same category fare even worse. For while less than one-third of the white families headed by women live in poverty, over half of families headed by nonwhite women have incomes of below government definitions of poverty. And as they confront the job market, black and Hispanic women also face very high unemployment rates.

Marcelina Maynard, a soft-spoken, 53-year-old immigrant from the Dominican Republic, has managed to find a job. She earns $129.80 a week as a maid at the Mayflower Hotel in Washington. On her day off, she adds another $3.50 an hour doing domestic work.

With the money, Mrs. Maynard supports three children who share her one-bedroom apartment in the capital and sends whatever is left to her disabled husband and three other children still in the Dominican Republic. She refuses to apply for government assistance; she fears that if she can't make it on her own, she will have difficulty bringing the rest of her family to America. "I tell my children that we have to take what comes," she says.

The problems of Mrs. Maynard and other "have-not" wives are compounded by sexual discrimination in hiring and pay. While women's earnings generally lag those of men in the same occupational group, the differential tends to widen at the lower end of the income scale.

At the top end, in "professional-technical" jobs, the median weekly income of full-time women workers was 73%

of men's pay in May 1976, according to the government. But the situation was worse in "clerical" jobs, where women earned 64% of what men did. It was worse still for women in "sales," whose incomes were only 45% of those of men in the same job category.

Faced with such difficulties in the job market, some low-income wives resent working women from more comfortable backgrounds. They contend that better-off women are taking jobs from people with greater financial need. Mrs. Filius, for instance, says it's "unfair" that some of her cleaning co-workers—married to skilled blue-collar men who bring home close to $20,000—should be able to "take off from work constantly" because they can get by with a smaller paycheck. "If they don't want to work, they should get out," she snaps.

Adds Carolyn Boone, a sales clerk whose blue-collar husband makes about $12,000: "I know women who earn more than my husband, and they don't need it." Prosperous working wives, she fumes, are "greedy" and "just blow their money."

Indeed, one well-to-do Pittsburgh woman—her husband is a successful physician—says she encountered such a reaction from female colleagues when she worked as a $14,000-a-year remedial-reading teacher. "People said to me, 'You don't need the job,'" she recalls. "They were angry, prejudiced." This "unpleasant" work environment was one reason the physician's wife left the job, and she now looks back in anger at "all the crap I had to put up with" from people who believed that a wealthy woman's place was in the home.

Between wealthy families and poor ones, of course, lie a great multitude struggling to maintain a middle-class existence despite inflation. Just how comfortable that existence is often depends on whether the wife works. Suzanne Pfaff's husband, for instance, makes a decent enough living—about $17,000 a year—as a foreman in a gear-cutting plant. And because it would "bother" her husband if she worked full time, Mrs. Pfaff holds part-time jobs as a sales clerk and as a cleaner at a church, which net her only about $50 a week.

Most of the time, Mrs. Pfaff says, she uses her money to "help with the little things" that her five children need.

But sometimes the budget is tight, and then her earnings are spent on groceries. "I don't know where we'd stand if I didn't bring home the extra $50," she says.

Among many young, college-educated couples, in fact, it's assumed these days that in order to get and keep middle-class status, the wife will pursue an active career and contribute a substantial paycheck over her working life.

Eileen and Robert Kalinoski, for example, are both lawyers in Pittsburgh. Mrs. Kalinoski, who says she would go "bananas" if she had to stay at home, is frustrated that her job as a law clerk to a local judge permits her to contribute only about one-third of the couple's $40,000 joint income. Still, her earnings allows the Kalinoskis to travel to Europe on vacation and to afford an expensive mortgage. "Middle-class life would be difficult on one income," she says.

Many lower-income wives, on the other hand, often feel uncomfortable with the idea that they *have* to work. A few, such as Ruth Baroni, even say that like their more prosperous counterparts, they work because they enjoy it. In Mrs. Baroni's eyes, the $9,100 she earns yearly doing custodial chores is "mad money"; she insists she could get by on her husband's $9,400 income as a tractor repairman. But she isn't going to try.

"I love to work," Mrs. Baroni says. "To be honest with you, when I'm home and I have the house all cleaned up, I smoke too much, I drink too much coffee and I watch TV all the time. There's too much idle time and it's just boring."

How Life Has Changed

Their teachers call them "latch-key" children. As young as six years old, they wear house keys around their necks and stay by themselves after school until Mom or Dad comes home from work.

The growing number of unsupervised youngsters in Morton Grove, Ill., an upper-middle-class Chicago suburb, distresses Barbara Blonz, a 35-year-old mother of two. So the energetic president of the League of Women Voters has asked her chapter to study Morton Grove's need for a day-care center.

But Mrs. Blonz doubts the project will succeed. She only as 20 active members, half the number available eight years ago. "I know what we should be doing as a league and how little we are doing—because we lack members," she says. "Everybody has gone back to work."

Sometimes, it does seem like every married woman is working. Actually, about 48% of all U.S. wives are employed or actively looking for jobs, a jump of 10 percentage points in just the last decade. And as Mrs. Blonz's complaint of too many latch-key children and too few volunteers suggests, the return of wives to the labor market touches life in communities throughout the country, affecting everything from the price of homes to the friendliness of the family next door.

In Morton Grove, population 27,000, signs of the trend abound. Eight years ago, according to U.S. Census figures, only one-third of the married women in town worked. Today, residents agree, over half of them are employed. Often former housewives with school-age children, they hold full or part-time jobs as nurses, teachers, interior decorators, secretaries, sales clerks and factory assemblers in Morton Grove or in nearby suburbs.

Like most men elsewhere, the husbands in Morton Grove tend to have better-paying jobs than their wives; they work as lawyers, accountants, sales managers and skilled tradesmen. But it's the combination of the two salaries that makes so many Morton Grove couples seem affluent. Median family income in Morton Grove is $27,370 a year, up from $16,500 in 1969, and about half the town's families earn $25,000 a year or more, estimates Pierre de Vise, assistant professor of urban planning and policy at the University of Illinois. Nationally, these couples would rank among the top 20% of all families in earning power.

This prosperity is reflected in the town. Once a sleepy village, Morton Grove boomed during the 1950s and 1960s as it picked up population from downtown Chicago, 16 miles away. Today, Morton Grove is a model of Midwestern suburbia.

Its residents, primarily of European descent, live in smartly painted homes on trimmed lots shaded by oak and maple trees. Local business is conducted along a 20-block commercial strip or at a nearby shopping center. A forest preserve provides recreation. There are about two dozen manufacturers each employing more than 100 workers, but the tallest structure in Morton Grove is a five-story apartment building.

It is in the daily activities of the people themselves, however, that the impact of the working wife on this town and communities like it can best be seen. Here, then, is a look at the way things go in Morton Grove these days. These events didn't actually occur on the same day, but they did take place over a period of several weeks. The mosaic of impressions that they give illustrates what a nationwide social phenomenon means in human terms.

EARLY MORNING: It is 7:45 a.m., and the Borg elementary school classrooms won't open for another 45 minutes. A sedan driven by a woman in a pantsuit pulls into the school parking lot, and two youngsters hop out. By 8:10, there are about 10 pupils, roughly seven to 11 years old, chatting or pacing back and forth. A student safety-patrol officer makes sure there isn't any horseplay.

Occasionally, a teacher or the principal also will come early to supervise these offspring of working mothers. At least once a week, school nurse Marilyn Hanson cares for two or three sick children all morning while she locates working mothers or fathers to take them home. "I don't feel I should be a baby sitter," Mrs. Hanson declares. Conway Dahmer, a sixth-grade teacher, concurs, remarking, "Parents are delegating more of their responsibilities to the school."

MID-MORNING: Morton Grove stores have little business at this hour. Neighborhoods also seem empty, with few parked cars and even fewer residents outside—even though the day is bright and sunny.

A deliveryman rings the doorbell at 6644 Church Street. "Your next-door neighbor isn't home. Could you keep these in your refrigerator?" he asks, gesturing at a box of frozen steaks. (Local repairmen know better: They get frequent requests nowadays to fix broken appliances after 4 p.m. or on Saturdays, because the customers are working wives.)

Edith Tragasz agrees to store the steaks for neighbor Kay Miller, a former housewife who has been the village's insurance administrator since 1973. The 28-year-old Mrs. Tragasz quit her job as a bank data-processing manager not long ago to have a baby. But she vividly recalls having her new lawnmower shipped to Chicago relatives because the store wouldn't deliver evenings or Saturdays, and few of her neighbors were home during the day.

The deserted neighborhoods appear to offer easy targets for burglars. Indeed, burglary is Morton Grove's fastest-growing crime. Some 60% of the 75 home burglaries in 1977 occurred between 8 a.m. and 6 p.m., and most involved households where "the husband and wife were both working," says Gerald R. Rossler, director of the Morton Grove police department's Crime Prevention Bureau. One ring of thieves committed or attempted two dozen daytime home burglaries over a five-month period.

Because many daytime burglars are teen-agers, the police department recently expanded its Youth Investigation Section to a full-time operation. And a citizens' "Mobil Eye" patrol has been created to cruise neighborhoods hit by thefts from homes.

NOON: The aroma of fresh-baked bread fills the air in an older brick ranch on Palma Lane. Barbara Blonz, the League of Women Voters president, tucks in the shirt of her squirming, six-year-old son, Alan. He dashes out the door to go to kindergarten and she yells, "If it's raining, I'll come pick you up later."

Then Mrs. Blonz takes a visitor on a drive through a wealthier, adjacent neighborhood. The large, split-level homes sell for $100,000 or more. Many have manicured lawns, sculptured bushes and boats parked in the driveway. The men who live here make so much money as lawyers or accountants, she says, that their wives usually work out of choice rather than necessity.

The sight of such fancy dwellings reminds Mrs. Blonz of how her family's life style has been crimped since she gave up full-time teaching eight years ago for motherhood. (But she herself was about to begin teaching part time for $6,000 annually to supplement the $20,000 a year that her husband, Steven, earns as an architect.)

"If I were still working full time," she muses, "we would have extra money for fun things, like a vacation for the two of us. We would probably go out to eat more often. And it wouldn't be such a hassle looking for boys' jeans for $8." She continues: "We don't live frivolously. We don't live high. Yet I get real depressed sometimes about not having enough money."

EARLY AFTERNOON: Two blocks from Mrs. Blonz's home, Mary Lou Flickinger is cutting short a coffee klatch with a neighbor, a housewife. "I have to run," the 27-year-old working mother explains. "I have to get dinner going."

Mrs. Flickinger works evenings and weekends, selling men's clothing at a store in nearby Skokie. Her husband, Michael, makes "between $10,000 and $15,000 a year" as an office manager; he cares for their children, aged five and seven, while she's on the job. Mrs. Flickinger's part-time employment boosts the family's income by one-third, and it's why she has a new refrigerator and a new stove.

"I still owe money on the refrigerator," the young woman observes. "But I'm buying better-quality food. And at least we don't have eggs, toast and coffee for dinner any more." Before returning to work in 1975, she occasionally served that regimen to save money.

LATE AFTERNOON: Psychiatric social worker Richard Zembron sits in the one-room office of Morton Grove Family Service, a counseling agency. He awaits a woman and her eight-year-old daughter, whose grades have been dropping and who has decided she hates school. A few months earlier, the mother took a full-time bookkeeping position, her first employment since the child's birth.

The little girl is acting out her anxiety. She needs reassurance that "Mommy still loves her," Mr. Zembron explains. "The problem isn't whether Mother works. It's how the family adjusts."

Around 5 p.m., Morton Grove's three main supermarkets fill up. Many shoppers are hurried, working wives like Sandy Kehr, a part-time receptionist, who says, "I try to get everything done at one stop." This is the busiest time of day at one store, Dominick's Finer Foods, and the time when "we sell a lot of frozen pizza. TV dinners and convenience food like lunch meat," Robert Karbowski, the manager, says. The women prefer "any quick meal, the kind of thing where they don't have to spend much time at the stove," he adds.

EARLY EVENING: The lines also grow long at the 10 hamburger, chicken and other fast-food restaurants in Morton Grove. (There weren't any 15 years ago.) At 6:30, Barry Marks, a 32-year-old data-processing consultant, picks up a pizza at a carryout place near his Morton Grove home. His wife Sandy, a junior-high-school English teacher, is busy feeding their infant son, and she feels too tired to cook.

Over at the real-estate firm of Nicholas J. Marino & Co., manager Joseph Moll pulls together his house listing for this evening's customer, a Chicago couple in their early 30s who now rent a home. They make between $30,000 and $35,000 annually from her teaching and his small manufacturing business. (Some weeks later, the Chicagoans buy a home in Morton Grove, paying "in the high 70s," Mr. Moll reports.)

They are rather typical. Two-income families accounted for 60% of the 120 mortgage loans (average amount: $40,000) made by First National Bank of Morton Grove in 1977; that's double the rate of a decade ago. Robert Young, a vice president, says. (The official adds that the presence of so many two-income families also has meant a marked increase in the size of checking and savings accounts, and that is one reason why the bank's total deposits have nearly tripled in the past 10 years to $87.4 million.)

Housing experts say a wife's income enables many couples to become first-time homeowners and some repeat purchasers to afford more expensive homes. Does this fuel inflation, too? If working couples couldn't pay the high prices, "houses wouldn't sell and prices would come down," Mr. Moll, the real-estate agent, contends.

Right now, that isn't happening. A three-bedroom ranch house purchased for $42,000 in 1968 currently sells for $80,000 to $90,000. Mr. Moll says. There aren't any Morton Grove homes on the market for less than $65,000, and new, custom-built houses sell for up to $250,000.

In addition to their willingness to pay such prices, Morton Grove's recent home buyers are also typical in another way: They have few or no children. The result is a sharp decline in public-school enrollment, which fell to about 1,700 pupils in 1977 from 3,250 a decade ago. This decline will force two of Morton Grove's eight public schools to close by 1980.

LATE EVENING: Working wives are a boon to Morton Grove clothing, sporting-goods and furniture stores, and therefore many will stay open until 9 or 10 o'clock tonight. Longtime residents say this wasn't the case 10 or 15 years ago. The local Fiat dealer also has joined the growing number of Morton Grove businesses that have Sunday hours. Dealership officials say the showroom now is crowded on Sundays, with many two-income couples among the buyers.

These couples not only shop different hours, but they also spend more. When Kromer Wolfgang opened his television sales and service shop in 1970, he sold few color-TV sets. Now, he says, the market for "big-screen black-and-white sets is dead in our area," and many Morton Grove families own three color sets. Working wives here "say the money they earn is their own to spend," Mr. Wolfgang observes, "often on a color TV for the kitchen."

This evening, 23-year-old Suzanne Ostergaard is at Goldblatt's department store for her weekly spree. "I'll spend whatever is in my wallet, anywhere from $40 to $60," declares the $9,600-a-year systems-control analyst. Adds her husband,

Russel, a $22,000-a-year tool-and-die apprentice: "We don't even have a credit card. We pay cash for everything." That includes a color-television set and a couch, bought after the childless couple purchased their first home in Morton Grove late in 1977.

The stores might be well-attended, but tonight's Parent Teachers Association meeting isn't. About 50 parents from three schools show up, and District 67 Superintendent William Stoutt blames the low turnout on the increase in working mothers. In the late 1960s, he says, "we used to have a full auditorium, with 300 parents, four times a year."

The PTA isn't alone. Other nonprofit women's groups in Morton Grove, ranging from the Garden Club to the American Legion Auxiliary, are hurting for members and leadership. "I think voluntary organizations are just going to disappear," says Mrs. Blonz, the League of Women Voters president.

Joyce Less is one former charity volunteer whose 1969 return to full-time teaching ended her outside activities. The 46-year-old mother of four prefers to spend her free time in family leisure activities. For instance, tonight she is seated in her elegantly decorated, colonial-style home, planning summer boating trips with her two teen-aged sons and husband Donald, a market-research executive. (The other two children are away at college.)

With a combined annual income of more than $50,000, "we are able to take vacations that we didn't before," such as annual winter trips to the Caribbean, Mrs. Less observes. "We're able to put the kids through college without sacrifice. And we're able to give our 22-year-old daughter a big wedding that we couldn't have done before."

In preparing the wedding-guest list, Mrs. Less noticed she wasn't inviting any neighbors, even though the family moved to this well-to-do section of Morton Grove six years ago. "I really don't know the people who live down the street," she confesses.

The lament is echoed again and again throughout the town. The day-time absence of employed wives, the few young children and the wide age gap between oldtimers and newcomers hampers socializing. "The phantom neighborhood" is how some residents refer to their block. "I have no time to socialize," asserts Rene Seyter, an officer at Second Federal Savings & Loan and a mother of two. "I work, and I'm very, very busy."

Increased anonymity and isolation are contrary to the ideal of friendly suburban living. As a result, some urban experts believe, the future may see two-income families begin to move out of places like Morton Grove and return to the city, especially if they don't have young children.

Regardless of where they live, however, an employed husband and wife do tend to center their social lives more around the office than the home. "The Joneses you keep up with will no longer be somebody near where you live," says John McKnight, associate director of Northwestern University's Center for Urban Affairs, "but somebody where you work."

Section VIII

How to Get *FAR* Ahead in Your Job

By Betty Lehan Harragan

A couple of years ago, I met four of the most successful women I know for a drink after work. Each is a line executive in a major corporation, and each works in a different industry. We were talking about (what else?) the problems unique to women as they move ahead in business. Inevitably, the discussion veered around to the mistakes that women make and how frequently they sabotage their own ambitions because of naive attitudes about the real world of working.

Finally, one of the executives burst out, "If only women would learn to read!" and all of us promptly concurred. What she meant, of course, was reading the business news: daily newspapers, national magazines and specialized industry publications that report financial, economic, trade and business news. The way she phrased it—"learn to read" —was tacitly understood by all. None of us had any connection with business publications, but all of us were avid readers of the half-dozen major periodicals plus assorted trade journals. We knew that it wasn't enough to merely absorb the printed word; one has to develop a critical sophistication to read behind the lines and extract the information that could apply directly to your personal job situation.

There are many reasons why the average working woman skips the business pages. The primary turn-off, however, is that so few see any relevance to their everyday job problems or to their career decisions. And they are right. Even though women are inching close to making up 50% of the American work force, most business and economic news leaves the impression that women are as much a staple as chocolate-covered grasshoppers. Despite an occasional article about the unprecedented flood of women into the paid labor market, economic forecasters have yet to include them as significant factors on the financial scene—except in their classic role as customers.

As producers and participants in the American economy, women haven't made the grade so far. Some would say, justifiably, that this fact is proof of continued sex-discrimination in the business community. In addition, many perceptive women question whether women *are* moving up into significant jobs. Could it be that millions of ambitious, striving women are being deflected into employment areas that won't change the existing male-dominated business milieu in any substantial way?

The answer is "yes." Not only can that happen, it is happening every day. Too many women jump to the unwarranted conclusion that competing with men is the most important criterion for moving ahead in a lifetime career pattern. Because of their unfamiliarity with business as a whole, they fail to notice that they must track and compete with the successful men, those who eventually achieve policy-making positions in the business hierarchy. These are the men whose opinions, decisions and actions are scrutinized in the business media. These are the executives whom upwardly mobile men watch and equally ambitious women must watch, too.

During the entire 20th Century, working women have been restricted to dead-end, low-status "jobs." As this book amply demonstrates, it is only within the past few years that intelligent, talented, ambitious women have been able to think in terms of a lifetime working "career" that implies a history of progress and improvement in their jobs. Otherwise, the influx of women into the labor force wouldn't have much meaning because the shortage of secretaries and clerical workers is so widely bemoaned that these traditional female occupations probably could absorb the entire influx. What worries the few male observers who exhibit any concern is that several million women no longer are content with traditional female jobs; these women are determined to fight for a place in the economic sun where their abilities can be tested and flourish.

For these career-oriented women, the business press

can serve as an introductory guide to the intricacies of business at levels far above anything with which they have daily contact. The business section of your daily newspaper will quickly teach you the most important fact that you need to know to get started on a serious career—that business is approached like a game. How can you tell? Because in every big newspaper in the country the daily business section is part of the sports section, or vice versa. Moreover, if you watch the reporting language in this twin section, you'll notice a startling similarity in terminology. Sometimes it's hard to tell, from page to page, whether you're reading about XYZ Corp. or the local team; both are said to be revising their game plan, putting their best hitters on the line, eyeing the opposition, going on the offensive or developing a first-rate, experienced team. Both are out to win.

Women wanting to play the business game seriously must also be out to win. To do that, you must keep the entire playing field in view and plan your moves in relation to the other players and to the timing of new opportunities. When men complain that women approach jobs "too personally," they often mean that women take too narrow a view of the corporation's demands, that they concentrate on one tiny activity—their own specific job—without seeing its relationship to the overall aims or problems of the organization. I see the disastrous results of this racehorse-with-blinders approach when talking to "successful" women about their jobs and their futures.

For instance, one extraordinary woman who has achieved the highest executive level ever reached by a female in her West Coast organization was justifiably confident because her reputation and performance were recognized as outstanding. Her future seemed secure and her complacency well founded until she was asked about published reports that her company was being reorganized. She was aware that two management-consultant firms had analyzed the company's structure, but she had paid scant attention to the final reports, which were readily available to her. In fact, both reports agreed on at least one recommendation: abolition of her department. The implications for her current job—not to mention her future—escaped her while she concentrated on maintaining her superior performance. It's unlikely that many men at her level would make such an error in a very tight game.

All too often, ambitious women direct superhuman efforts into activity that is essentially pointless in the context of the corporation's overriding concerns. Regular reading of business publications—if it does nothing else—will reveal that industries are very different and that companies within the same classification can be quite diverse. And although all business enterprises aren't alike, it isn't unusual to find capable women butting their heads against hopeless situations simply because they stumbled into the wrong field. In such cases, attempts to remedy their deficiencies by improving their personalities, appearance or management style won't help. The problem is more basic.

For example, one financial analyst was devastated when her boss said her reports were too "flamboyant." She worked for what every reader of business pages knows is one of the most staid, conservative, big-business-oriented banks. She has a witty, creative, innovative mind, plus boundless energy and enthusiasm for her work. Her talents are ideally suited for a marketing-oriented financial institution or, better yet, a high-pressure consumer-product manufacturer. Yet she spent years perfecting technical and personal skills in a bank that needed her attributes as much as it needed a giraffe. Although there was absolutely nothing wrong with her personality and she wasn't flamboyant in any derogatory sense, she simply worked for the wrong kind of company and didn't know it. (Nor, incidentally, did her superior, who condescendingly concluded that "women" aren't any good in institutional banking. Had any of her bosses assessed the problem accurately, they could have steered her to a more-appropriate employer and hired for themselves a female analyst temperamentally inclined toward their manner of operation).

When it comes to moving ahead in business, women are pretty much left to their own devices. There are, however, some broad guidelines. First of all, make sure there is someplace to go—some real opportunity—before expending extraordinary efforts. At present, most women are in entry-level jobs merely because they are so new to the nonclerical environment. And the comparatively few experienced women who have attained supervisory or executive positions are often at entry-level management—in effect, trainees. (We all know of the handful of genuine management women, starting with Katharine Graham of the Washington Post and ending with Jane Cahill Pfeiffer of NBC; so there isn't any point in belaboring the obvious.)

Unfortunately, most management-trainee women today are located in staff service departments, which offer limited opportunities for advancement. Despite steady progression up the hierarchical ladder, such women will never reach policy-making or power positions for the self-evident (to men) reason that staff executives never hold decision-making power. Power positions develop out of operations experience and "line" manager training. Probably 99% of ambitious women, including MBA graduates, don't understand this crucial distinction in business structure. During the past year, I have put the same question to some 15,000 to 20,000 women, all across the country, who define themselves as "management aspirants." The question is: "How many of you are in line jobs?" The universal response: "What is a line job?"

As a rule-of-thumb, line jobs—from which women have traditionally been excluded—are located in the profit centers of business operations. "Staff" jobs, in contrast, are in the service departments that supplement the work of line managers. Because staff departments don't generate income (quite the reverse; they are considered overhead or expenses), staff employes are most vulnerable to cutbacks, termination or reduction—all euphemisms for being fired. This is one reason female unemployment soars in an economic crunch; staff departments are the first ones cut, and these are precisely the areas in which women, especially professional and executive women, are likely to be found.

Although many of the most interesting jobs in industry are professional staff positions, the lack of power assigned to them puts definite limitations on the upward mobility of women in general as well as of individuals. Being named head of the personnel department, for example, certainly is a major jump for a woman, but it's also the end of the road on the promotional track. The same is true of other corporate staff departments: public relations, communications, research, customer relations, consumer affairs, accounting, data processing, management-information systems, planning departments and so on. If you are moving up in one of these staff departments (and want to stay there), it's important to understand the functions of staff and gear your behavior accordingly. No matter how high you go, your job is to provide information or ideas to line executives who make the key decisions. Your "power" is limited to persuasion, influence or recommendation; you haven't any recourse if your best work is ignored, tabled or rejected. That's the way the ball bounces in this court.

The ambiguity inherent in line-and-staff structure is disturbing to many professional men, but women who believe that can "change the system" are deluding themselves. Indeed, many women lose good jobs by pressuring or ignoring superiors after these executives have made a final, irrevocable decision—which they have the power to make regardless of what you think or how important your project seemed to you. This system is ingrained in the corporate structure. If it ever changes, the change must be ordered by those holding the power to do so, and practically none of them are female.

So, ambitious young women aiming for power must either start in, or get transferred to, line operations. These are the departments that directly affect the company's income. Basically, there are two kinds: those that sell or market the company's products or services, and those that produce the output that is sold. It isn't any accident that women have been excluded—and still are discouraged from precisely these business areas—marketing and production—because experience in one or both usually is needed to qualify for senior management. In this connection the women's penetration into blue-collar jobs is an important breakthrough. Many women taking these so-called—and well-named—nontraditional jobs probably haven't any intention of aspiring to the company presidency, but if they change their minds (as many will, once they perceive the opportunities), they will have accumulated some line experience. Even in this age of MBA credentials, many companies still insist on technical or production background for top executives, and almost all require sales or marketing experience. The reason women encounter so much masculine resistance in these job areas is because these positions open the door to the senior-management staircase.

If you're uncertain about the line operations in your organization (and they aren't always easy to spot in service industries), begin to study promotion announcements and read business biographies of upper-level executives. Carefully note the jobs that they have held and in which departments or geographic regions they have worked—and you'll invariably find the "line." You'll also find that potentially successful individuals move a lot to various jobs or departments, but that they stay on the line track!

If I seem to be overemphasizing the line and staff differentiation, it's partly because I've run into distressing examples of what can happen to women who don't know whether they are in line or staff positions. A number of women who somehow started in line jobs have been shunted off into staff dead-ends with offers of a "great promotion." In every case, these women "had what it takes" to move ahead, reliable observers say. But suddenly the unexpectedly successful female plant manager is "promoted" to head a new one-person headquarters department designed to keep track of the consumer movement. Or a production supervisor accepts a fancy title and new job that traps her into an employe-training function under the Human Resources umbrella. Such mistakes aren't necessarily fatal to a career, but they waste several important years and make it much harder to move into marketing— where the major action takes place.

Another way to switch from staff to line operations is to change companies. A professional specialty that is pure staff in large corporations can be a line function in a service firm where that specialty is the company's primary business focus. In industrial or consumer corporations, for example, advertising is a staff department, but in an advertising agency some of the jobs, specifically account management, are in the line. Attorneys in a corporate-counsel office are staff, but the same attorneys in a law firm have a shot at an eventual partnership. Corporate accountants are staff, but accountants in a nationwide auditing firm can be line. Overspecialization needn't be an unalloyed handicap. The trick is to locate your-self advantageously by joining the right gaming table.

* * *

Business stories have one common denominator: mon-ey. All business organizations need to make money because this is almost always the sole reason for their existence. If a company fails to make money, it will eventually go bankrupt. Because of that unvarying standard, every job is judged and rewarded in direct ratio to how much it contributes to the overall accumulation of profits. In practice, this formula has faults, because everybody knows that many companies have plenty of deadheads who collect exorbitant salaries for pro-ducing mighty little. Nevertheless, the formula holds sway, and nothing will benefit most working women more than knowledge of financial terminology and monetary activities. Even if you don't understand a word of it, economic news and information can help solve your primary job problem—get-ting paid what you're worth for the job you perform.

Women tend to be inordinately lax in grasping the fun-damental principle that a job is a simple contract to exchange specified services for a stipulated amount of money. Thus your job itself is a financial transaction between you and your employer. If you were a sales rep and sold two units of your company's product for the listed price, but then delivered three units at no additional charge—just to show what a nice person you were or how grateful you felt toward the customer —you would lose that job mighty soon, to put it mildly. Yet women do essentially the same thing to themselves when they take on additional job duties or absorb another job on top of their original one without asking for a pay raise or a raise plus a promotion. "Niceness" and "gratitude" are exem-plary qualities under certain conditions, but they never su-persede money in the pragmatic business world.

Moreover, one subject businessmen studiously avoid tackling is the ubiquitous practice of underpaying women. So every employed woman should take the initiative in negotiat-ing a higher salary and not allow underpayment of women to continue indefinitely. Economists commonly rationalize the wide gap between male and female earnings with the absurd assertion that over 80% of employed women are unskilled. They never mention that 100% of men in the work force were equally unskilled the year they got their first job. After 10 or 20 years' experience, women usually are still arbitrarily classed as unskilled, while many men are upper management. It pays for women to remember that skill level is an attribute of the job description, not of the abilities of the person holding that job. Superior performance in an "unskilled" classification doesn't change it to a "skilled" job. What moves you ahead is transfer or promotion to a properly labeled job category. Then, even if your performance is minimal, you are qualified for subsequent upgrading because your "skills" are appreciating.

The most effective way to ensure a decent job future is to study your job description and evaluate its contribution to the company's financial objectives. When your performance advances those objectives, let your boss know you know it and press for adequate remuneration. Adopt the accepted economic game rule (i.e., don't give away the company's product for nothing) and don't give away your own talents and services for anything except dollars and cents. When reading business publications, hone in on all items having to do with compensation plans, wage administration and executive salaries. If that doesn't help you understand that money is just another impersonal commodity in the business-financial mix, watch labor union negotiations with top management. You'll never see the union leaders reducing their discussion to how loyal Joe Doakes is or what a nice guy Charlie Six-Pack is. Money negotiations are unrelated to employes' personalities; don't fall in the trap of thinking that you have to be perfect before asking for a raise.

In the final analysis, there is only one language that successful businessmen understand—the language of money. The reward system in a hierarchy is based on salary and status; this is the scoreboard in the business game. Career-committed women must accept this focus and put all their business relationships on a purely financial basis.

* * *

Once you become a steady reader of the business press, you will find many subtle innuendoes and hidden mes-

sages that serve as invaluable tip-offs to your own career decisions. This book is a good elementary primer in that respect.

Take the subject of flexible or part-time hours, which
often are billed as evidence that women are forcing business
to change its ways. True, in the sense that employers have
finally recognized that educated housewives can be valuable
workers at a fraction of the pay and minus costly fringe benefits. But does that mean that full-time career women will benefit from this "improvement"? Hardly; you'll note that non-
standard work schedules are informally called "mother's
hours." In short, if you switch to part-time work, you will be
categorized according to parental status rather than business
status.

Nowadays women also are often treated as part of a
revolutionary economic package—the dual-income family.
This idea, too, is fraught with dangers for the ambitious
woman who lets it go unchallenged. Once she is stereotyped
as nothing more than a voluntary contributor to the family
coffers, the career woman won't be taken seriously as a business competitor. She's apt to get the same response that a
product supervisor in a leading cosmetic company got just recently when she argued for a raise: "But you don't need it,
your husband makes good money, and it will only put you in
a higher tax bracket."

Higher tax brackets are rapidly taking over—both at
home and at work—as reasons for women to be happy with
where they are in the salary schedules and not to push ahead
to higher-paying positions. One way to solve this problem is
for working women to establish their independent financial
status by not filing joint income-tax returns. Let your husband take care of his income, expenses, deductions and net
tax—and you take care of yours. That way you'll know who
owns what, who pays for what, who is responsible for child
care and household help, who has the better medical and retirement programs. You might pay a few dollars more in taxes this way (but not necessarily). Even so, that's mighty
cheap tuition to learn the nitty-gritty elements of independent financial planning.

But there's a much stronger reason for women to become economically independent. Can anyone guarantee that the slender thread of financial dependence upon a husband's income never will be broken—by illness, unemployment, divorce, desertion or death? If a male boss ever mentions your husband's income in relation to your salary, ask him if he will cosign a legal note to be personally responsible for your husband's monetary debt to you. (I think you'll get the deserved raise with no more such nonsense from him.)

*   *   *

So far women haven't had much significant impact on the business financial and economic system. But they will. The shape of the resulting changes has yet to be foreshadowed clearly in any crystal ball. However well-intentioned, male experts cannot accurately predict how women will respond when half of the human population, who have been confined to upholstered social prison cells, are exposed to the great wide world of society, companionship, politics and business. Women can't predict this future, either, because we don't know each other well enough. However, one trend is clearly discernible, especially in this book. Women from all-walks of life, in every economic circumstance, belonging to every racial or ethnic group, and living in every lifestyle are individually moving in roughly the same direction. They are joining the paid labor force with the same determination to get ahead according to their own interests as did the men preceding them.

The future is not assured, but the game is bound to be chaotic, exciting and challenging.

Sources

The following list gives the authors and titles of all the Wall Street Journal articles on which this book is based.

BLUNDELL, William E., "Women at Work: Chat With 11 Women Finds Anger at Sexism, Hope for Better Jobs," Sept. 5, 1978.

BRALOVE, Mary, "A Cold Shoulder: Career Women Decry Sexual Harassment by Bosses and Clients," Jan. 29, 1976.

BRONSON, Gail, "Bitter Reaction: Issue of Fetal Damage Stirs Women Workers at Chemical Plants," Feb. 9, 1979.

DRINKHALL, Jim, "Ladies of the Bar: Women Attorneys, Now Over 9% of Profession, Keep Making Gains in All Areas of Legal Work," May 31, 1978.

EVANS, Christopher A., "Sandy Biggest: Search for Fulfillment," Feb. 7, 1977.

FALK, Carol H., "Backtracking on Job Bias?", Feb. 9, 1978.

GALLESE, Liz Roman, "Blue-Collar Women: More Female Workers Get Skilled-Trade Jobs, But Problems Remain," Nov. 13, 1978.

—"Charm Courses Are Passe at the Boston 'Y'," Sept. 14, 1978.

—"Going It Alone: Juggling Kids and Job Is Routine for Mother Who Is a Breadwinner," July 27, 1976.

—"Job Harvest: Women and City Dwellers Learn About Farms; Agriculture-School Enrollments Rise Rapidly," Feb. 14, 1978.

—"Moving Experience: Women Managers Say Job Transfers Present a Growing Dilemma," May 4, 1978.

GETSCHOW, George, "Women in the Pits: Kentucky Mother, 29, Endures Dirt, Danger to Work as Coal Miner," Nov. 29, 1976.

GOTTSCHALK, Earl C. Jr., "Women at Work: Day Care Is Booming, but Experts Are Split Over Its Effect on Kids," Sept. 15, 1978.

GRAHAM, Ellen, "Ad Lib: Advertisers Take Aim at a Neglected Market: The Working Woman," July 5, 1977.

HILL, G. Christian, "Topers and Tipplers Tend to Be Tippers, Wowing Waitresses," April 5, 1978.

HYATT, James C., "Early Warning: Protection for Unborn? Work-Safety Issue Isn't as Simple as It Sounds,' Aug. 2, 1977.

IGNATIUS, David, "Women at Work: The Rich Get Richer as Well-to-Do Wives Enter the Labor Force," Sept. 8, 1978.

JASEN, Georgette, "Ma Bell's Daughters: Women Got Big Gains in '73 AT&T Job Pact, but Sexism Cry Persists," Feb. 28, 1978.

KRONHOLZ, June, "Women at Work: Management Practices Change to Reflect Role of Women Employes," Sept. 13, 1978.

LABOR LETTER, selected items from the weekly feature in the Wall Street Journal.

LEFF, Laurel, "Feminist Flop? Despite High Hopes, Women's Banks Find Financial Seas Rough," Dec. 22, 1978.

—"Rough Tough Males Who Sell Autos Fall for Feminine Touch," Aug. 5, 1977.

LUBLIN, Joann S., "Careers in Collision: Working Couples Find an Increasing Chance of Conflicts in Jobs," Nov. 18, 1977.

—"Getting Organized: More Women Enroll in Unions, Win Office and Push for Changes," Jan. 15, 1979.

—"Secretaries' Revolt: Female Office Workers Form Groups to Fight Sex Bias, Petty Chores," Feb. 24, 1978.

—"The Managers: Mrs. Lowe Has to Deal With Stress and Sexism as Bank-Branch Head," April 26, 1977.

—"The Rural Wife: While Keeping House, Donna Keppy Ranks as a Partner on Farm," June 2, 1975.

—"Women at Work: Life in Morton Grove Hasn't Been the Same Since Wives Took Jobs," Sept. 22, 1978.

MALABRE, Alfred L. Jr., "Women at Work: As Their Ranks Swell, Women Holding Jobs Reshape U.S. Society," Aug. 28, 1978.

MAY, Roger B., "The Venturers: Joan Massey Struggles to Keep an Idea Alive on Bare-Bones Capital," Nov. 14, 1977.

MORGENTHALER, Eric, "Women of the World: More U.S. Firms Put Females in Key Posts in Foreign Countries," March 16, 1978.

NISSEN, Beth, "Woman to Woman: Mary Kay Sales Agents Zero In on Prospects in Their Living Rooms," Sept. 28, 1978.

OTTEN, Alan L., "Two-Career Couples," July 29, 1976.

RICKLEFS, Roger, "Antibias Inc.: Small Firms Specialize in Helping Companies Find Blacks, Women," Sept. 20, 1977.

SANGER, Elizabeth, "Women Pilots Find Acceptance Is Slow of Their Role Aloft," July 19, 1978.

SEASE, Douglas R., "Women at Work," Marital Relationships Often Undergo Strain When Wives Get Jobs," Sept. 10, 1978.

YAEGER, Deborah Sue, "Women at Work: Many Companies Find Employed Women Are a High-Class Market," Aug. 31, 1978.